# Everyday Politics in the Libyan Arab Jamahiriya

*Modern Intellectual and Political History of the Middle East*
Fred H. Lawson, *Series Editor*

**Select Titles in Modern Intellectual and Political History of the Middle East**

*The Autocratic Parliament: Power and Legitimacy in Egypt, 1866–2011*
Irene Weipert-Fenner

*Figures That Speak: The Vocabulary of Turkish Nationalism*
Matthew deTar

*Iran's Experiment with Parliamentary Governance: The Second Majles, 1909–1911*
Mangol Bayat

*Killing Contention: Demobilization in Morocco during the Arab Spring*
Sammy Zeyad Badran

*Islam, Revival, and Reform: Redefining Tradition for the Twenty-First Century*
Natana J. DeLong-Bas, ed.

*Sayyid Qutb: An Intellectual Biography*
Giedrė Šabasevičiūtė

*Watermelon Democracy: Egypt's Turbulent Transition*
Joshua Stacher

*Why Alliances Fail: Islamist and Leftist Coalitions in North Africa*
Matt Buehler

For a full list of titles in this series,
visit https://press.syr.edu/supressbook-series/modern
-intellectual-and-political-history-of-the-middle-east/.

# Everyday Politics in the Libyan Arab Jamahiriya

**Matteo Capasso**

Syracuse University Press

*For the good of Libya*
*and its future generations*

# Contents

# Acknowledgments

This book would not have been possible without all the stories, anecdotes, and jokes that Libyans have shared with me. I am deeply grateful to Younis Lahwej, Mustafa Younis, Abdelatif Talouba, and Murad Baour, who always encouraged me to pursue this project, while pushing me to question its findings.

This project originated at the School of Government and International Affairs at Durham University, UK, and continued with the postdoctoral program at the European University Institute, Florence, and the University of Turin, Italy. The final product was possible thanks to their financial support and intellectual engagement with their faculty.

A special thanks goes to Eric Hooglund for his constant and patient mentorship throughout every stage of my academic career. Also, I am highly indebted to Matteo Legrenzi for his unique strategic advice on the academic profession. More scholars than I can list have helped me to refine some of the ideas discussed in this book. Special mentions go to Anna Baldinetti, Federica Bicchi, Irene Bono, Aida Hozic, Ali Kadri, Emma Murphy, and Gabriella Sanchez. Thanks to the Syracuse University Press editorial team for having supported and believed in this project, together with the two anonymous reviewers.

I also want to thank my parents, Concetta and Antonio, for the love and support throughout the years. A special note to all my friends, especially Waed, for providing much-needed breaks and encouragements. My greatest thanks go to my partner, Walaa, whose unmatchable support, love, and patience have made this book possible.

# Everyday Politics in the Libyan Arab Jamahiriya

# 1

# Mapping the Everyday

We came, we saw, he died.
Hillary Rodham Clinton, 2011

After the brutal capture and killing of Muammar Qaddafi in October 2011, the US secretary of state, Hillary Rodham Clinton, used these words to comment on the alleged success of the NATO-led military operation in support of the Libyan protests, also known as the 17 February Revolution (CBS News 2011). The events began eight months earlier, when Libyans marched into the streets to protest against the regime, emulating the actions that had characterized the course of events in its neighboring countries—Tunisia and Egypt—since late 2010.[1] In this case, people took to the streets of Benghazi to protest the arrest of Fathi Terbil, the lawyer representing the families of the disappeared victims of the infamous state-led killings in the Abu Salim prison in 1996 (Human Rights Watch 2006; Zarrugh 2018). While the protesters' demands included the lawyer's release as well as justice and transparency regarding the unknown fates of their loved ones, their protests also offered an opportunity to voice a more widespread societal discontent around worsening economic conditions and political freedom (Prashad 2012; Cole and McQuinn 2015). However, they soon escalated into open and violent confrontation. Some protesters torched police stations and besieged the city's airport in Benghazi as well as army barracks, where they obtained weapons (CNN 2011). In Bayda

---

1. The book refers to the political authorities in charge of the Libyan Arab Jamahiriya interchangeably as the Libyan regime or government.

and the port town of Tobruk, they forced out those who were considered regime loyalists, while in Zintan they set fire to a police station and the premises of security forces (Alaaldin 2012). On February 15, 2011, the rebels captured, tortured, and killed a Black lieutenant, Hisham al-Shoushan, accused of being a mercenary soldier working for the regime. Hanged by his feet and whiplashed by protesters in public, al-Shoushan's fabricated accusations were also widely recirculated by the Qatari-based television channel Al-Jazeera (AfricaGateNews 2020).

The regime, for their part, sought to contain the unrest by various means, including mass shootings, arrests, and peaceful calls to the protesters to return to their homes. More importantly, at the international level, in less than ten days since the start of the protests, major Western governments such as the United States, the UK, and France had already started to call upon Qaddafi, asking him to step down "now, without further violence or delay" (Clinton 2011). Breaking any diplomatic relations with the Libyan regime, on February 27, 2011, they recognized the nascent National Transitional Council (NTC), which was formed to act as the executive and political face of the rebels, taking up administrative roles, distributing weapons, and paying salaries (Bartu 2015).

Therefore, as the regime seemed to have regained control of the areas held by rebels, reaching the outskirts of the city of Benghazi, a moral consensus grew among many Western countries regarding the necessity to contain Qaddafi's "killing of his own people" (*Telegraph* 2011) and avoid an impending genocide (Obama 2011). On March 13, 2011, the United Nations Security Council (UNSC) passed Resolution 1973 (UN Security Council 2011a, 2011b), calling for an immediate ceasefire, establishing a no-fly zone over Libya, and authorizing the use of "all necessary measures" to protect civilian-held areas. A few days later, an international coalition of eighteen countries initiated the military operation Odyssey Dawn, initially lead by US African Command (AFRICOM) and then by the North Atlantic Treaty Organization (NATO), in support of the rebels. The UN-authorized humanitarian intervention was deemed necessary to support a popular uprising that aimed to overthrow a ruler who had governed Libya in an authoritarian, if not a dictatorial, fashion for more than forty years (O'Sullivan 2017; Pack 2014; Becker and Shane 2016). By protecting the lives of the Libyan people, the humanitarian intervention paved the way for a democratic government, and, in fact, elections took place in 2012. Nonetheless, the country descended into further destruction and internecine violence. Those armed groups—also known as militias—that had contributed to the fall of the regime did not acknowledge the results of the elections and began fighting against each other. To this day, while alliances and actors have shifted several times, the civil war and its related violence has not ended. Libya is a failed state.

At such a critical juncture for the past, present, and future of Libya, post-2011 fragmentation, destruction, and violence are interpreted as stemming from a domestic and traditional weakness of Libya and its people. Libya's long rejection of modern state structures, which, at its best, Qaddafi's rule pursued, now poses a major challenge for the country. An oversimplified version of this argument, which is often used to make the country legible to nonexperts, stresses Libya's unchanging nature. As Italian journalist and renowned expert on Libya Michela Mercuri (2017, 11) writes, "Contemporary Libya is a place where everything moves, but nothing changes, a country that seems to be stubbornly fighting against itself." From the Ottoman times to the present, Libya has been traditionally represented as a society without a state. One hundred and fifty years of the country's political history are encapsulated as the result of an historical battle between the center and the periphery (Pack 2014). Beginning with the Ottomans and extending to the Qaddafi regime and afterward, in Libya peripheral forces have always rejected an institutionalized central power. This proves not only that Libya's twentieth-century history has differed from other despotic Arab regimes but also that its trajectory brought about the creation of an accidental state (Laessing 2020). In other words, comprehending Libya's destruction now requires us to brush up on its history of statelessness and the return of tribal structures and their related dynamics.

This book aims to reconstruct the intricate political dynamics in the Libyan Arab Jamahiriya leading up to 2011. Drawing directly from the voices and lives of Libyans, it weaves the threads linking the sphere of the quotidian to the regional and international. The book leads up to a unique and timely analysis of the 2011 events that witnessed the fall of the regime, demonstrating how a popular movement for freedom against an increasingly repressive regime turned into a melodrama of violence and war. In doing so, it demonstrates how those academic frames used to interpret the country's events in 2011 have contributed to obscuring the interdependence between everyday local and global dynamics, including constant Western politico-military interference in the country and the consolidation of capitalist modernity worldwide.

The term "statelessness" derives from the anthropological work of John Davis, who adopted the concept to describe the development of modern Libya based on two main factors. First, he linked statelessness to the historical incapacity of the colonial authorities to establish hegemonic institutions in the eyes of the colonized population. Second, the presence of a tribal structure in Libyan society allowed Qaddafi to reject conventional notions of the state—that is, buying off people's legitimacy through the use of hydrocarbon revenues (Davis 1987). The history of the Libyan polity, in other words, had not "encrusted the state with respectability, nor given it any cloak of inevitability" (41). The launch of the al-Fātiḥ Revolution in 1969 and the subsequent establishment of the Jamahiriya in 1977 dovetailed with a more general path that had characterized Libya's historical development since the defeat of the Ottoman Empire in the early part of the twentieth century—in other words, the absence of a modern institutional framework, or, more simply, statelessness (Vandewalle 2006; Martinez 2007; Bensaâd 2012; Geha 2014; St John 2015).[2] In such a scenario, where statelessness represented both an historical anomaly and the continuity of Libya's rulers, who were unwilling to establish a modern state, the regime of Qaddafi only reaffirmed this understanding of the country's history, adding another shard to the mosaic of statelessness.

2. From 1969 to 1977, the country was named the Libyan Arab Republic. In 1977, it became the Socialist People's Libyan Arab Jamahiriya, and, in 1986, the Great Socialist People's Libyan Arab Jamahiriya. Muammar Qaddafi coined this term, which is a neologism combining two Arabic words: *jamāhīr* (masses) and *jumhuriyya* (republic), meaning "republic of the masses."

To further strengthen this argument, statelessness is often associated with the authoritarian, quixotic, idiosyncratic, or bizarre ideas of Qaddafi (Vandewalle 1995, 2006; Parteger 2012). The absence of state institutions in Libya come hand in hand with a focus on his eccentric and authoritarian theoretical experimentations (Capasso 2014). In such a scenario, a stateless Libya that rejects the modern structures of the state and instead is governed by an irrational man also became a menace to the stability of the international order. There is, in fact, another and important concept that scholars have attached to the study of the Jamahiriya, this time to describe its status in the international arena: that of the rogue state (Zoubir 2002; Miles 2003; Parteger 2005; Onderco 2014), or, in other variations, the outlaw state; pariah state (Martinez 2007; Oakes 2011); irrational state (Dror 1971; Mandel 1987); quasi-state (Jackson 1990); or terrorist state (Lake 1994; Martinez 2007). Libya—or, to be more precise, Qaddafi's Libya—was considered a state that nurtured and supported international terrorism, relentlessly pursuing the creation of weapons of mass destruction (WMD), ultimately threatening the world's peace and stability.

This conceptual tryptic—statelessness, authoritarianism, and rogueness—has not only acted as a powerful and enduring reference used to characterize the diverse stages of political development that Libya has undergone but has also contributed to set the scene for making sense of the 2011 events that took place there. In doing so, one comes to realize the convenient and reductive clichés adopted to decipher the turbulent fall of the Jamahiriya and the ensuing conflict. To keep framing and tracing these dynamics in such terms obscures rather than clarifies the multiple forces at work that shaped the political development of the Libyan Arab Jamahiriya and its aftermath.

Reflecting on the work of those who view the social history of Libya as a variation on the theme of statelessness, the Libyan scholar Ali Ahmida argues that the absence of a centralized state does not necessarily constitute a sign of a country's weakness; rather, it indicates the existence of different regional social formations whose structural institutions also represent a type of state formation (2005, 69). Therefore, the first problematic aspect lies in the normative way in which the state has been approached as the normal and unchanging repository of power. Ahmida's reflections are pertinent because they indicate how scholars have failed to understand the specificities of Libya's political development.

Yet there are other problematic assumptions connected to the same tryptic. Explaining the statelessness of Libya as a weakness entails an overfocus on the role, figure, ideas, and speeches of Qaddafi, thus reflecting an idea of power as culminating and residing in one man. Reminiscent of Orientalist writings, this concentration of power signals the lack of a normal, democratic, and functioning political order that inevitably leads up to the emergence of non-Eurocentric, thus deviant, forms of authority. Interestingly, this argument builds on the use of two self-reinforcing notions that come to occupy the empty space coinciding with the absence of liberal-democratic state structures. On one side of the spectrum, it is possible to find the figure of one man, the authoritarian ruler who uses the population to realize his own whims: Qaddafi. On the other, the category of "tribes" routinely reemerges to describe the social configuration of the country. These notions do not work in contradictory ways; rather, they are part of the same unit of analysis that reinforces the unruly and undemocratic character of these states. For instance, historically, the notion of a stateless Libya has emerged from the country's tribal character, in an unmodern organization of life that has constantly rejected the modern state. In this regard, the figure of the authoritarian ruler appears as somewhat required, because it shows a capacity to manipulate and rein in tribes, while governing without any accountability toward them. Scholars and analysts have taken the part (Qaddafi) for the whole (Libya), assuming that there was no Libya-ness beyond the macrohistorical metanarrative of Qaddafi-ness. The ideas and personality of Qaddafi obscured Libya's complexity, and one Libyan became the symbol for all Libyans (Capasso and Cherstich 2014). This turned Libya into a perfect terrain for studying authoritarianism and other types of regime behavior.

However, when the radical pulse of the protests began to sweep throughout the entire Arab region in late 2010, the empirical and theoretical certainties that such an overemphasis on authoritarianism and its resilience had produced were suddenly and radically questioned. The people had not simply shown a desire to improve their actual living conditions;

their actions forced scholars to revisit numerous conceptual assumptions. How was it possible that thousands of people decided to rebel in the streets, to protest their authoritarian governments? How did we miss those seeds of discontent and radical action? To put it another way, scholars had forgotten to pay attention to the "quiet encroachment" in the lives of ordinary people (Bayat 2009), and, thus, the way people negotiate, accept, or challenge the yoke of domination, even in repressive political settings (Ismail 2006; Navaro-Yashin 2002; Wedeen 1999).

This book loosely situates its inquiry within those latter parameters, as it aims to retrieve the lost voices of ordinary Libyans, which are almost completely absent in the academic scholarship on the Jamahiriya. There are studies that rely on sociopolitical approaches and offer a more nuanced understanding of the politics in the Jamahiriya. Focusing on the processes of elite formations (Ouannes 2009) or questions of political culture (Obeidi 2001), ideology (Stocker 2012), or legitimacy (al-Werfalli 2011), they move beyond the notion of a state-lacking society, as well as the emphasis on the one-man role. They do not provide a chronological history of Libya, but peruse the country from below, thereby seeking the views, opinions, and experiences of Libyans through questionnaire, surveys, and, at times, interviews. For instance, when academic studies reduce the Jamahiriya's anti-imperialist ideology to a rogue state and Qaddafi's ideas to extravagant whims, they underestimate the role such discourses have played at both the everyday and national level. In other words, they do not take into account how people experienced and related to those values, and how the regime tried to pursue policies in subservience to those ideas (Obeidi 2001). Similarly, to claim that tribal dynamics prevent the creation of a central/national structure means ignoring how tribalism reemerged or was accommodated in the everyday life of people. It means overseeing its elastic and changing structure and uses (Cherstich 2014).

This book proposes to study the main modalities of political interaction in the everyday lives of Libyans, showing how these shaped and affected their relationship with their government, and vice versa. Through the direct narratives of Libyans, this book peruses the political valence of everyday beliefs,[3] emotions,[4] and practices, and how those quotidian forms and modes of interactions can help us better understand the politics of the country and the events of 2011.[5]

At the same time, the book remains careful not to rely entirely on some of the inherent consequences that such a renewed focus on the everyday has triggered. Initially, as mentioned above, scholarship focused on describing Libya as another authoritarian government in the Middle East and North Africa region, whereby people lacked either agency or the means to reflect critically on the values and policies of the regime. After 2011, the surge of studies on protests and revolts flipped the authoritarian picture upside-down. In every act or ordinary practice, there was now a tendency to trace those seeds of agency and resistance that had been overlooked for a very long time.[6] Both conceptualizations, I argue, offer a mutually reinforcing representation of the Arab region in general and of

---

3. When analyzing questions of political power and authority, Žižek (1987) argues that power acquires its force by operating upon how people act in everyday life. What matters is that people keep acting and moving strictly within the set of the dominant symbolical and rhetorical parameters, even if they do so in pretense and dissimulation. They should comply with it, but there is no obligation to believe in it if one acts *as if* one believes in it (19). In this way, the hierarchical order is reproduced, while subjects fail to act out their grievances and to challenge authority (Wedeen 1999; Navaro-Yashin 2002; Wedeen 2019).

4. I take fantasies, aspirations, and fears (Ahmed 2004, 2010) as elements that reveal the ways people interact with political structures, shaping their actions and subjectivities (Davies 2015; Duffy 2017; Kleist and Jansen 2016). They can contest the political status quo because they manifest what people hope for (Fischer 2014); yet these same emotional states and everyday affects can also help regulate present quotidian life because they create possibilities for governing peoples' behavior (Berlant 2011).

5. I explore how political power operates through the creation of repeated conduct and normalized behaviors, also known as disciplinary mechanisms, or *dispositifs* (Foucault 1993, 149).

6. The book also pays particular attention to the ways popular culture (e.g., humor, satire, tricksterism) can mock the fictitious grounds of official codes, unveiling the discrepancy between public and hidden transcripts of power, or the existing conditions of ordinary life (Mbembe 2001; Scott 1990). Yet this focus has not translated into a constant—if not obsessive—search for political resistance.

Libya in particular that is problematic, failing to provide more nuanced sketches of gradual political development.

It is certainly true that the roots of these binary categories go much deeper, because they originate in academic regimes of knowledge aligned with the logic of, for instance, the Cold War (Bilgin and Morton 2004). The idea of rogue states, in fact, is a remnant of those academic analyses that aimed to reproduce the hegemonic pretensions of the United States. At the same time, the overemphasis on the agency and power of the people (Tripp 2014) led scholars to dismiss a bit too quickly the impact of global and structural factors. In this binary reversal, the everyday has rightly gained prominence and become a privileged site for studying politics, yet remains disconnected from long-standing international dynamics of politics (Armbrust 2019; Chalcraft 2016) and political economy (Abdelrahman 2017; Ayeb and Bush 2019; Bogaert 2018; Hanieh 2018; Kadri 2015, 2019) that shaped and influenced not only people's everyday lives, but also the outcomes of many of those 2011 uprisings.

By focusing on the everyday, this book undermines the idea that politics should be solely studied through the presence—or absence—of institutions, or the agency of the people. Nonetheless, it maintains the necessary tension between everyday life and national and international politics. My recourse to this vocabulary is guided by the need to decenter the master narrative that depicted Libya as a one-man show, an authoritarian and stateless society, a terrorist state, which triggered the disappearance of Libyans from their own history and the world stage. Instead, the book takes the everyday as a site for the study of the politics of the Libyan Arab Jamahiriya, acknowledging their often contradictory, polarizing, and ambiguous nature. It discusses those ordinary beliefs, emotions, and practices that could simultaneously challenge the stability of the regime while paving the way for the cruel outcome of the events of 2011, as chapter 5 will show. It explores how forms of control, violence, and surveillance, so deeply entrenched in the everyday lives of Libyans, cannot simply be translated into the formation of an umpteenth authoritarian regime in the Arab region. Rather, a focus on the everyday forces one to read questions of violence and surveillance in a wider and historical context of international violence and changing geopolitical conditions, including threats of war, the rise of political Islam, and international sanctions, to which Libya was not immune.

On such a premise, the following provides a brief historical prologue that permits the reader to comprehend where and when this journey into the everyday starts in the last two turbulent decades of the Jamahiriya. In doing so, it avoids a priori negative representations of the Libyan regime, such as "forty-two years of dictatorship," without falling into the trap of romanticizing.

## Situating al-Fātiḥ and Its Defeat

On September 1, 1969, a group of seventy young officers in the armed forces overthrew King Idris al-Senusi in a bloodless coup d'état that launched al-Fātiḥ (The Opening) Revolution. This military operation, which had the code name "Jerusalem"—chosen to remember the fall of the holy Old City of Jerusalem just two years earlier under Zionist-Israeli occupation and to honor the Palestinian cause—was primarily a response to a set of social and political problems that the monarchy had not been able to resolve. These problems were the consequences of Libya's violent early twentieth-century history as well as the socioeconomic impact of its emergence as an oil-producing and exporting country in the 1950s and 1960s. Libya's political turmoil began in 1912, when Italy invaded what at the time was a relatively prosperous Ottoman province. Resistance to the Italian effort to colonize Libya continued for more than twenty years (Ryan 2018), with considerable destruction and loss of life; severe repression of the native Libyan population continued during the 1930s, after Italian forces had "pacified" the country (Ahmida 1994, 2005). In fact, the Italian colonial genocide resulted "in a loss of 83,000 Libyan citizens as the population declined from 225,000 to 142,000 citizens. Some 110,000 civilians were forced to march from their homes to the harsh desert and then were interned in horrific concentration camps. Between 60,000 and 70,000, mostly rural people (including men, women, elderly, and children) and their 600,000 animals were starved and died of diseases" (Ahmida 2020, 3). World War II brought more devastation to Libya, as both French and British forces invaded to oust the Italians. Once the

Allied powers defeated Italy (1943–44), Libya was de facto partitioned into three provinces with diverging political interests: Cyrenaica, Tripolitania, and Fezzan.

The Allies occupying Libya had no shared vision for the country. French forces in Fezzan in the south and adjacent to France's African colonies in the Saharan region seemed to want to stay indefinitely, while the British in Cyrenaica and Tripolitania ruled those provinces in accordance with the Hague Convention of 1907 regulating military occupation. The United Nations decided to intervene in 1949 by appointing Adrian Pelt as UN commissioner with the task of designing a plan for the creation of an independent and unified Libyan state. His plan officially came into existence in 1951, when the United Kingdom of Libya was proclaimed under the rule of Idris al-Senusi. However, a newfound national unity struggled to take root in Libya, due to the fact that the political process was largely dictated by external powers with little input from local actors and forces (Baldinetti 2012, 15). For these reasons, King Idris enjoyed relatively strong support only in the eastern part of Libya, in the region of Cyrenaica (Ouannes 2009, 41). Moreover, although the monarchical constitution offered a broad spectrum of civil and social rights, two fundamental characteristics of postindependence Libya—elections and the federal system—did not last long. When the first free general elections were held in 1952, political parties from the opposition accused the monarchy of electoral fraud, supported by the British government. The monarchy reacted by suspending all political parties and, in 1964, abolishing the federal system altogether.

Following the discovery of oil in Libya, a relatively rapid economic growth occurred and changed the basis of its society. These changes brought about the emergence of new social groups that no longer related to each other based on kinship, as had the traditional elites, but on professional relations and—most importantly—ideological beliefs.[7] The failing response of the monarchy to those dynamics ultimately explains its demise.

7. Al-Barbar (1994) provides a detailed explanation of those rapid social and economic changes that reconfigured the monarchy and caused its crisis of legitimacy.

The consequent emergence of new social groups due to the discovery of oil did not translate into the establishment of a wider and more inclusive process of political participation. Rather, the monarchy decided to centralize its control, assigning to the national government "the sole right for all transactions involving finance, transportation and, most important, oil and taxation" (Al-Barbar 1994, 65). However, the dependence of the monarchy on foreign technical assistance for oil extraction and production further eroded its ideological legitimacy in the eyes of the population. When the king made the unpopular move of conceding the military base of Wheelus Field to the US government, his decision further signaled the country's ideological distance from Pan-Arab sentiment in the region, especially after the humiliating defeat of the Arabs in the 1967 war.[8] A similar ideological distance emerged routinely within the education system, where the reliance on Egyptian teachers and materials influenced the development of Pan-Arab ideas and beliefs among students (Obeidi 2001, 37). In 1962, numerous student-led riots were organized in Tripoli and Benghazi opposing the traditional tribal ruling elite and demanding the recovery of the two Western military bases of Wheelus Field and El-Adem. Recognizing the country's dilemmas, King Idris and his narrow circle—known as the royal palace—tried to legitimize their own authority. They built a patronage structure aimed at integrating the regional leaders into the governmental apparatus (Djaziri 1996, 53). However, social discontent increased as a result of two main factors: first, the emergence of newly enriched social classes that, far from serving the state, used it to their advantage (64); and, second, the start of the 1967 war, which confirmed the interference of the West in the country's political affairs. While virtually the entire Arab world sided with Egypt and its allies against Israel's preemptive attack, the Libyan monarchy maintained a neutral position.

8. Pan-Arabism is an ideological and political movement aiming to unify all present-day Arab nations and Arab-speaking regions into a singular, unified state stretching from the Atlantic Ocean to the Persian Gulf. It is also worthwhile to stress that the ideological relevance of Pan-Arabism comes in relation to Arab Socialism. For a general understanding, see definitions of Arab Socialism and Pan-Arabism in Ness and Cope (2017, 812–17, 915–16).

More importantly, the defeat of the Arab countries by Israel, which ended up conquering the rest of Palestine—including the Gaza Strip and West Bank/East Jerusalem, plus Golan Heights and Sinai Peninsula—simultaneously represented a major blow and a trigger for action to the young Libyan nationalist and Pan-Arab officers. The sense of humiliation, frustration, and helplessness that spread throughout the Arab world in the aftermath of the 1967 Six-Day War led these young military officers to desire profound change. While blaming the military failure on the foreign presence in the region, the officers perceived the Libyan monarchy as an anachronistic institution that had accepted the Western presence for too long and thus contributed to an unfinished process of independence for Libya (Khadduri 1963).

Therefore, the 1969 revolution came about as a reaction to the unresolved and growing crisis of legitimacy of the Sanusi monarchy, whose close and strategic alliance to Western countries clashed with the mounting Pan-Arab and anticolonial ideals spreading throughout the region. Hence, the revolution interacted with multiple levels of power, including national, regional, and global. The interlayering of these levels not only prompted the revolution but also provided a guiding rationale for the officers in developing their policies. Initially, the group of Free Officers, as a collective, oversaw the initial takeover and political development of the country. Since the officers wanted to break with the country's monarchical past, shaping Libya according to their ideological and political commitments, the first years of the al-Fātiḥ Revolution were characterized by what Mansour El-Kikhia (1997, 67) labeled the Egyptianization of Libya. The Revolutionary Command Council (RCC) remodeled the Libyan political system into the unique party formula of the Arab Socialist Union (ASU) and signed a union declaration with Egypt, adopting its flag and anthem (42).[9] Subsequently, the RCC expelled Italian nationals, confiscating their assets (40), and shut down the Western military bases in the country. Also, the newly established military committee completely

9. The Egyptian president Gamal Abdel Nasser created the Arab Socialist Union Party based on the principles of Pan-Arabism and Socialism (Ouannes 2009, 115).

renegotiated the existing agreements on oil production and profit with major Western companies, which considerably tipped the balance of power in Libya's favor.[10] By pursuing a policy of production cuts and increase in oil prices, the Libyan government laid the basis for other oil producers both to renegotiate their agreements with foreign companies (Blair 1978, 223–30) as well as to turn oil into a political weapon, which Libya used to seek revolutionary goals in the realm of foreign policy, such as pressuring Western countries to liberate Palestine (Stork 1975).

From an economic perspective, the RCC did not hesitate to take upon itself the challenge of initiating an internally induced, independent path to economic development, whose objectives consisted in rejecting foreign domination and overcoming the economic obstacles that existed during monarchical rule. In 1973, the oil industry was nationalized, and in 1977, economic measures were introduced to improve the lives of the most marginalized segments of society with the establishment of the Jamahiriya. The launch of the Republic of the Masses did not arrive in a vacuum; rather, it built upon the previously launched program of the 1973 Cultural Revolution, which had catalyzed the political and economic transformation of Libyan society in line with the directives outlined in the Third Universal Theory, also known as "the Green Book."[11] Consisting of three pamphlets, the Green Book was published in full in 1981 and aimed to offer a solution to the political, economic, and social problems of democracy. Its central tenet was the theory of direct democracy, proposing that "ordinary citizens can directly manage their lives and devise their own solution to economic and social problems" (Vandewalle 2006, 102) through a dual and complementary process. This consisted of renouncing any form of

10. For more information on the Tripoli Agreements, see Waddams (1980); Yergin (1991, 578); and Parra (2004, 132).

11. The four points were: (1) changing the country's name from the Libyan Arab Republic to the Socialist People's Libyan Arab Jamahiriya; (2) adopting the Qur'an as the law of society; (3) establishing popular, direct authority through a system culminating in the General People's Congress; and (4) assigning responsibility for defending the homeland to every man and woman through general military training as a normal practice (Berween 2003, 59).

representation or delegation of their authority, while recognizing the need for popular organization at every level of society (Al Gathafi 2005, 17).

Although ideological ferment played a major role in guiding the political experimentation of the Libyan leadership, the concomitant rise of oil prices and revenues, which had been pushed by the United States as a strategy to counter the international power of Europe and Japan (Oppenheim, 1976), also contributed. Oil prices, in fact, had quadrupled between 1973 and 1974, while in 1979 the rise in domestic production and the concomitant Iranian revolution increased the annual income to a record $71 billion (Villa 2012, 70). The oil boom of the second half of the 1970s therefore allowed the Libyan government to take a bolder step, with the aim of eliminating private property and employment. Those measures also included the introduction of a program of land reform in 1978 (A. A. Abdussalam 1985, 78), and, in 1986, land ownership was abolished altogether. Another important economic reform entailed the abolition of the role of traders. The revolutionary government pursued the return of the ownership of production to the people by replacing the concept of "wage-earners" with "partners" (Al Gathafi 2005, 33). The liberation of the workers represented a crucial step in the realization of the Libyan revolution (Centro Studi Libro Verde 1984, 198–210), since the workers had to become aware of the difficulties in carrying out the fight against exploitation and the "legal codification of free work"—that is, wages—which was only a license for capitalists to rob workers of their productivity (194). The workers' takeover of the factories was fully planned at both practical and ideological levels. People "knew exactly where to go [because] it had been prepared down to the last detail" (Naur 1986, 94–96), and the takeover was the most fundamental step for the subsequent creation of the Revolutionary Committees. The creation of popular committees ushered in a new system of democratic representation.

By the mid-1980s, these same maneuvers boosted economic development in Libya and raised the general standard of living. The rate of infant mortality witnessed a massive reduction, the average intake of calories per day was the highest among the members of the Organization of Arab Petroleum Exporting countries (Naur 1986, 140), and life expectancy had increased from fifty-five to sixty-four years old over the course of eleven years (World Bank DataBank n.d.). The government had fulfilled many of its promises, transforming slums and unhealthy dwellings into modern tenements (Otman and Karlberg 2007, 112), building a wide range of infrastructure and construction projects, such as an artificial river, transport and communication networks, and providing free healthcare and education (112). These policies translated into a large consensus around and support for a model of political and economic development that challenged the idea of a state-centric and market-oriented world political system.

At the political level, the subordination of economic policies to the achievement of anti-imperialist goals translated into the active support of the Libyan government for a wide range of revolutionary, socialist, and independent movements across the world, as well as the pursuit of Arab unity, backing for the liberation of Palestine, and the establishment of regional alliances with neighboring states (Lahwej 1998). Even though their ideological motivations and ultimate political ambitions varied, all of those movements were seen as a direct challenge to the hegemony of the main Western geopolitical powers (the United States, the UK, and France) and their proxy allies (mainly Israel and Saudi Arabia).[12] As Adom Gotachew (2019, 5) aptly describes, postcolonial "nationalism in the age of decolonization continued to confront the legacies of imperial hierarchy with a demand for the radical reconstitution of the international order." That is, national independence was understood as a revolutionary project that required remaking the relations of domination that sustained the international order.

However, it did not take long before the United States and its allies unleashed a set of measures—including conspiracies, gunboat diplomacy, bribes, economic sanctions, and military bombings—designed to undermine the achievements and ambitions of the Libyan postcolonial revolution. Two major historical processes marked the gradual defeat of al-Fātiḥ: first, the long military confrontation in Chad; and, second, the imposition of international sanctions in 1992. Those processes culminated in a massive military-ideological defeat for the Libyan revolution,

---

12. Libya was accused of supporting numerous so-called terrorist organizations worldwide. For a comprehensive list of the groups that Libya supported, see Jureńczyk (2018).

whose consequences reverberated across all levels of society, and led to major changes in the political-economic structure of the Libyan regime. In 1973, when the Chadian Civil War began, Libya entered the conflict in support of the anti-French group Front de Libération Nationale du Tchad (FROLINAT) and occupied the bordering area of the Azouzou Strip in order to claim it back (see chapter 2). In response, Chad soon became a perfect territory of international struggle between Libya and its allied groups against Western-led geopolitical forces and their regional and local allies—Egypt, Israel, Saudi Arabia and Sudan (Toaldo 2013, 136–38).[13] The draining military conflict, which ended with the defeat of the Libyan regime in 1987, forced the regime to reconsider its international and regional ambitions. The military and ideological defeat in Chad, however, was soon followed by the imposition of international sanctions in 1992 after three years of investigation into the 1988 bombing of Pan Am Flight 103 over Lockerbie, Scotland, which had caused the death of 270 people. The UNSC imposed an air and arms embargo and a ban on the sale of oil equipment and called on Libya "to cease all forms of terrorist action and assistance to terrorist groups" (UNSC 1992).

While overreliance on oil had shown the enormous limitations faced in building a self-sustaining and productive society by the 1980s, the multilateral UN sanctions further damaged living conditions. In response, the Libyan regime, which had already announced a first wave of economic liberalization (*infitāḥ*) in 1987, launched a second wave of privatization in the 1990s, allowing private businesses to resume and initiate, for instance, the creation of private commercial banks. More importantly, this second wave of economic liberalization not only marked the abandonment of those egalitarian economic principles that had characterized the al-Fātiḥ Revolution since 1969 but also witnessed the country's progressive loss of autonomy over its economic policies. Like many other Arab republics, those shifts marked the emergence of a merchant/comprador class (Kadri 2015, 2016), which kept extracting wealth from national resources without reinvesting it for

13. In 1982, the United States intentionally relied on Saudi Arabia financial funds to bribe several African countries in order to deprive Qaddafi of the Organization of African Unity (OAU) chairmanship. See Lahwej (1998, 258-61).

the country's development. At the same time, international sanctions were leading to the steady rise of inflation, the underperformance of the public sector, the rise of smuggling, and the emergence of black markets and, thus, a thriving informal economy (Abdussalam 2006, 101–2).

Overall, economic inequalities became more visible in society and only further widened the inequality gap, resulting in popular discontent, which in turn developed into armed popular rebellions, such as the attempted coup d'état of a group of army officers in 1993. Moreover, those lower classes left out of the country's wealth either increasingly aspired to develop the Western patterns of consumption and values embraced by the elites (see chapter 4) or distinguished themselves by becoming more inclined to support religious-based political groups (see chapter 2). Therefore, the most visible axis of confrontation became the Islamist mobilization in the eastern part of the country from the mid-1990s, supported by Western governments. An important threat witnessed the complicity of two British secret intelligence agencies supporting the Islamist group al-Jāmaʻa al-Islāmiyya al-Muqātila (Libyan Islamic Fighting Force), which unsuccessfully challenged the regime throughout the 1990s.

As chapter 2 will discuss, those years of international isolation, leading to popular unrest and armed struggle, inevitably made the Libyan government tighten security and its control over the population, such as the violent repression of the Abu Salim prison revolt in 1996 (Zarrugh 2018). Simultaneously, to maintain its power, the government began developing new alliances and mechanisms, the most emblematic of which was the creation of the Popular Social Leadership in 1993, established to grant a role for "respected natural leaders"—that is, tribal chiefs. This move sanctioned the merger of formal political structures with informal alliances and more broadly resulted in the institutionalization of personalized politics and patrimonialism. The pursuit of private profit and personal gains—thus corruption—became one of the most important elements that undeniably deepened the crisis of confidence in the political system, translating into political apathy and alienation (see chapter 3).

Military and ideological defeat generated a massive reconfiguration of the material, ideological, and state structure of the regime, making it increasingly repressive and perceived by the population as domestically illegitimate. The state-led development experienced in the early years of the revolution was gradually transmuted into neopatrimonial development, and a class of military-turned-merchants emerged, propagating the importance of modernizing and privatizing the country as opposed to what was considered the rigidity and banality of radical-revolutionary struggle. This process best captures the internal elite division and class restructuring that reigned supreme in Libya in 2004, when the country emerged from its international isolation. Two groups faced each other: the so-called technocrats or reformers, guided by Saif al-Islam and Shukri Ghanem, who were trying to reapproach the United States; and the "old guard," representing the inner circle of Qaddafi's affiliates. Despite Qaddafi having continuously pushed for strong regional cooperation with African countries, which was crucial for Libya to break the UN embargo in the 1990s, his anti-imperialist claims had lost relevance among the population. On the contrary, they were now seen as a diversion from the urgent problems of economic inequality. Therefore, while the corrupt practices of dividing the spoils of public wealth had been institutionalized, unemployment had reached levels of 20–25 percent in the 2000s (St. John 2008). Like many other countries in the Arab region, growing societal discontent over socioeconomic conditions, corruption, and police violence acted as fuel for the protests that took place in 2011.

It is in the last turbulent decades of the Jamahiriya, when Libya gradually abandoned its revolutionary ambitions and contradictory changes were shaking the entire political edifice, that this book starts its journey into the everyday lives of Libyans.

## Collecting Memories in Turbulent Times

This book relies on the collection of oral histories, or what I call "narratives": semistructured, in-depth interviews with sixty-six Libyan nationals, mainly residing in Italy and the United Kingdom.[14] These Libyans were

14. I started meeting them while I was a graduate student at Durham University, during which time I traveled to numerous cities in England, including Huddersfield, Hull, Manchester, Newcastle, Nottingham, Reading, and Sheffield. I also did research in Italy,

between twenty and sixty years old, all men except for three women, and the entire group had left Libya in the aftermath of 2011.[15] From working-to middle-class backgrounds, all participants were working or studying abroad. Those who were studying were either learning English or pursuing academic degrees in undergraduate or graduate programs.

Overall, it did not take long for me to realize that the first reaction of my interlocutors, when answering questions about the past, involved positioning themselves vis-à-vis the events of 2011, whose political nature remains highly contested—a theme discussed at length in chapter 5. The 2011 events had split the population into two major groups: those who were regime supporters, and revolutionaries. This translated into me finding myself in between the two sides, often looking for ways to fend off interviewees' intentions in using the interview as a means not only to express their political opinions about the highly contested nature of 2011 but also to convince me that these were the *facts*. The dangerous implications of this could be seen in the way each question about the past sparked a comparison with the present and the difficulties of imagining a future. At the same time, while this constant polarization characterized the beginning of (almost) every encounter I had, it does not mean that any appreciative opinion or indictment of the Jamahiriya is necessarily indicative of one's political allegiance (or lack of allegiance) to the past regime. On the contrary, once the initial Manichean position shattered, interlocutors went beyond such polarizing logic, when discussing politics and its modalities of interaction in the everyday. While this could appear natural, it cannot be emphasized more strongly, since readers—and scholars—might feel the unnecessary urge to compartmentalize those narratives on one side or the other of the political spectrum.

Moreover, these exchanges prompted me to ponder whether the interviewer could occupy a position that does not clearly support either the "pro-regime" or "revolutionary" vision. As a way out of this dilemma, I

---

interacting with the Libyan nationals residing in Perugia and studying at the University for Foreigners of Perugia.

15. At the time of writing, three of them have died as collateral victims of airstrikes in 2020, once they returned to Libya.

capitalized on my position as outsider, which allowed me to play the role of the devil's advocate and challenge interviewees over their assumptions toward the divisive logic of the post-2011 events. Specifically, I began posing questions to each side, using arguments I had learned from the opposing one. Once again, though, this approach had its (dis)advantages: it reproduced uncritically the present violence in the country. Yet it enabled us, in conversation, to peer into the past with different eyes, unveiling more commonalities than differences that many Libyans shared when remembering their lives under the Jamahiriya.

This process forced me to reflect on my own positionality as a foreign and Western researcher (chapter 2), acknowledging the importance of studying the history of Western geopolitical and economic interference in the Arab region and Libya. I began to wonder how one can formulate a form of political solidarity with the struggle of Libyans and, more widely, the Global South. The dynamics that shaped the fall of the regime—including the protests, the NATO-led intervention, and the regime's anti-imperialist discourse—influenced my personal and analytical understanding of what forms of political solidarity can emerge, issues I engage with in this book's conclusion.

The remarkable recurrence of such a divisive logic, at least at the start of the interviews, also explains the necessity of undertaking this research outside of Libya. While this external position presents a major limitation to the research, because it restricted access to ethnographic material, it also provided an invaluable chance for both interviewer and interviewees to reflect on past political history by going beyond the imposing and divisive logic of the civil war. The story of Ahmed and Salah, both young men in their mid-twenties, captures the relevance of thinking inward about the past when a space to bridge grievances is created. While Ahmed was a member of the regime's army and fought for six months against the rebels, Salah worked as a nurse, helping those rebels who were injured during the clashes. Being abroad allowed me to witness how these men were able to meet, have dinner together, laugh, and challenge their assumptions. However, this chance seemed more a temporary privilege than a long-term opportunity. It remains, in fact, emblematic of the general silence that answered my own question, as written in my field notes in 2015: "I wonder what happens if each one of you goes back to Libya, sticking to his own close community of people. Would you still be able to argue with each other calmly, as you are doing today?"

One important limitation concerns this inquiry: the question of gender. I am a male researcher who was granted the opportunity to interact with male interviewees almost exclusively, apart from three women. Most of the male interviewees introduced me to other male friends or relatives, but they seemed extremely reluctant to have a male stranger interview their female relatives or wives. Particularly representative of this was the way Ismail responded when I asked whether the everyday life of women, and their opinions, differed: "There is no need to talk to my wife, I know what she thinks. Just ask me" (interview 2015). Such an attitude neither encouraged nor facilitated access to female interviewees. Nonetheless, the empirical richness of the inquiry evolved in relation to those male interviewees with whom a process of bonding and trust was more easily established.

While collecting these stories and writing this book, I felt it was important to intervene and construct at times a contextual background, a narrative of events that would enable the reader to place certain political moments or developments in an (inter)national picture. The challenge, therefore, was to recognize those different levels, allowing them to interact while maintaining the primacy of the oral sources. In doing so, the structure of the book implied a departure from conventional accounts of Libyan history that provide a linear chronological account of its political and social changes; rather, the chapters are organized according to the main modalities of everyday political interaction that emerged throughout the research.

**Structure of the Book**

This book's main concern is to understand the everyday politics that shaped the last two turbulent decades of the Libyan Arab Jamahiriya. While the book is divided into four main chapters, each offering a unique and vivid look at the diverse modalities of political interaction that characterized the country, these chapters need to be read as if in a state of perpetual dialogue—in other words, they constantly crosscut, interact, and speak back to each other.

Chapter 2 builds on the interviewees' uneasiness with a foreign, Western researcher. Starting from both their suspicion toward my research and their interest in understanding its guiding rationale, this chapter explores the violent role that Western geopolitical forces played in the process of state formation in Libya under the Jamahiriya. The key element of this discussion lies in the way violence and suspicion became crucial elements of this power struggle, which reverberated in the everyday lives of Libyans. The chapter goes on to discuss the rise, under threat of war and international sanctions, of the Islamist opposition in Libya, which the regime countered with violence and surveillance, framing all those who opposed and criticized its policies as "enemies of the revolution." It investigates the gradual formation of a culture of fear, which passed from fathers to sons, and explores the role of informants, the quotidian practice of reporting and its multiple uses that accrued in the quotidian sphere.

Chapter 3 unpacks three subthemes that focus on people's everyday experiences of the structure and ideological symbols of the Jamahiriya itself. The chapter outlines the contradictory and complex meanings assigned to the figure of Qaddafi, simultaneously a father and a dictator. Then it reflects on the role that dissimulative practices had in the everyday, showing how they reshaped the relationship between individuals, state, and society, which increasingly assumed a transactional nature. Building on those insights, the chapter's last section provides a lengthy discussion of the key role played by corruption, a quotidian culture in which patronage, tribalism, bribes, and favors spread from the regime through society both vertically and horizontally.

Chapter 4 departs from conceptual readings that highlight the unique role of oil revenues and its negative role in shaping Libya's economy. The chapter discusses the emergence of a popular desire for consumerist goods and traces the development a widespread fantasy of building a Dubai in Libya, which implicitly contested the anti-imperialist and Pan-African ambitions of the regime. As these fantasies sustained a quest for a capitalist modernity, they failed to reflect on how the latter had progressively contributed to the demise of the country's infrastructures. In such a scenario, it discusses the ascendant political role of Qaddafi's son, Saif al-Islam, who seemed able to magnetize those aspirations, building on the way Libyans experienced and rationalized his proposals to modernize the country.

Chapter 5 interrogates the extent to which people's interpretations of the causes and effects of the 2011 event, their use of certain political discourses to make sense of a moment that has marked Libya's history, have entered (or not) into a critical dialogue vis-à-vis the anatomy of everyday politics that characterized the country. It reflects on how these two main narratives (*ṭaḥālib* and *jurdhān*) replicated the inevitable effects triggered by the geopolitical violence that fell on the country via the NATO-led intervention and prevented a (self)critical understanding of how Libya got to this point.

In Chapter 6, I reflect on the overall journey of the book and provide some concluding remarks on the opportunities offered by the everyday as both an analytical and political tool to move beyond predominant paradigms across the fields of area studies, international relations, and transnational political solidarity.

# 2

# Violence, Fear, and Surveillance

Why are you interested in Libya?
Why are you studying Libya?
interviews, 2015–17

I always believed that any topic of research could stimulate curiosity among those with whom one interacts. For this study, however, the questions quoted above did not simply inspire curiosity but filtrated a recurring tendency: interlocutors took for granted that an Italian who studied Libya did so because of Italy's infamous colonial past in that country in the early twentieth century. Whether they silently assumed or bluntly stated as much, many Libyans evidently believed that Italians were and still are interested in the politics of their country, particularly in its oil resources. However, as I tried to explain that my research did not align or collaborate with foreign and neocolonial interests, I came to the realization that such attitudes contained a much more political meaning. This meaning closely related to the recurrent appearance of suspicion and fear as everyday forms of political interaction. To study the everyday meant posing intrusive questions about my interviewees' personal lives; it meant, for them, sharing details with somebody who, despite being a researcher, remained nonetheless a stranger, if not an agent. It may sound odd that they perceived little or no difference between a researcher and an alleged agent of the security service of a Western government. Such statements should not be considered unusual. Here is how Ahmed, a man in his early fifties who used to work as a security staff member at Tripoli airport, began our interview in 2015, on a very inquisitive note:

25

AHMED: You are Italian, and you study in Durham about Libya. Well, you could easily be an agent of the secret services [*mukhābarāt*].

ME: But, my friend, I just told you that I am having many problems getting people to trust me.

AHMED: It does not matter if you are from the secret services, they could use your research. Anyway, I do not care about all this ... CIA, MI6 ... if they needed to know something about me, I am sure they already know everything. So, what do you want to ask me?

This conversation, which took place in a little café much frequented by Libyans in Sheffield, was neither the first nor the last time in which one of my interlocutors raised concern over the broader scope of my research. Many Libyans, in fact, did not just question what had brought me to study the politics of their country; some went as far as to avoid establishing any contacts, preferring "not to get involved." The feeling of suspicion was so widespread that, at times, people would completely disappear or avoid answering my calls, despite having initially agreed to meet. Those situations arose both in the UK and Italy. For instance, when I explained to another interviewee, Omar, the difficulties encountered in convincing the large community of Libyan nationals living in Perugia to speak about their everyday lives, he offered to help and made some phone calls to smooth out the process. A couple of days later, he contacted me and explained: "I spoke with a couple of them on the phone and they all seem to believe you are from the intelligence ... that you are an agent" (interview 2015).

Following conventional literature on the Jamahiriya, one would expect that the fall of the long-standing authoritarian regime would have eased people's preoccupations, making them willing to talk about politics. Yet it was not until I met Latif, a retired government functionary in his late fifties, that I started comprehending that the social and political nature of this widespread sense of mistrust did not cohere with the authoritarian hypothesis. Discussing my early concerns over the difficulties that I had encountered while trying to establish contact with Libyan nationals in the UK, Latif unhesitatingly replied, "Most of them do not speak to you because they are afraid. This is the Libyan mentality. You need to understand our history!" (interview 2015).

Latif put into words what I had felt since my first encounters with Libyan interlocutors, yet without explaining in depth the constitutive elements of what he called the "Libyan mentality." His words nonetheless prompted me to start gauging carefully what factors had contributed to make fear and violence main elements of everyday politics in the Jamahiriya to such an extent that they continued to influence present exchanges. Therefore, it became important to step back and turn my gaze inward, thus looking at the nature of the interaction between the Libyan government and Western geopolitical forces, which I—willingly or not—represented to several of my interlocutors.

## Geopolitical Violence

The political history of al-Fātiḥ, and thus the Jamahiriya, cannot be considered apart from the long-sustained military, economic, and diplomatic interference of Western countries in the Arab region in the last two centuries, as well as the consolidation of global capitalism as a main system of economic production. As mentioned in the previous chapter, the 1969 revolution had taken place in a climate of immense frustration among Libyans—and most of the Arab world—about their pro-Western governments and the broader Western presence in the region. Not only did anticolonial and Pan-Arab ideas represented the popular sentiments of average Libyans at the time, but the military operation of the Free Officers had perfectly captured and embraced them. No longer willing to remain helpless, the officers overthrew King Idris and emulated the gestures and ideals of the Egyptian leader Gamal Abdel Nasser. Their quest for independence aimed to install a government that challenged the existing balance vis-à-vis anti-imperialist, particularly Western, powers that wanted to control and expand their interests in Libya, Africa, and the Arab region as a whole (Otayek 1986). What animated the al-Fātiḥ Revolution were strong anticolonial and revolutionary ideals, the political significance of which translated into a revolutionary practice and discourse ready to assert itself via any means, including violence. This phase of ideological ferment in Libya cohered with a wider postcolonial moment in Asia and Africa (Gotachew 2019). The political ambition of Third World countries entailed the reclamation of their full sovereignty over national resources as a right to self-determination, which had also led to the official call for a New International Economic Order in 1974 (Dietrich 2017). For those countries, as for Libya, anti-imperialism meant winning back the power to imagine alternative paths to development and regional cooperation, to regain the power to shape one's economy, culture, and society. The group of revolutionary officers was ready to undertake this battle at all three interrelated levels: ideological, military, and economic. As such, anti-imperialist policies not only contributed heavily to the development of its national and international politics but also had a direct impact on the Libyan people's everyday lives (Mattes 1987; Obeidi 2001).

One of the very early actions that the Libyan regime undertook as a way to break from what it considered a military occupation of its territory was to demand the immediate closure of the English military bases in Tobruk and El-Adem, and of the American base in Wheelus Field (Dietrich 2021). Such measures were followed by the nationalization of the oil industry, as the Revolutionary Command Council aimed to use oil as a foreign policy tool to pressure the West (Lahwej 1998). In June 1973, for instance, while announcing the nationalization of several American oil companies, Qaddafi adamantly refused to kowtow to the interests of American imperialism: "The Americans think that they dominate the World with their fleets and their military bases; constantly defying the wishes of the people of the World. . . . America continues to support Israel to humiliate the Arabs. American imperialism now takes the form of limitless aid to monopolistic oil companies, which refuse to recognise our rights. . . . American imperialism has passed all bounds. It is time for us to give a vigorous slap to the impassive and insolent face of America" (Lahwej 1998, 199).[1]

The Libyan regime perceived Western—particularly American imperialism—as an obstacle to the freedom and development of the Arab region, especially in light of staunch US support for the Israeli-Zionist colonial expansion in Palestine. The United States for its part saw Qaddafi

---

1. Qaddafi's speech at the third anniversary of the evacuation of the American troops from the Wheelus Air Base, Tripoli, al-Fajar al-Jadid, June 12, 1973 (Lahwej 1998). Permission granted by translator.

as a "despotic and authoritarian ruler," the "most prominent supporter of terrorist activities," and Libya as a "stockpile of weaponry" (ElWarfally 1994, 165). As a 1981 article in the *New York Times* described him, "Qaddafi systematically supports rebellion and terrorism throughout the Arab world, from the Polisario gunning for the King of Morocco to the Palestinian Arabs gunning for the Egyptian President" (Safire 1981).

These dynamics were accentuated when the Libyan ideological rationale began to translate into an active sponsorship of the use of revolutionary violence worldwide. The groups supported included the Palestine Liberation Organization (PLO), the Irish Republican Army (IRA), and various African, Asian, and South American separatist and revolutionary groups, such as the Sandinistas in Nicaragua.[2] It is analytically simplistic to interpret the actions of the Libyan regime in terms of madness and rogueness without considering the ideological tenets that boosted its rise. Rather, as a declassified CIA memo from the 1980s perfectly captures, for Qaddafi anticolonial struggle meant "providing military and financial aid to radical regimes," since his commitment of political, economic, and military resources focused on "undermining US and other Western interests in Third World as he sees these as the main barrier to his radical and expansionist goals" (Central Intelligence Agency [1986] 2011). By acknowledging the political valence of anticolonial ideas to the practices of the Libyan regime since the early years of al-Fātiḥ, one can identify a guiding rationale that not only appears logical but also defies stereotypes and aligns with many other revolutionary movements and figures in Africa, such as the Algerian National Liberation Front (FLN) and the Ghanaian leader Nkrumah (Ahlman 2010).

Inevitably, the contest for power escalated between the Libyan regime and Western countries, which were unwilling to sit back and watch the Libyan revolutionaries attempt to promote a vision of unity among Arab countries or support revolutionary groups whose struggle entailed

2. Recent unclassified documents revealed that over three periods (1973–75, 1985–86, and 1988–90), the Libyan government paid over a total of $12,655,863 to the IRA. All of the money was paid in cash, with no bank accounts used (McCullagh, McMorrow, and McCarthy 2021).

a confrontation with Western powers. Their responses gradually developed into a set of measures and rationales that aimed to discipline the Libyan regime, thus destabilizing and containing its political ambitions, which imperiled Western hegemony in the African and Arab region. Such attempts date back to the "Hilton Assignment" in the early 1970s, when the British government and its intelligence agency, MI6, designed a plan to overthrow the Libyan revolutionary leadership. The UK never implemented the assignment, since the US government rejected it after Libya decided not to align with the Soviet Union and thus did not represent a direct threat (Seale and McConville 1973; Davis 1990, 33–34; Dorril 2002, 735–38). Nonetheless, it did not take long before the relationship devolved into a full-scale military confrontation marked by two specific events: the crises in the Gulf of Sidra, and the Chadian Civil War. In both cases, what often guided the actions of the Libyan regime was a willingness to confront the colonial power whose dominance had shaped the country, including its territorial borders.

In 1973, the regime unilaterally proclaimed the Gulf of Sidra an integral part of Libyan territory based on security reasons, and a historic claim to the bay. The claim contravened international law—that is, the International Convention on the Territorial Sea and the Contiguous Zone, which did not allow such unilateral moves. The immediate reaction of the US government was to challenge such a proclamation, yet it did not do so when, in 1977, the Italian government announced the complete closure of and their control over the Gulf of Taranto for the same reasons (Francioni 1980). As Francioni (1984, 323) notes, no objections were raised because "the main factor behind the closing of this Gulf appears to be to secure the Gulf from the unwelcome visits of non-NATO naval units." In the Libyan case, between 1977 and 1981, the US Navy began conducting large-scale maneuvers in the area until, in August 1981, a military confrontation between the Libyan and American air forces took place, resulting in casualties on both sides (Ratner 1984). The regime in Tripoli deemed those military exercises a manifestation of aggressive American intentions, while the US government claimed them to be a simple military routine, even though the American press had often quoted President Reagan's willingness to demonstrate US military might to potential "trouble makers" (66).

The incident did not escalate further because the international (particularly European) community remained largely silent. The dispute over the Gulf of Sidra, moreover, provided two other opportunities for a military confrontation between the United States and Libya, on March 24, 1986 and January 4, 1989 (Silj 1993). On both occasions, while the United States continued to undertake military training within the designated "line of death," the Libyan regime considered those exercises as proof of the US government's determination to strike their country militarily.

Together with the events in the Gulf of Sidra, the US-Libya military engagement also took place via a proxy war in Chad. In fact, when in 1973 the Chadian Civil War started, Libya soon entered the conflict in support of the anti-French group Front de Libération Nationale du Tchad (FROLINAT) and occupied the border area of the Azouzou Strip to reclaim it. Its claim to the territory drew on a rejection of the power relations behind colonial border formation and was allegedly linked to its own peculiar experiences of state formation that fell back on the heritage of the Senusi Order (Burgi 2009, 139).[3] Inevitably, Chad turned into a territory of international struggle between Libya and Western states, especially the United States, France, and Israel (Toaldo 2013, 136–38). In 1979, the United States decided to add Libya to its list of states sponsoring terrorism, and in 1982 imposed economic sanctions; meanwhile, it provided military aid and training to Hissène Habré—who came to rule Chad until 1991—in order to defeat the Libyan-backed groups. The United States also started to create an army of "Libyan Contras" (Human Rights Watch 2016) out of those former soldiers who had been captured as prisoners of war (Nolutshungu 1996, 310); some sources suggested their number was as many as 2,500 soldiers (48). The proactive Western role in Chad aimed to limit Libya's role in the region by supporting the National Front of Salvation for Libya (NFSL), a splinter group of the Muslim Brotherhood, founded in Sudan in 1981 and operating in exile (1992).

3. The legal documents handed to the International Court of Justice in 1993 by which Libya and Chad agreed to peacefully settle their grievances over the Azouzou Strip also demonstrate how the Libyan regime built a legal argument drawing on a rejection of colonial treaties and borders.

During those years, and particularly under the leadership of President Ronald Reagan (1981–89), US government plans to overthrow the Libyan regime intensified. The United States designed the so-called Flower plan, which included two different options for striking Libya: either a covert operation to overthrow Qaddafi with the help of Egypt and the NSFL, or a preemptive military strike in concert with Egypt, which had long abandoned Nasser's ideals and normalized its relationship with Israel under the leadership of Anwar Sadat (Toaldo 2013). Although neither of these two operations materialized, on April 15, 1986, the United States launched "El Dorado Canyon," authorizing the shelling of the cities Benghazi and Tripoli, including the direct bombing of the residence of the Libyan leader in Bab al-Aziziya (Davis 1990, 133–71; Bacevich 2016) under the pretext of "fighting international terrorism" (ElWarfally 1989, 167). What triggered the El Dorado Canyon operation was a terrorist attack that had taken place on April 5, 1986, at the LaBelle discotheque in Berlin, where two Americans and one Turkish woman died (Malinarich 2001). For the US government, it took barely ten days to indict the Libyan regime as responsible for the attack, citing the existence of indisputable proof related to a coded communication between the Libyan embassy in East Berlin and Tripoli. It nevertheless took fifteen years and the fall of the Berlin Wall for German prosecutors to establish that there was no proof "that Colonel Qaddafi was behind the attack—a failure which the court blamed on the 'limited willingness' of the German and US governments to share intelligence" (2001).

The alleged proof, in fact, failed to appear in court and reveal the direct involvement of the Libyan leader when a proper investigation was undertaken in 2001. A German public television documentary aired on Zweites Deutsches Fernsehen (ZDF) Television (WSWS 1998) in August 1988 proposed instead to explain the slow proceedings of the investigation by providing a much murkier picture than the indisputable one that the US government had offered. The journalistic account refuted the American explanation, as it appeared that there might have been a connection between one of the bombers and the Israeli security agency Mossad. In presenting these conflicting stories and the investigation's failure to assign direct responsibility to the Libyan regime, I do not aim to establish the real culprit of the attack on the LaBelle discotheque, but, rather, to show the eagerness of the United States to resort to the use of military violence against the Libyan regime with or without tangible proof. These facts demonstrate how US distrust of the Libyan regime ignited the use of violence against a state considered an international sponsor of terrorist activities. The American investigative journalist Seymour Hersh (1987) concluded after three months of interviews with more than seventy current and former officials in the White House, the State Department, the Central Intelligence Agency, the National Security Agency, and the Pentagon that the assassination of Qaddafi was the primary goal of the Libyan bombing in 1986. Therefore, acknowledging the political struggle that characterized the relationship between the Libyan regime and the West helps to explain how violence and fear became main modalities of political interaction between the global and the everyday.

The political and military struggle between Libya and Western countries reached a major crisis after three years of investigation into the December 1988 bombing of Pan Am Flight 103 over Lockerbie, Scotland. Undoubtedly, the Lockerbie incident represented a fundamental turning point in the history of Libya, together with the military defeat in Chad, and its impact triggered consequences that transformed the regime, as well as Libyan society, in multiple ways. The initial findings of the three-year investigation into the bombing assigned responsibility to a Palestinian leftist group, Popular Front for the Liberation of Palestine–General Command, which had previously carried out similar operations and received support from the governments of Syria and Iran (Köchler and Subler 2002). In 1991, however, the direction of the investigation switched completely, with the discovery of new evidence that pointed to the sole involvement of two Libyan individuals. The attack on Pan Am 103 was now presented as a direct response of the Libyan regime to the US bombings in 1986.

Following this decision, France also reached the same conclusion about the explosion of another flight, UTA 772 DC in the skies of Niger in September 1989, and condemned the Libyan regime. In this case, France accused Libya of targeting the French flight in response to France's support for Chadian forces fighting against the Libyan Army. The Libyan regime initially denounced both accusations as outrageous, yet it proposed to allow the two Libyan individuals accused in the Pan Am bombing to be tried in a "neutral" country under a Scottish court, in accordance with international law (Rubin 1993). The UK and US governments, however, rejected the proposal outright, deeming it a sign of obstructionism and refusal by the Libyan regime to hand over the two suspects. The Libyan proposal was eventually accepted in 1997, but, earlier, the United States and the UK had pressured the UN Security Council to pass economic sanctions against Libya (Rubin 1993, 15; United Nations Security Council 1992). The resolution, which took effect in 1992, imposed an air and arms embargo and a ban on the sale of oil equipment to Libya and called on Libya "to cease all forms of terrorist action and assistance to terrorist groups" (United Nations Security Council 1992).

As with the Berlin bombings, the conviction of Libyan Abdelbaset Ali al-Megrahi in 2001 as the individual responsible for the explosion had numerous flaws. Analysts, journalists, and UN mission observers (Lahwej 1998, 323–73; Ashton 2013; Wolchover 2016) have questioned the trial procedures and the validity of the evidence that identified Megrahi and thus Libya as the sole culprits. Within hours of the explosion, for instance, the CIA had interfered with evidence, and reports cast doubt on its main source, FBI agent Thomas Thurman. Thurman, in fact, had been officially accused—and later barred from FBI laboratories for this reason—of not having formal scientific qualifications and of fabricating evidence throughout his career (Péan 2001, 91–100; Peirce 2009). Moreover, a scholarly analysis by Kevin Bannon (2020) raises two other points: first, he challenges the decision of the Scottish court to convict Megrahi because of incomplete and discordant statements from the prosecution's key witness, a Maltese shopkeeper named Tony Gauci. As official documents show, Gauci was later paid a reward by the US Department of Justice "in excess of $2m" (Ashton 2013) for his assistance with the investigation (Bannon 2020). Second, Bannon highlights the failure of the British legal team defending Megrahi to counter Gauci's contradictory and unsubstantiated claims. Such criticisms resonated with the report of Hans Kochler, UN-appointed human rights observer at the trial, who criticized the lack of "consistency and legal credibility" of the court's verdict (Kochler 2002,

2003). On such grounds, Gareth Peirce, the famous UK defense lawyer who uncovered the notorious miscarriages of justice that followed the IRA bombings of the mid-1970s and kept innocent people in prison for more than fifteen years, described the trial of Megrahi as the "death of justice" (Peirce 2009).

Ultimately, Lockerbie became another important—if not the most crucial—episode in the struggle that characterized the Libyan regime's challenge to the dominant structures of the Western global order which led to its gradual defeat. Lockerbie tells the story of the willingness of powerful Western states to harshly discipline the Libyan regime, even in the absence of substantive proof. Hence, when Latif describes the "Libyan mentality" as one of everyday distrust, which many of my interviewees had demonstrated toward the topic of this research and myself, the political trajectory of the Jamahiriya vis-à-vis the West becomes the first crucial layer to uncover. Understanding the mentality pointed at by Latif requires a perusal of the enduring role of anticolonial struggle and ideology, and the consequent role of violence in shaping the regime's relation with Western powers. It requires comprehending how violence, fear, and surveillance unfolded and defined the political identity, discourse, and policies of the Libyan regime, both internationally and locally.

## Looking for *Zanādīq*

International sanctions, a sponsored coup d'état, military support for opposition groups, and direct bombings against the Libyan leadership not only put increased pressure on the revolution but also translated into more repressive means of governing the population and controlling the regime's alleged enemies. Already in the late 1970s, the Libyan regime called upon dissidents to return home and instructed the Libyan People's Bureaus (embassies) to facilitate their return (Lahwej 1998). The regime considered many of those opponents "collaborators" with Western powers, since they had left their country and enjoyed Western protection as well as access to media channels to discredit the Jamahiriya, thus working against Libya's national interests. The regime had serious concerns about the active role of political groups in exile working with Western countries to destabilize Libya.[4] In February 1980, an official campaign was launched against the "stray dogs" (kilāb ḍālla) (Lahwej 1998, 319–20) that aimed to "physically liquidate" all Libyan dissidents who resided abroad. The Revolutionary Committee members took responsibility for carrying out such assassinations. During the 1980s, the display of public violence in trials and executions became an important instrument of state's control of the population, as Essam recounted to me: "I remember I was a kid, precisely when my family was breaking the fast during Ramadan, we switched on the TV and they were showing some people being hanged. My father immediately switched the TV off. Nothing happened randomly. Qaddafi planned it. He knew that everybody was going to be there, looking at the television, because it is a moment where you sit down with your family, and he really wanted everybody to see it" (interview 2015).

In 1984, during the Muslim holy month of Ramadan, the Libyan regime televised the public execution of Sadiq Hamed Shwehdi together with other eleven men, considered political opponents, in a basketball arena at the University of Benghazi.[5] The public hangings in 1984 were not, however, the first public demonstration of government power

4. For instance, an article appeared in June 2011 in *Der Spiegel* pointing to the existence of a close relationship between the leader of Libyan opposition group Al-Burkān—a Ragab Zatout; a hefty German millionaire, Hilmar Hein; and an American security agency. Their relationship traced back to 1978 in Derna, where the two came to know each other in business, which quickly turned into a partnership aimed at destabilizing and overthrowing the Libyan regime through the provision of fake passports and weapons. Hein was arrested in 1985 by the German authorities after one of his employees went to the police and revealed his company's involvement in assassination attempts on the former Libyan ambassador in Vienna, Iss al-Din al-Ghadamsi, that same year. Hein was sentenced to seven years in prison and found guilty of helping setting up the attack on the Libyan embassy in Bonn in 1984. See Gebauer et al. (2011); and Meyer (2012).

5. Other executions also took place in 1984, such as the hangings of Ali Sassi Zekri and Ahmad Sulaiman in the city of Nalut on February 2, 1984 (ImazighenLibya 2013b), and the execution of Muhammad Saeed al-Shabani in the city of Nafusa Mountain on April 6, 1984 (ImazighenLibya 2013a). In 1997, during the month of Ramadan, six military officers and two civilians were also executed; see Ronen (1997); and Zucchino (2011).

unleashed against those who opposed its revolutionary legitimacy. Many of my interlocutors, for instance, still remembered the reaction of the regime to the student unrest at the Universities of Benghazi and Tripoli in January and April 1976, protesting against Qaddafi's call to take over the universities in order to turn student unions into revolutionary organizations. The regime responded by establishing a military court to stage the public execution of several of those students on April 7, 1977. Over several years, "the 7th of April" assumed a symbolic status for both the regime, which organized street marches against the enemies of the revolution on this day, and political opponents, who celebrated the occasion in memory of grief and resistance.[6] By having the accused men publicly aver that Western countries supported their subversive political activities, the regime turned these confessions into enforcers of its discourse, thus showing its righteous mistrust toward the West and supporting its national agenda.

This deadly combination of violence, fear, and surveillance consolidated further in the 1990s, when the government began facing lower levels of domestic support. Together with the detrimental socioeconomic effects of UN-imposed multilateral sanctions, another source of popular discontent related to the intervention in Chad (Joffé 1981; Gatron 1989; Wright 1989; Koskenniemi 1994), which had turned into a thirteen-year military debacle (1973–87) and resulted in the deaths of almost two thousand Libyans (Vandewalle 2012, 132). At this point, the regime met resistance, as several groups tried to challenge its power. In 1993, for instance, forty-two officers mainly from the Warfalla tribe in Bani Walid, located 150 kilometers southeast of Tripoli, attempted a military coup against the leadership. However, the regime intercepted the coup before its implementation, forcing the same tribe to execute or otherwise punish those officers who had tried to rebel.[7]

6. For more information on the political relevance of this day, see al-Watanona (n.d.); United Nations High Commissioner for Refugees (2003); and Hagger (2009, 107–8).

7. As for Bani Walid and Derna, the regime also imposed an economic embargo on these cities suspected of harboring political opponents. Several interviewees recounted how the regime prevented these town's inhabitants from carrying out activities (i.e.,

The most important threat involved the complicity of two British secret intelligence agencies—MI6 and MI5[8]—supporting the Islamist group al-Jāmaʻa al-Islāmiyya al-Muqātila (Libyan Islamic Fighting Force), which unsuccessfully challenged the regime throughout the 1990s ( Coles 2016, 28–29; Dorril 2002, 793–95).[9] This group mainly consisted of the so-called Libyan-Afghans, Islamist jihadi fighters who had fled Libya in the 1980s to join the mujahedeen in Afghanistan and fight against the Soviets. Coming back to Libya in the 1990s, the group mounted a steady armed resistance to the regime with the firm goal of eliminating the Libyan leader (Ronen 2002).[10] Eastern Libya became the main theater for those

---

building and repairing) that could ameliorate its infrastructure, if not cutting off electricity and water supplies altogether.

8. According to ex-M15 officer David Shayler, the most important LIFG's military operation—a failed attempt to assassinate Qaddafi in February 1996 that killed several of his bodyguards—had been financed by British intelligence to the tune of $160,000. While these allegations have never been independently confirmed, the group was tolerated to a degree by Western foreign intelligence services because it was an enemy of the Libyan regime (Ibrahim 2020). Nonetheless, it has been confirmed that the UK allowed LIFG to develop a base of logistical support and fundraising on its own soil, particularly in the city of Manchester (Brisard, Dasquie, and Madsen 2002; Gambill 2005; Machon 2005).

9. Throughout the 1990s, the British city of Manchester had become the main operative base of the LIFG. As I discovered during my visit to the Libyan community there, many Libyans avoided interacting with me because they had been directly recruited by the British government to return and fight against the regime in 2011. In fact, "the British government operated an 'open door' policy that allowed Libyan exiles and British-Libyan citizens living in the UK to join the 2011 war" (Curtis 2018). It is worthwhile to point out the story of two brothers—Salman and Ramadan Abedi, as well as Rachid Reouane, who fought in Libya alongside Islamist militias. Upon their return to the UK, they all carried out terrorist attacks. While Salman Abedi blew himself up during a concert in Manchester, killing twenty-three people, Reouane killed eight people in London (Thomas-Johnson and Hooper 2018).

10. While in Afghanistan, the group never officially joined the ranks of al-Qaʻida. It appears that a change of strategy only took place in 2007 due to two main events. First, the change was a response to the attempt of the Libyan government, under the auspices of Saif al-Islam's foundation, to develop a peaceful agreement with imprisoned and exiled members of the group. Second, it related to the UK extradition of two of the group's main leaders as part of the rendition program, in which Libya participated (Cobain 2015). At

violent clashes, particularly the city of Derna and the Green Mountains, where most of the LIFG militants either resided or were hiding.

In the struggle against the *zindīq* (pl. *zanādīq*)—meaning "heretic," a word used to label all Islamist-inspired groups—the regime responded with a surge of restrictive measures, ranging from increased violence to stricter surveillance—for instance, the establishment of a special intelligence agency, the Office Fighting Heretics (Maktab Mukāfaḥat al-Zandaqa). On several occasions, the Libyan leader associated those heretics with animals who should be slaughtered, exhorting the population to liquidate them. On July 19, 1990, Qaddafi said: "If you find among you one who says: *da'wa* or *jihad* or . . . *ikhwan*, then you should cut off his head and throw it in the street as if you found a wolf, a fox or a scorpion" (Amnesty International 1991).[11] Similarly, in May 1993, he declared: "If you know anyone who is one of them [*zanādīq*], then he should be killed and liquidated exactly like a dog—without a trial. Do not be afraid. Nobody will arrest you or put you on trial if you kill a heretic" (Ronen 1993, 538–39).

In such a climate, the government ended up relying on the use of aerial bombardment to put an end to the fight against the LIFG, in the areas surrounding Derna. Moreover, in 1996, 1,200 inmates disappeared from the Abu Salim prison after riots over worsening food ratios and medical conditions broke out, and as late as 2011 the authorities had failed to provide a clear explanation of their fate (Zarrugh 2018). Therefore, violence and surveillance seeped into the everyday lives of people, with the city of Derna becoming a primary target. Hussein, for instance, recounted what happened in the aftermath of the capture and killing of those groups: "The regime tied their dead bodies to cars, touring them around the city, and forcing people to watch. They would go to the owners of the shops, to the people working in the banks, and force them to come outside, into the

---

that point, disagreement and a split in the ranks brought Abu al-Libi to announce the group's allegiance to al-Qaʿida (see also Ghubara 2019).

11. These three terms are all connected to Islamic-inspired religious groups: *da'wa* (preaching of Islam), *jihad* (holy struggle), and *ikhwan* (meaning brotherhood, in relation to the Muslim Brotherhood).

streets, in order to watch such disgusting scenes. My father watched this scene, I did not but I know about it because everybody in Derna knows about it." The display of their bodies, as Hussein described, functioned together with other mechanisms of control, including the normalization of language imposed to refer to these groups: "We could not refer to the picture of those men, who were wanted by the regime, with their names, but we had to say, 'This is the picture of a *zindīq*'" (interview 2015).

Salah also recounted an anecdote from the aftermath of an attack in Derna on a car belonging to the regime's security forces. The internal intelligence (*al-Amn al-Dākhilī*) showed up at his house, took his father, and jailed him for a month because he owned the same car as the attackers: "My father had a Mitsubishi and, two weeks earlier, he had brought the car to the mechanic in order to change its color. As soon as he went to pick up the car and came back home, the internal intelligence arrived at my house to seize the car and arrest him . . . He stayed in prison for almost a month" (interview 2015). Although an unhappy coincidence might explain why the regime jailed Salah's father, this episode also shows how surveillance functions not at the level of what one does but of what one might do. It tends to decollectivize people, breaking their solidarities, while simultaneously individualizing the author of the act and alarmingly expanding the regime's grip on the potentialities rather than materialities of people's actions.

The regime's crackdown on the Islamist opposition created a climate of surveillance, where those people who seemed to embrace a too extreme lifestyle often ended up either behind bars or under severe scrutiny. The secret services made use of tiny quotidian details to identify potential enemies, and the hunt for *zanādīq* became synonymous with "to grow a beard" or "to pray at dawn" (*fajr*). This is the story of Abdul Hakim, in 1999 a student at the University of Derna, where the security situation of the town remained unsettled due to the ongoing clashes between regime forces and Islamist groups. One day, a man started tailing him as he was going back home. In a state of panic, Abdul Hakim immediately realized that the man worked for a security-related agency and soon found out why he had been stopped: "My heart was pumping so much; I was so scared. He introduced himself as a member of the security service and then said:

'Your trousers are shorter than usual, and you have some beard'" (interview 2015).

The length of a pair of trousers and the presence of facial hair turned Abdul Hakim into a potential enemy of the revolution to be scrutinized. Why? It is important to note that Abdul Hakim's encounter takes place in Derna, a city the regime besieged and embargoed during the fighting against the LIFG, and that the security agent applied certain filters ("shorter than usual trousers"; "some beard") as way to identify "extremely religious" people who would thus be inclined to support Islamist groups. For devout Muslim men, whose lifestyle strictly follows the sayings—called Hadith—attributed to the Prophet Muhammed, it is considered *harām*, prohibited by religion, to let any garment they wear hang down beneath their ankles, as would be the case with fashionable European trousers.[12] Similarly, it is possible to find religious obligations attributed to the Prophet that require Muslim men to grow their beards (BBC News 2010).

In this process, the state's control was imposed directly on subjects via their quotidian habits and ways of dressing. The most powerful effect of such a modality of political interaction was its capacity to discipline people, who started internalizing those practices and regulating themselves without the need for intervention by an external body, as the story of Mansour indicates. Moving from adolescence to adulthood, Mansour passed from smoking two packs of cigarettes per day, detesting religion and prayer, to what he calls "a more balanced" lifestyle. He decided to quit smoking, grow a beard, and attend the mosque. These everyday changes, however, did not pass unnoticed, and some people began suspecting what might have triggered them: "One day, an old woman, a neighbor who used to come and talk to my mother every day comes to my house [pausing while laughing], and says to my mum: 'What happened to Mansour? Why is he not smoking anymore? I noticed he is growing a beard, going to the mosque. . . . Listen to me, tell him to start smoking again and forget about all this, it's better for him' [big laugh]" (interview 2015).

12. Those religious prescriptions appear in the hadiths—678, 686, 694, 696, 697, 743, 744—attributed to Sahih al-Bukhari (n.d.).

All these regime-sponsored measures operated at different levels, often creating complementary, as well as contradictory, results. First, they were used to counter an alleged foreign-funded opposition threat, thus annihilating possible attempts to destabilize the country, its sovereignty, and its political leadership. Second, they aimed to undermine any form of local support for the group, thus governing the behavior and actions of the population toward the *zanādīq*. In fact, people took upon themselves certain practices of surveillance, so that even neighbors interfered in the private lives of others. This aspect of everyday politics in the Jamahiriya becomes even clearer when one realizes how it impinged upon and insinuated itself into people's private and domestic spaces, influencing family dynamics and passing from one generation to the next.

### From Fathers to Sons

> A father is walking around the street with his child. Suddenly, the child points at a poster of Qaddafi and, in front of passersby, says, "Dad, that's the man you always spit on whenever you see him on the TV." Looking at the passersby, the father replies, "Does anybody know who this child belongs to?"
> interview with Mustapha, 2015

This joke serves as a prelude to explaining how the effects of surveillance on people's lives reconfigured the relationship between fathers and sons, and, thus, a generational attachment to the political sphere. As soon as the child reveals the action of his father in front of passersby, the latter quickly and publicly misrecognizes him. The joke captures how the pervasive atmosphere of control in the Jamahiriya would make anybody turn against their closest family members. The recurrence of childhood memories describing how fear and surveillance seeped into the most private environments, such as house and family, indicate how an older generation of fathers taught sons to be afraid and to avoid politics. As Ali recounted: "Our parents used not to speak about politics in front of us. When—as children—we used to say something wrong, they would warn us not to repeat that in front of other children. They would tell us:

'They might take us away! They might bring us to prison! Don't say those things!' Even as children, we had to be very careful, fear was everywhere. It was like a big prison" (interview 2014). Ali's depiction of the everyday as an experience of omnipresent fear, a "big prison," shows how the state combined the use of brutal force with surveillance, leading to a growing sense of fear.

Another interlocutor, Rajab, described this sense of surveillance as part of the walls of his house: "When there were the anniversaries of Qaddafi's revolution, he always gave speeches and we always listened to them, but you could not criticize him, not even in front of your mother or your father. Maybe there was somebody behind the wall—they would say—listening to us in that moment" (interview 2015). Such a sense of surveillance creates a situation in which people feel constantly observed without knowing it to be true or being able to prove otherwise. Surveillance emerged as both an effect and a supporting mechanism of the regime's increasing adoption of measures used to control the population (Khalili and Schwedler 2010). Rajab's narrative echoes many other narratives containing descriptions of fathers who would admonish their children to be careful and avoid dangerous situations.

Emad, for instance, described the reaction of his father when he, as a kid, started playing a cassette of a very famous Egyptian cleric, Shaykh Abd al-Hamid Kishk, at such a high volume that anybody in the street could hear it. The father, who was sitting outside the house, instantly came in, slapped Emad and shut everything down, saying, "Would you like me to be killed?" Although Emad—being just a child—could not comprehend what was happening, he reflected on the reasons that led his father to react in such a manner: "He felt responsible for protecting his family. I am sure he was speaking about politics with his friends, but not with us . . . As children, we grew up being afraid of the regime . . . If a difference exists with the new generation, it is that they are much more confident than we are. We were taught to be afraid" (interview 2015).

Emad's narrative contains several important points. First, the reaction of his father to the loud sound of a tape playing a speech from Shaykh Abd al-Hamid Kishk (Hammond 2007, 90) stresses the Jamahiriya's perception of Islamist-related ideological and political activities.[13] In this case, the transgressive nature of Shaykh Abd al-Hamid Kishk's tape was defined by his speeches and sermons, in which he used to criticize the formation and condition of Arab secular states such as the Jamahiriya.[14] Second, this narrative underlines how the older generation of fathers taught their children to be fearful of discussing politics. People both internalized fear and transmitted it to their children.

These self-censorship mechanisms concerned any possible action that—as Hamza discussed—related to politics: "As a grown-up, I now understand why my father—with a cousin of the same age—always used to speak quietly, away from anybody else. When I tried to get close to them, he used to say 'Hamza, go away!' Back then, I could not understand why I could sit with them sometimes and not other times . . . because they were talking about politics" (interview 2015). Hamza's father's spatial distance from his son and his murmured talk (which one can also interpret them as measures taken to protect the child), stem from a sense of fear that can discipline and control subjects (Ahmed 2004). Reflecting upon his father's behavior in retrospect, Hamza pointed out how the political nature of fear enabled a subject to foresee the future, thus linking fear to the anticipation of hurt and injury. As a result, fear as an everyday experience characterized the interactions of people in their most private spheres, occupying a central place in quotidian family exchanges. The governing power of fear, its capacity to censor people's ideas and subjugate their behavior, could potentially entail any aspects of life, including seemingly funny and innocuous comments.

Every night at 9 p.m., Jamahiriya state television broadcasted a program in which a presenter read extracts from the Green Book. As Nabil said, Qaddafi's philosophical pamphlet at times contained obvious ideas, such as "Women are female; men are male" or "Men do not have a

---

13. As Hirschkind (2001) also describes, the practice of listening to speeches or sermons by politically contested clerics not only applies to Libya but was also diffused throughout the region.

14. Many of Shaykh Abd al-Hamid Kishk's sermons that openly criticize Qaddafi's politics can still be found on YouTube (Shayk Kishk Channel 2014).

menstruation cycle" (Al Gathafi 2005, 65). These moments vexed Nabil, who would then approach his father and ask about the usefulness of such teachings: "'Why can't Libyan people understand this? Why do we need to listen to it every night?' Do you know what my father always replied? 'Nabil, do not dare to speak like that!' He was afraid, careful because our neighbor was a police officer. Maybe, if we spoke louder, he could hear us" (interview 2015). An interaction between a son and his father, characterized as "careful" and "afraid," captures how criticisms and challenges to the ideas and stature of Qaddafi crossed red lines fraught with danger. While the consequences of such actions did not necessarily materialize into punishment such as torture or imprisonment, the unspoken power of fear seeped into everyday life, dictating how people could act toward the regime, which, in turn, influenced how they interacted with each other.

Mukhtar also recounted a story from his school days in the 1980s. During a lecture in the module reserved for the study of the Green Book, the teacher compared Qaddafi and his companions to the Prophet Muhammed and the Sahabah. Mukhtar intervened and reprimanded the teacher for such a comment, because it contradicted one of the basic teachings of the Holy Qur'an, which states that no human can assume the status of the Prophet. While the teacher initially remained silent, an unpleasant surprise was waiting for Mukhtar at home: "As soon as I came home, my father already knew what had happened in school. They had already notified him, and he told me not to do such thing ever again. He really shouted at me. I was terrified because he already knew what happened" (interview 2015).

In this case, the father did not simply suggest that Mukhtar remain silent; rather, he rebuked his son aloud and punished him. Overall, one would be tempted to argue that these narratives reveal the authoritarian—if not totalitarian—nature of the regime, as expressed in an emerging culture of fear in the everyday. As I have argued, however, it would be an analytical error, for several reasons, to uncritically adopt the authoritarian hypothesis. First, while it is important to acknowledge that violence and fear permeated the everyday, one should also trace their unfolding vis-à-vis the geopolitical violence and assault to which Libya—like many other countries of the Global South—had not been immune. Second, as the following section will unpack, the expansion of a tighter system of surveillance worked in directions that did not necessarily align with the intended goals pursued by the regime—namely, stability and control. While Libyans could avoid reporting somebody they knew, they could also exploit the same system in their own interest.

### *Taqrīr* or *Tiltāl*

During the Jamahiriya, multiple security, police, and military agencies existed and functioned simultaneously: the Armed Forces; the People's Resistance Forces (Quwwāt al-Muqāwama al-Sha'biyya); the Police (Shurṭa), which became the People's Security Forces (Quwwāt al-Amn al-Sha'bī) in 1985; the Jamahiriya Security organization (Haï'at Amn Jamahiriya), divided into Internal Security (al-Amn al-Dākhilī) and External Security (al-Amn al-Khārijī); the Military Secret Service (al-Istikhbārāt al-Askarīa); the Revolutionary Committees (al-Lijān al-Thawriyya); the Revolutionary Guard (al-Ḥaras al-Thawrī); the People's Guard (al-Ḥaras al-Sha'bī), which included the Loyal Security Fighters; the Purification Committees (Lijān al-Taṭhīr); and the Office Fighting Heretics (Maktab Mukāfaḥat al-Zandaqa).[15] Despite a lack of numerical data indicating how many people actually worked for these agencies, *taqrīr* (report) became, according to my interlocutors, one of the most important activities associated with the everyday propagation of violence, fear, and surveillance. This took place on such a scale that, when I started inquiring what people were reporting and who was working as an informant, Ismail's answer was: "Everybody was reporting. We had many people who were invisible. Sometimes they would pray in the mosque beside me, but they were working in the Revolutionary Committees and you did not know. The regime had an invisible army of normal people and they were working very well" (interview 2015).

15. For a contextualized description of each agency, apart from the last one, which is absent from his study, see Mattes (2004); and, for a specific look at the role of the Revolutionary Committees, see Mattes (1995).

As mentioned previously, one of the most powerful effects of surveillance is its ability to blur the boundaries between reality and imagination. It does not matter who carries out the act of reporting because anybody can become a potential object of observation or an informant at any point in time.[16] Emad further reflected upon these aspects: "There were true stories, and there were things that people imagined . . . because they were afraid. At times, they imagined that somebody was listening to their conversations behind the wall. These stories are like rumors (*ishā'āt*)" (interview 2015).

Spreading tributary-like into every aspect of society, surveillance influenced how emotional states such as fear reinforced the control of the state over people's lives. Yet, if anybody could become an informant, then why did none of my interlocutors, when asked, ever admit to being one? At best, they referred to a friend they knew who had worked as an informant. Certainly, I was aware that there were questions related to the political present and the ongoing war in response to which interlocutors preferred not to offer too much information about their past. However, these important questions remained: Who was reporting whom? Were these people working as security agents? What were they reporting? As details began to materialize, answers to these questions provided a more ambiguous picture, revealing the multiple uses and meanings of *taqrīr*.

In the aftermath of the events of 2011, with the fall of the Jamahiriya, some of my interlocutors had managed to get hold of intelligence reports. For instance, Younis, who had strongly opposed the regime of Qaddafi, was baffled to discover that people seemed to report on each other for the most trivial reasons: "It was about a woman who reported, guess who? Her

16. The French philosopher Michel Foucault refers to a structure of surveillance capable of embroiling everyone in a reign of terror as the Panopticon, in which "it does not matter who exercises power . . . [because] any individual, taken almost at random, can operate this machine" (1993, 202). In her study on security and surveillance in Gaza under Egyptian rule, Feldman (2015, 58) also draws attention to this same aspect, stressing how "everybody knows that surveillance is happening, but they can't always pinpoint exactly when or by whom."

husband! [pause] To the Internal Security. She had written, 'My husband has a farm with two camels, but he owns three shops selling milk from camels, and so on . . . How can he run three shops if he only owns two camels?' Why would you report your husband? Maybe she had some personal problems with him. Nonetheless, she wrote to the Internal Security. Can you imagine? It's crazy. You could not even trust your family members" (interview 2015).

The shock of Younis also echoed what Wael expressed in relation to some reports he discovered after the fall of the Jamahiriya. The first report alerted the authorities to a schoolteacher who organized football practice between classes. In it, the informant wrote that the teacher labeled each football team by numbers rather than using revolutionary language: "What the informant wrote was: 'I have seen the schedule, and they never called the teams al-Fātiḥ, al-Ittiḥād, and so on.' The informant meant that the teacher never used Qaddafi's revolutionary language. Then he added, 'See the attached schedule of the games.' What is that supposed to mean?" Wael also referred to a report where the informant raises doubt over the growth of facial hair on a man whose father opposed the regime: "The informant wrote: 'He was Dr. Mustapha's son, and he is growing a beard. He might have become Salafi or something; we should put our eyes on him.' Anybody could write something about you, for any reason" (interview 2015).

As these discussions developed, many interviewees engaged in a debate over the question of loyalty of informants toward the regime. Everyday reality called into question to what extent loyalty to and identification with the ideals of the regime guided a person to *taqrīr*, to report, to work as an informant. There were, in fact, numerous reasons why someone would report on someone else's activities, and Libyans possessed a unique set of words, mostly deriving from dialect, to describe those who wrote reports not as informants but in search of benefits, favors, or advantages. The most frequently recurring word was *tiltāl* (informant), but other words were also repeated, such as *guwwād* (pimp); *zimzāk*, *liggāg* or *firmāt* (informant), and *antīna*, the latter in particular referring to someone who is always listening to other people's conversations and is thus untrustworthy.[17] Despite its variations, the term *tiltāl* is one of those distinctive words that are so intimate a part of Libyan culture that they can be only rendered in its own language; in fact, they are not just synonyms for "informant." Most importantly, they provide insight into how and why people acknowledged and participated in the structure of surveillance.

For instance, Abdul Aziz described *tiltāl* as "someone who informs the regime that Matteo, every day, comes to that café and drinks cappuccino. Is it important? No! But he wants to show that he also writes reports for the regime, he wants to be on the safe side" (interview 2015). For Abdul Aziz, *tiltāl* means somebody who writes reports not to harm fellow citizens but to protect himself, showing his loyalty toward the regime. People might act in this way to engage preemptively with surveillance in an attempt to avoid interdiction; thus reporting becomes a defensive tactic. The social awareness of such overreaching surveillance had two main interrelated effects:[18] first, it enabled people to exert influence, reorienting the use of those same everyday practices utilized to control them; and, second, it hindered the creation of political organization and obstructed the possibility of sociality by turning a neighbor (or a wife) into a security agent.[19]

Ihsan further illustrated the meaning of *tiltāl*, relying on a Libyan saying: "Someone who knows from where to eat the shoulder's meat" (interview 2015). This culinary metaphor, which describes the shoulder's meat both in terms of its delicacy to the palate and the difficulty of eating it, describes the *tiltāl* as a clever and opportunistic person, someone who reports to gain something in return. In addition, Ali told me that,

17. As Ismail explained: "They used to say: 'Don't look at him, don't speak close to him because he is *antīna*'" (interview 2015).

18. Those agents assigned to a *murabbaʿ* (square/area) were also in charge of probing the population's mood. This practice, for instance, resembled what Katherine Verdery (2014, 163) calls "mood reports" in Romania under Ceausescu.

19. I am borrowing this term from the work of Ahmed (2006), who describes orientations as those spaces people occupy in relation to objects and people. By studying orientations, we can understand the web of political dynamics and social relations that define certain orientations (e.g., sexual, political) and the way people can reorient them.

for some people, working as an informant could provide an opportunity for social mobility: "*Tiltāl* is one of those guys who does things just for future benefits. He provides information for free to get something back" (interview 2016). Ashraf provided a similar definition, emphasizing the gap between working as an informant and demonstrating loyalty toward the regime: "It means informant! But if I tell you that someone is *tiltāl* it does not mean that he is supporting the regime. *Zimzāk* is the same thing" (interview 2015).

Through the initial image of "the invisible army," the Jamahiriya resembled more of a police state, where a secret security complex runs silently and invisibly throughout the entire social fabric in search of the enemies of the revolution. By zooming in and out of the everyday, however, we can grasp how surveillance and violence functioned in multiple and complex ways, which defy the monolithic use of notions like authoritarianism. My interlocutors instead suggest that Libyans also got something out of the system—that is, there was some level of social support for the regime as well as willingness to utilize surveillance mechanisms to pursue personal benefits. As Younis explained, the system had "two sides": "There were people loyal to the regime, upon which the regime relied, but there were others who worked for these institutions only for their personal interests. So, when they were told to arrest somebody close to them, they would go and tell them, 'Look, don't go to the mosque these particular days because someone will write a report on you. They will arrest somebody at *fajr.*' . . . It is a two-way system" (interview 2015).

The meanings and uses of *taqrīr* as a common, mundane practice of everyday life were constantly negotiated. Surveillance could also be practiced for one's own benefit, without necessarily requiring one to be a staunch supporter of the regime. More importantly, a complete new and local vocabulary emerged that reveals a growing chasm between individual actions and the idea of the collective good. In other words, the use of surveillance for personal advantage negated the core philosophical principle of the Jamahiriya: the role and action of the masses as a collective. While the Green Book trumpeted the advent of a "society controlled by the masses in whose hands power, wealth, and arms should be placed" (Al Gathafi 2005, 74), the rationality of surveillance that governed Libyan society worked against this same philosophical idea, atomizing society. The growing mismatches between everyday practices and the regime's calls for egalitarianism brought about a growing sense of political alienation, which increasingly distanced the population from the ideological tenets of the regime, favoring instead a culture of individualism, the pursuit of self-interest, and private profit. It is crucial to understand these processes because, as the following chapters will clarify, they reflect heightening contradictions, both ideological and material, at all levels of society. All of them, in aggregate, contributed to the gradual transformation of the regime that, under geopolitical threat of war and sanctions, turned increasingly repressive and, for a great part of the population, domestically illegitimate.

Interestingly, as Libya reached the early 2000s, the ambivalent nature of everyday reporting mirrored the fractions within the regime, which emerged as the country hoped to break out of international isolation. In other words, while the uses of surveillance and reporting partly diminished because the geopolitical threat of war was fading away, they now captured the growing divisions at the level of the elite, between reformists, led by Saif al-Islam, and the old guard, closer to Qaddafi, each one having a different vision for the future of Libya.

## Full Circle

> In the 80s, the regime was very strong, and I call this period "closed minded." Nobody who had different ideas was acceptable. In the 90s, if the person was going to the mosque three to four times per day or to pray at *fajr*, they would put him in prison. Then, the situation changed. It got much better when Libya tried to return to the global arena.
>
> interview with Omar, 2015

Omar's words capture the feelings of many interlocutors toward the changing approach of the regime vis-à-vis dissent and political opposition, stressing how the "the situation changed, it got much better" when the Jamahiriya's long period of international isolation ended. After almost a decade of UN-imposed economic sanctions, which started in the early

1990s, and a tug-of-war with the West over Lockerbie, the internal stability of the regime only looked shakier. The economy suffered from the impact of international sanctions, which had triggered profound social consequences. As mentioned in the previous chapter, socioeconomic difficulties under the weight of sanctions led to several cycles of economic liberalization, which triggered the steady rise of inflation, the underperformance of the public sector, and—most importantly—increasing inequality. As in many other Arab republics, those shifts marked the emergence of a merchant/comprador class (Kadri 2015, 2016), which kept extracting wealth from national resources without reinvesting it for the development of the country. In other words, these changes marked a reversal of the progressive and redistributive policies of the previous decades (see chapter 4). As part and parcel of this process, the Jamahiriya began normalizing its relationship with the West to stabilize its position domestically and internationally. In April 1999 it surrendered the two Lockerbie suspects in accordance with the requests of the United States and the UK. Europe quickly welcomed Qaddafi back as a legitimate counterpart, while the US government preferred to continue to delay the normalization of its diplomatic relationship with the Libyan government (St. John 2004; Zoubir 2006; Ochman 2006; Schwartz 2007). European countries such as Italy, France, and the UK were more eager to accept Libya's rehabilitation due to the strategic location of the country in the Mediterranean. They favored a normalization of Libya's international position because it allowed them to control and negotiate the influx of African migrants, guaranteed a large oil production, and provided opportunities for new financial investments such as arms and technology sales, as well as the development of the tourism, education, and industrial sectors (Genugten 2016, 135). Moreover, in 2000 the UK passed a Terrorist Act listing the LIFG as a terrorist group, thus complying with the request of the Libyan regime, only a few years after British intelligence agencies had helped the group organize a military coup against Qaddafi (Bright 2004).

A major turning point for the rapprochement between Libya and the West took place in the aftermath of the September 11, 2001, terrorist attacks by al-Qa'ida on the World Trade Center in New York. In response, the US government launched the war on terror and, after invading

Afghanistan in 2001, brought down the Iraqi regime of Saddam Hussein in March 2003. Notably, on December 19, 2003, Qaddafi decided to announce publicly that Libya was abandoning its WMD program (BBC News n.d.; Zoubir 2002). In addition to the WMD requisite, Washington also wanted Tripoli to end its sponsorship of terrorism as well as accept responsibility and pay compensation for Lockerbie (Moss 2010). Once Libya accepted these conditions, the United States followed other European states in dropping all economic sanctions and officially reengaging with the Jamahiriya (Kaplan 2007). Not only did this rapprochement reactivated diplomatic and economic ties, but the two countries also achieved major results at the level of counterterrorism cooperation. For instance, the Jamahiriya started providing essential information on the numerous Libyans with ties to al-Qa'ida, while the US government designated the LIFG as a terrorist organization in 2004.[20] Together with the UK, all three countries cooperated in a program of extraordinary rendition, transferring suspects from one country to another by means that bypassed all judicial and administrative due process (Amnesty International 2006). Inevitably, Libyan internal stability benefited from these actions.

In such a situation, fear and surveillance also appeared to undergo a process of change that mirrored the political atmosphere of the country in the first decade of the twenty-first century. Another interviewee, Ali, compared the 1990s as a period where "just a word could have killed you" to the late 2000s, when the intensity of overarching surveillance began to wane: "Since the mid-2000s everybody was talking about Qaddafi, people were cursing him. Even the security organizations, such as the Revolutionary Committees, did not really care or worry about what was being said or who was talking about Qaddafi. You could talk about whatever you wanted to talk about" (interview 2015).

Libya's political rapprochement with the West also improved the domestic perception of surveillance, since actions that had seemed unconceivable in the recent past, such as criticizing or challenging Qaddafi, had

---

20. It is also important to note that, according to the "Sinjar Records" (Felter and Fishman 2007), a list of documents listing all the foreign fighters joining al-Qa'ida in Iraq via Syria in 2007, a large percentage were Libyans coming from the city of Derna.

for many become acceptable. Those narratives, however, do not provide a full picture of how Libyans experienced surveillance at the beginning of the twenty-first century, since many continued to encounter it as a modality of political interaction in their everyday lives.

For instance, the professional experiences of my interlocutors Murad and Ibrahim, which took place in 2003 and 2006, respectively, tell us otherwise. In the first case, Murad clarified that his research did not contain any criticism of the regime; it merely showed that since 1981 the regime had not raised public salaries, while the cost of living had risen by 200 percent (Otman and Karlberg 2007).[21] There was great dissatisfaction among Libyans concerning Law No. 15 of 1981, which was introduced to regulate the salaries of civil servants, substantively freezing them, with only very minimal increases.[22] Therefore, his recommendations to the regime were to upgrade public salaries in two phases: 100 percent immediately and 100 percent gradually. As he reached the end of his presentation, a man approached and spoke to him in a threatening tone: "This guy—probably from the security—was not even listening to me. He wanted to switch the focus from research to politics and he came to me saying: 'Why are you saying this? Are you against the government? Salaries are controlled by a resolution of the government in 1981'" (interview 2015).

Murad appeared frustrated because, no matter what his research work indicated, the man was "not even listening to me" but only interested in his political views about the regime. In other words, he experienced this moment of everyday life as a reminder of a never-ending machinery of surveillance. Similarly, Ibrahim recounted the day he gave a presentation on the lack of jobs and the rise of unemployment in Libya, which was welcomed by a threatening set of questions: "Why are you doing this? Are you against Qaddafi?" (interview 2015).

21. For an explanation of Law No. 15 of 1981, see Otman and Karlberg (2007, 132); on the increase of public sector wage vis-à-vis decrease of state subsidies, see (2007, 142–43).

22. At the time, one of the proposed measures by NASCo to overcome this problem was to reduce the amount of state subsidies and convert them into cash, using it to improve the salaries of public officials (Otman and Karlberg 2007, 145).

Both stories seemingly convey that surveillance remained active and functioning in the 2000s. These episodes, however, also reveal a gradual change of the substance and matter of surveillance; in other words the terrain of scrutiny, if compared to the past decade, had now changed and revealed a different type of anxiety within the regime. No longer linked to the Islamist-inspired opposition, Ibrahim and Murad delivered presentations on the economic needs of the country, thus positioning themselves in a larger, ongoing debate on economic reform and the status of human rights in Libya. Their suggestions were nonetheless treated as possible threats to or criticisms of the regime because, as I argue, they mirrored an underlying struggle that reflected the national reconfiguration of the political elites, who pursued conflicting (inter)national policies for the future of Libya (see chapter 4).

At the international level, the regime took important steps in order to ameliorate its isolation. Saif al-Islam relentlessly pursued open diplomacy toward Western governments, the United States *in primis*, to make Libya a country of primary interest to foreign investors. In 2003, for instance, he wrote an article on "Middle East Policy" suggesting that Libya was "now ready to transform decades of mutual antagonism into an era of genuine friendship" (Al-Qadhafi 2003, 44) with the United States. Inviting a US-based consultancy firm, Monitor Group, Saif promoted a plan to transform Libya into the Dubai of North Africa, thus embracing a more neoliberal model of economic development, requiring a closer alliance with the United States. At the same time, the regime continued to mistrust the interference of Western powers in the country's national affairs, and the pragmatic rapprochement came hand in hand with a public stance that remained in part attached to those same anticolonial values that had characterized Libya since 1969. In 2009, Qaddafi gave a two-hour speech at the UN New York Summit proposing to rename the UN Security Council the "Terror Council." Throughout its last decade, the Libyan regime had often requested guarantees of its sovereignty when signing a friendship agreement with Italy and a Joint Letter of Peace and Security with the UK government (United Nations Security Council 2006). The letter recalled both countries' mutual commitment to refrain from "organizing, assisting or participating in acts of civil strife or terrorism" and "the threat or use of force against the territorial integrity or political independence of either State, or in any other manner inconsistent with the purposes of the United Nations" (2006). At the domestic level, these tensions therefore translated into a growing obstructionism by the so-called old guard, a group of powerful revolutionary members belonging to the military-security apparatus of the regime, who refused to embrace fully the policies of Washington and felt threatened by Saif al-Islam's proposed plans to reform the country. For these reasons, I argue that people's perception and experience of fear and surveillance mirrors this contradictory last decade of the Jamahiriya.

Another story, from Nuri, illuminates this point, especially as Nuri identified himself as both a member of the Revolutionary Committees (RC), a very powerful organization closely affiliated to the leadership, and as a strong supporter of the Jamahiriya. During the early 2000s, while he was traveling back and forth between Libya and Italy, he had taken part in a routine meeting of the RC in Tripoli. Since those meetings also entailed the discussion of people's perception of the regime's policies, Nuri thought it appropriate to point out to his colleagues that Qaddafi's constant appearances on television via speeches and news outlets posed a concrete risk: they could make the population grow disaffected and bored, thus losing interest in the importance of his political messages. Despite conveying his thoughts for the "good of the country," as he told me, two nights later members of the RC paid him a visit and took him to jail. They wanted to find out whether he was planning any subversive activities against the country. Apart from spending a couple of days in jail for no apparent reason, nothing else had happened, but, as he comprehended after this experience: "Do you understand now? You could not criticise him [Qaddafi], not even among us [the RC]" (interview 2017).

It is essential to grasp these dynamics, because they show how quotidian modalities of political interaction emerged in interaction and collusion with the national reconfiguration of elites, and geopolitical changes. As shown earlier, the increasingly repressive turn of the regime requires us to understand how international forces interacted with the mundane, as the threat of war and sanctions characterized the relationship between

Libya and the Western geopolitical order. At the same time, the reduced level of surveillance in people's everyday lives also necessitates an examination of the international dynamics that characterized the Jamahiriya vis-à-vis the West and their effects on its circulation in the late 2000s. In this way, the inquiry into the role of fear, violence, and surveillance under the Jamahiriya comes full circle, showing the multilayered forces at work that enable us to delineate a modality of political interaction and its rationalities. As chapter 5 will show, these (inter)national political dynamics linked to the consolidation of everyday violence and surveillance in the Jamahiriya were so entrenched that Libyans quickly turned to them to frame the events of 2011.

## Rethinking the Boundaries of Authoritarianism

When thinking about violence, fear, and surveillance in the Arab region, one is tempted to identify the Jamahiriya as an authoritarian—almost dictatorial—regime, locking people's everyday lives into a grid of total control and domination for forty-two years. Libya and Libyans appear not only stateless but also powerless in relation to a one-man regime that subjugated and dominated them. My research, however, challenges the core of the stateless paradigm while urging readers not to view the Libyan regime as simply an authoritarian structure of power. To do so makes it easy to ignore how everyday politics interacted with the international sphere. As international sanctions and military bombings curbed the regime's ambitions, violence internally impeded the emergence of relations of trust, legitimacy, and solidarity that could nourish Libyan society, replaced instead by increasing fear and surveillance.

As in many other Arab states, anticolonial ideals and practices lay at the foundation of the state formation process, thus occupying a major role in the political discourse of both al-Fātiḥ and the Jamahiriya. The desire to confront the past brutality of Western colonialism was not limited to the ideological discourse or Qaddafi's rhetoric; it found additional expression in a series of political decisions from the earliest stages of al-Fātiḥ, which undermined the supremacy of Western powers both in Libya and throughout the Arab region. The boldness of the Libyan regime inevitably produced a power struggle with the West that had a significant impact on the unfolding of violence, fear, and surveillance within the country. Threatened and assaulted militarily by the West, the Libyan government began perceiving any internal challenge to its authority as a Western-sponsored attempt to overthrow the revolutionary legitimacy of al-Fātiḥ.

In such a situation, the hunt for the enemies of the revolution generated the construction of a society with an increasingly blurred distinction between the private and public spheres, where violence and surveillance could—and did—invade domestic and familial spaces. When some Islamist groups started mobilizing in the mid-1990s, supported by many Western governments, the ceremonial display of violence that followed, via televised executions or trials, had a lasting impact on society. People not only internalized fear and violence but also transmitted those values to their children. Operating at an emotional level, fear determined how people oriented themselves toward the future in the everyday: first, by pitting subjects against each other in suspicion, reinforcing the regime's control over the population; and, second, by obscuring any possibility of distinguishing between real and imagined threats and dangers. In other words, people's mundane interactions mirrored state-led paranoia and persecution of any potential criticism and opposition.

Just as the regime's surveillance of people's actions shaped their interpersonal relationships, so did private citizens with their reporting practices (*taqrīr* and *tiltāl*). The anatomy of the everyday forces us to rethink the political boundaries of authoritarian control because the expansion of surveillance to the most minute aspects of life conferred to those quotidian practices a sort of power that they otherwise would not have had. In this situation, people participated in and manipulated the system either for their own benefit or as a defensive tactic, thus hoping to evade the grid of surveillance. Those insights question the existence of a single point—Big Brother or authority—from which punitive measures emanated. It was not a one-man regime surveilling the entire population; rather, violence, fear, and surveillance impregnated the politics of the Jamahiriya, spreading from the international through the national, ultimately reaching the everyday lives of Libyans. In the dimension of the quotidian, surveillance entailed a network of bosses, peers, and individuals, real or imagined, who could inhabit the proximate environment, individuals' most intimate spaces. Ultimately, this demonstrates that everyday practices of political control and domination are always influenced by and entangled with international politics and geopolitical dynamics. That said, these quotidian interactions with surveillance linked and contributed to the emergence of a strong culture of corruption. The political valence of this process lies in the way it fostered a quotidian culture based on the pursuit of individual benefit that ultimately led to a backlash against the ideology of the masses and revolution that was supposed to guide peoples' everyday lives.

# 3

# Alienation, Corruption, and Humor

Following the launch of the Cultural Revolution in 1973 and the Republic of the Masses in 1977, the Libyan government established a set of symbolic and ritualistic measures to accompany the implementation of a set of radical economic and political policies. It developed elaborate strategies to propagate its revolutionary vision across society to promote the main values of freedom from and unity against colonial and imperialist powers; reinforcing the concept of the nation over that of tribalism; and supporting Arab socialism (Al Gathafi 2005; Del Monte 2015; Kadri 2016). These strategies included the use of radio messages, newspapers, television programs, patriotic songs, educational curricula, and national holidays, all of which honored historical landmarks and aimed to maintain the population's support for the revolution.[1] September 1, for instance, became the anniversary day on which the al-Fātiḥ Revolution was celebrated, while every year on March 28 and June 11 the regime celebrated the evacuation of the military bases of El-Adem and Wheelus Field by British and American troops in 1970. Similarly, October 7, the date in 1970 on which Italian-owned assets were confiscated and the remaining Italian communities expelled, was made a national holiday (St. John 1983). Those symbolic occasions commemorated wider power struggles that marked the history of Libya, shaped the ideology of the regime, and demonstrated its determination to challenge the hegemony of Western-colonial powers and their state/market-centered vision of the world. However, as the regime fell

---

1. Ritchie (2013) provides a good overview of the relations between television programs and politics under the Jamahiriya.

under the grip of UN international sanctions following the military defeat in Chad, many of its economic and political stances were reversed, and, in turn, people's everyday interactions with those rituals changed. In fact, the government's discussions around the liberalization of the economy coincided with a gradual retreat from a number of policies that, despite their numerous limitations, had achieved more progressive results in the previous decade. The everyday also interacted with these changes, and a perusal of people's interactions with those symbols and rituals reveals a larger picture of increasing corruption and political alienation.

## Madman and Tyrant, Leader and Father

> We know that this mad dog of the Middle East has a goal of world revolution, Muslim fundamentalist revolution, which is targeted on many of his own Arab compatriots.
> Ronald Reagan, 1986

> Qaddafi was the man, he was magic . . . I mean, this was how we thought about him. At that time, we did not feel that it was a silly thing to go and see Qaddafi alive. It was very cool to see him.
> interview with Anas, 2015

Juxtaposing those two quotes—one from US president Ronald Reagan and the other by one of my interlocutors, makes crystal clear how contradictory the figure of Qaddafi can be. Those seemingly opposite judgments were perfectly reconciled in the everyday lives of many Libyans. Was he an exceptional leader, or a ruthless dictator? To read these two statements at face value, one might assume that the interviewee was either praising or opposing the Libyan leader, thus being pro- or anti-regime. Such an approach, however, would not only obscure our comprehension but also offer a merely partial picture of the otherwise manifold cultural and material meanings that Qaddafi captured in the quotidian sphere. In other words, Qaddafi functioned as a "nodal point" (Laclau and Mouffe 1985) of the everyday, a central figure around which everyday actions were oriented and emotions articulated, becoming intelligible only if tied to wider political dynamics, national and international.

For instance, the unique political trajectory of Libya and the Jamahiriya is often associated with such adjectives as "authoritarian," "quixotic," "idiosyncratic," or "bizarre" (Vandewalle 1995, 2006; Parteger 2012), particularly when used to describe the ideas and personality of its leader. As the argument goes, the authoritarian Qaddafi compensates for the perennial absence of state institutions—thus, democracy—in Libya. Unsurprisingly, such claims resonate with those cultural and political narratives in many Western countries that have depicted Qaddadfi's "mad" and "evil" personality. For instance, the quote from Ronald Reagan refers to him as the "mad dog of the Middle East," a crazy leader aiming to radicalize the entire region with his revolutionary ideas. Media pundits preferred catchier, yet more absurd, depictions, such as a "tent-loving dictator who travels with camels and virgin guards" (Roper 2009), or a power-hungry, narcissistic and psychopathic tyrant (Fallon 2011). Another interesting Western representation is the use of Qaddafi's picture, along with that of Saddam Hussein of Iraq, by the Swiss Center for Women, for a campaign raising awareness about domestic violence against women (Publicis Communications Schweiz AG 2016). The billboard, which depicts a woman standing behind a seated Qaddafi, who holds a book (most likely the Qu'ran) in his right hand, conveys its main message via the sentence "If your partner turns out to be a tyrant" (2016).

Similarly, the Hollywood movie *The Dictator*, whose main character—a childish, tyrannical, sexist, anti-Western, and anti-Semitic despot who surrounds himself with female bodyguards—is explicitly based, as the same director admitted, on the Libyan leader (Eden 2011). After Qaddafi's brutal killing in 2011, French journalist Annick Cojean published a book, *Gaddafi's Harem: The Story of A Young Woman and the Abuses of Power in Libya* (2013), in which she recounts the bottomless sexual appetite and evil deeds of the Libyan leader as related by a Libyan teenager who claimed to have been one of several young women kept as sex slaves for him. Despite the seemingly progressive ideas about the role of women in society that had characterized the early years of the revolution, such as allowing them to join the army (Graeff-Wassink 1993), Cojean represents Qaddafi as a man who enjoyed the darkest carnal pleasures, including systematically raping men, women, and children as part of a quest for absolute power.[2] The linkage between Qaddafi and orgies was also made in the Italian media in 2010, relating to the organized erotic meetings, also called "bunga-bunga," of the then prime minister of Italy Silvio Berlusconi. According to one of the women who participated, and to whom Berlusconi referred to as the "niece of Mubarak" because of her Arab origins, the term "bunga-bunga" had been suggested by Qaddafi, who was said to practice similar sexual rituals. Unsurprisingly, this connection was never confirmed.[3]

Investigating the centrality of gender and sexuality to the war on terror, Jasbir Puar and Amit Rai (2002, 119) describe the use of the notion of monstrosity as a "regulatory construct of modernity that imbricates not only sexuality, but also questions of culture and race." They argue that Western cultural and political narratives tend to dwell on the sexual desires of their "terrorist enemies" to simplify complex power struggles, exclude questions of political economy, and—most importantly—attempt to master forms of political dissent by resorting to a banal and often dichotomous scheme of classification. Overall, these racialized, sexualized, and gendered assumptions evince the existence of a core difference from the ways in which the state-society relationship unfolds in the modern and democratic West vis-à-vis Libya.[4] In this regard, as Joseph

2. The same pseudojournalist (Cojean 2014) offers a similar portrait of Bashar Hafez al-Assad in the case of Syria, describing mass rapes as the main reason for the violent turn of the initial protest in Syria in 2011. This theme also resonates with a post-2011 Libyan series called *Phobia*, in which Qaddafi is represented as an evil and bloodthirsty monster; episodes of the series are available on YouTube (LibyaTV 2013).

3. What is known conclusively is that Berlusconi in 2009 had used the word "bunga-bunga" when retelling a joke in front of a crowd about two male officials from the opposition party going to Africa. Kidnapped by an African tribe, they are asked to choose between death and bunga-bunga, which turns out to be collective sodomy. In a post-2011 variation, Berlusconi repeated the same joke, this time with the two officials kidnapped by a Libyan "rebel" tribe (Colaprico, D'Avanzo, and Randacio 2011; Huffington Post 2015; Il Sussidiario 2010).

4. These racial tropes are used to render Libya legible. As Manchanda (2020) emphasizes, the act of representing (the other) is inherently one of conferring difference and creating distance. In its attempt to either capture or re-create reality, representation

Massad (2015) points out, Islam occupies a constitutive role in the formation of the set of ideas supporting Western liberal modernity, which remains, at its premise, Orientalist. Thus, Western anxieties over Muslim sexual desires translate at the geopolitical level. Overall, such discourses reduce questions of contestation and opposition to dominant structures through a taxonomy that demeans the moral attitudes and values of the latter, thus othering the opponent with respect to issues of sexuality, race, and religion. These questions, as will be argued in chapter 5, will reappear prominently on the stage of Libyan politics in 2011 in reference to, for example, the humanitarian intervention, the regime, the West, and African mercenaries.

As such, the narratives of my interlocutors challenge those representations and caricatures used to downplay the political significance of Qaddafi's actions, while preferring to label him as "mad" or "extravagant." For example, in 2008, the Italian government apologized to the Libyan people for the atrocities committed during its colonial rule and accepted the Libyan government's demand that they compensate the country (Pisa 2008). In 2009, after forty years in power, Qaddafi visited Italy for the first time and met with Prime Minister Berlusconi to sign the "Friendship, Partnership, and Cooperation Agreement" (Kashiem 2010) as a form of historical reconciliation between the two countries. My interlocutor Ahmed explained that Qaddafi landed in Rome dressed in a military uniform and later requested to meet two hundred Italian women in order to explain to them Islamic cultural values. Unsurprisingly, the media interpreted his actions as an umpteenth attempt to convert those women to Islam (Al-Arabiya 2009; Hooper 2009; Kington 2009). Ahmed, however, indicated that Qaddafi simply reenacted Italian colonial history upside-down; hence, his actions conveyed a subtler and much more political meaning, one that was purposely ignored by Western and Italian media, since it required acknowledging and vilifying their countries' past atrocities. When Benito Mussolini visited Libya, presenting himself as the

---

reifies its object, gives shape to it, and sets it apart, both temporally and spatially, from the speaking subject.

"protector of Islam," he traveled from Tobruk to Benghazi in a convertible car, and when he arrived in Derna on March 17, 1937, he requested to be greeted by almost three hundred Libyan women.[5] In regard to this point, as the Libyan scholar Mustapha Younis (2014) explains, this gesture of fascist propaganda either aligned with or aimed to imitate other colonial powers in recognizing the importance of the position of women in society, thus using them as an instrument of mobilization to infiltrate fascist culture into Libyan society. Later, he delivered a speech in the main square of Benghazi praising the Fascist empire (Wright 2005). Ahmed elucidates that Qaddafi's arrival in Italy merely replicated Mussolini's grand arrival in Libya. First, he landed in Rome wearing a military uniform with a pinned photo of Omar al-Mukhtar, the indigenous leader of the Libyan resistance against Italian colonization who was later hanged in 1931.[6] Second, he delivered two speeches in Rome, in Sala Zuccari and Piazza del Campidoglio, respectively, where Mussolini also used to address the Italian people, discussing the dangers of US interference in the Arab region, as well as the limits of parliamentary democracy. Finally, he paraded in a convertible through the streets of Rome, and asked to meet hundreds of Italian women. For these reasons, Ahmed concluded: "Do you understand? Qaddafi knew our history, he was a very smart, an exceptional leader" (interview 2015).

People revered Qaddafi's political acumen and considered him a "very smart" and "exceptional" man, aware of the suffering that colonial powers had inflicted on the Libyan and Arab people, which demonstrated the underlying political motives that had always guided the actions of the Libyan leader with respect to Western countries. In a similar fashion, rumors and unconfirmed stories represented another social element used to explain Qaddafi's actions and interpret his extravagant gestures and conducts as originating from his political intelligence: "Once I heard that Qaddafi delayed the landing of the Jordanian king's airplane, who was on

5. Burdett (2010) provides a scholarly and historical detailed discussion of Mussolini's visit to Libya.

6. The grandson of Omar al-Mukhtar also flew to Italy as part of the Libyan delegation.

an official visit to Libya, because he was punishing the king for having signed an agreement with Israel" (interview 2016). On another occasion, Qaddafi was said to have been disrespecting the English prime minister Tony Blair throughout the course of their meeting: "I heard that Qaddafi sat with the naked sole of his foot facing Blair. This is a sign of disrespect in Libyan culture, but Tony Blair could not understand it. Qaddafi was very smart" (interview 2015).

My interviewee Nuri offered a similar episode, recounting Qaddafi's first visit to France, specifically to Versailles, where he was asked to sign the royal guestbook of the lavish royal palace and wrote "We are here" (interview 2017). Apparently, Qaddafi wrote the sentence to replicate the actions of the French general and first high commissioner for the French Mandates of Syria and Greater Lebanon, Henri Gouraud, in 1920, when he made his first visit to the newly occupied city of Damascus and pronounced those words while standing on the tomb of Saladin.[7] These narratives express admiration of Qaddafi's persona and gestures, due to his ability to stand up to any international leader. They represent Qaddafi as a metaman with a unique attachment to and knowledge of Libyan and Arab history and tradition, eager to liberate the country from colonial and imperial yokes. Speaking of him in such terms therefore translates into an appreciation of his ability to give Libya a sense of national unity and independence vis-à-vis international powers. It is important to reiterate that these sentiments expressed by the interviewees did not necessarily align with the regime, but they were due to their perception of the loss of these values (national sovereignty, foreign interference, etc.) in the aftermath of 2011, deemed as a selling-off of the country to the West (interviews 2015–17).

Qaddafi's exceptional grandeur enabled a predisposition on the part of my interlocutors to describe him as possessing a supernatural and

---

7. For a good historical recount of this episode, see Provence (2017, 3) who writes that "once in Damascus Gouraud went directly to the tomb of Saladin. In the garden outside the small tomb building, Gouraud delivered a speech in which he ignored the small crowd of anxious Damascene onlookers before him, and instead addressed Saladin directly, proclaiming, 'arise Saladin, we have returned, and my presence here consecrates the victory of the Cross over the Crescent'."

metaphysical dimension, thereby portraying him as immortal. Several spoke about Qaddafi's abilities to survive numerous attempts on his life, such as during a planned visit to his father's tomb. On that occasion, Qaddafi canceled the visit at the last minute, "as if he knew that somebody had planted a bomb there." Another interlocutor, Latif, offered an exemplary narrative depicting Qaddafi as an ethereal, all-knowing, and God-like figure. One day, Latif's cousin, who worked as a security guard for the regime, joined a convoy of twelve cars being sent to Derna to fight the Islamist groups that had started rebelling against the regime. Latif told me that, when the convoy reached the bridge of Wadi al-Kuf, Qaddafi ordered it to stop because he wanted to observe Derna through a pair of binoculars. While all the guards stayed where they were, only Qaddafi and Latif's cousin stepped out of the cars: "Now, think about what kind of personality Qaddafi had! As they were out, my cousin started thinking to himself: 'The only thing I did in my life has been working for this man, and he messed up so much in the world. What if I push him down now?'" As soon as the cousin started entertaining these dangerous thoughts: "Qaddafi turned around, looked deeply into his eyes, and said, 'What are you doing here?' My cousin replied, 'I am with you, in case you need something.' But Qaddafi told him to sit in the last car of the convoy and drive back to his house. He told him to leave . . . Qaddafi was not normal, he was very charismatic . . . but also intelligent, superior in a way. He could read into your eyes" (interview 2017).

The magnitude of Qaddafi's charisma expanded to those aspects of surveillance and discipline of the self that also defined everyday life in the Jamahiriya. Qaddafi's immortal character included a capacity to penetrate and understand people's deepest and obscurest thoughts ("He could read into your eyes"), thereby anticipating any threats to his life. A famous popular joke reinforces this aspect, trivializing any attempt to kill or plot against him: "Qaddafi, Jallud and Younis are standing on the top of al-Fātiḥ Tower in Tripoli. While Qaddafi stands in front of them looking at the city, Younis and Jallud begin arguing about whether and who should push him down. 'You do it!' 'No, c'mon! You do it!' In the end, Jallud decides to push him down, but Qaddafi flies away" (interviews 2015). It does not matter how hard Qaddafi's closest affiliates are trying to plot his killing: he flies and survives. The joke depicts Qaddafi as a man who, in surviving assassination attempts, could abandon the sphere of the terrestrial and reach a metaphysical dimension.[8]

Numerous labels and names were used to describe Qaddafi, including "leader," "brother," "teacher," "engineer," "warrior," and "my love."[9] The Libyan leader not only invaded materially the sphere of the everyday life through his portraits, speeches, and quotes appearing on billboards, office walls, television programs,[10] banknotes, stamps, T-shirts, and watches.[11] Qaddafi also was perceived as an intangible leader, as "more than a man," whose traits astonished and fascinated people to such an extent that everybody would grab a chance to see him alive.[12] The sensory experience of seeing him allowed people to associate a material body with a man whose presence was otherwise perceived as both volatile and pervasive in everyday life.

Every year on September 1, the regime celebrated the anniversary of the al-Fātiḥ Revolution. People gathered in the main squares of their towns and cities while Qaddafi delivered an hours-long speech televised nationwide and as numerous other activities aimed at celebrating the revolution took place. Farag, for instance, told me that on one of these anniversaries of the revolution, the news spread that Qaddafi and his convoy was passing through Misrata via Tripoli Street. As soon as he and his friends heard this, they rushed to attend the event because they "wanted to see Qaddafi from close up." As Farag recounted, "The security level was higher than ever," the extraordinary presence of police officers obstructed their view,

8. See Schatzberg's (2001) comparative analysis of African leaders, where he argues that their persona is often associated with the capacity to muster or play with occult practices.

9. The interviewees mentioned how all those words were used to address Qaddafi.

10. Varzi (2006) makes a similar argument on the case of postrevolution Iran.

11. Stocker (2012, 96–136) carefully reconstructs the regime's numerous rituals and efforts to occupy and control symbolic space in Libya.

12. Similarly, Khosrokhavar (1993, 209) describes the role of Ayatollah Ruhollah Khomeini in the aftermath of the Iranian Revolution in 1979: "The Guide is between human and super-human, between real and metaphysical; he is more than a man" (my translation).

and nobody was allowed to leave the sidewalk. A fleet of huge black cars—Toyota Land Cruisers—with tinted windows arrived, making it impossible for onlookers to find out which car the leader was in, yet people kept cheering, hoping to see him in the flesh. The background story already reveals the emotional potency of Qaddafi's cult of personality. Farag, however, further confirmed its magnitude when he paused to reflect on those moments: "At that time, it was a silly thing to do but, as students, we really planned to see him alive, from close up" (interview 2015).

It is evident that such ceremonies functioned as a tool to make visible the regime's dominance ("higher level of security") and unity ("big cars, many people"), while centering the emotionality of the social toward the persona of the leader. However, the everyday is not a site of total control and domination; rather—as I argued in the previous chapter—subjects neither blindly supported such ceremonies and rituals nor refused to passively accept them.[13] Farag's narrative captures a quotidian experience of the magical aura surrounding Qaddafi, revealing the role played by emotions in mediating subjective and social experience.[14] Statements like "We wanted to see him close" tell us how Farag's wonder and awe circulated and reinforced an existing perception of the leader in the Jamahiriya. Such emotions moved people, physically and emotionally, because people imagined the leader as a man possessing special characteristics. However, Qaddafi could not be special or exceptional without the enactment of these rituals.

Khaled, in reflecting on his graduate years at the University of al-Fātiḥ in Tripoli as a law student, offered a similar story. Describing an occasion when Qaddafi was invited to give a speech to the University of Tripoli in 2005, Khaled admitted: "It didn't matter if he was a good or bad leader. Qaddafi was a leader, he was everywhere, in streets, in international news, on dinars, in books . . . I had a chance to see him alive, and so I went to sit

13. Either way, these rituals contributed to reproducing the banality and mundanity of the leader's magnitude. See also Navaro-Yashin (2002, 129), who makes a similar argument in the case of Turkey.

14. The economy and circulation of emotions produces boundaries, thus structures of power. As Ahmed (2004, 71) writes, "Emotions may involve 'being moved' for some precisely by fixing others as 'having' certain characteristics."

in the hall. Everybody wanted to see him close up" (interview 2015). The centering of public emotions in the persona of the leader functions as a reminder of hierarchies in society. Nonetheless, I argue that the desire to "see him close up" also demonstrates how people actively supported and reinforced the exceptional qualities of Qaddafi through their mundane behaviors. This aspect is linked, in fact, to the more concrete picture of the leader that my interlocutors offered, framing its legitimacy in those gendered terms that characterize patriarchal family life: Qaddafi as the father.

Undoubtedly, many popular songs praised Qaddafi as "our father" (abūnā), "my love" (ḥabībī), or "the light in the midst of the darkness."[15] The title of one song in particular that began circulating in 2011 exemplified the paternal structure of society and its legitimacy: "We are one family and he is our father" (4Gaddafi 2012). Although the lyrics of the song never mention the identity of the father, the overall message of this regime jingle is clear: Qaddafi is the father, and the family is called to respect his role and authority. In 2011, during an interview in which Qaddafi was asked to comment on the reasons for the ongoing protests, he replied, "Against me for what? I am not the president. They love me, all my people are with me. They all love me! They will die to protect me, my people" (BBC News 2011).

Qaddafi's answer does not show how "unfit and disconnected from reality he is" (Al-Arabiya 2011) as stated by the then US secretary of state Condoleeza Rice.[16] Rather, his reply reveals how the relationship of love and dependency that tied ruler and ruled resembled a father-family connection. The statement "They all love me" simply demonstrates that the image of the father was well established, since economic and emotional dependency connected the ruled to the rulers, like the father to his children. Qaddafi, therefore, was often depicted by my interlocutors as a father figure who provided for his people:

15. Some popular songs praising Qaddafi are available online (mp3libya 2013; Green Rebel 2013).

16. See also an article from the *Telegraph*, where Qaddafi's words are described as part of "a typical flourish of the dictator's bizarre, saber-rattling and increasingly self-delusional rhetoric" (Ford-Rojas 2011).

I am proud and honored to have lived twenty-three years of my life under Qaddafi.

I am proud to have had him as a father.

He took care of us like a father! (interviews 2015–16)

Other interviewees described him as the father who betrayed his family:

Think as if your father has money and he is not giving it to you and your brothers . . . but to someone else.

It's like knowing that your father has so much money, but he is spending this money outside the house, not for his family. (interviews 2015)

While interpretations vary on the ways in which the father provided for the family and offered protection, the adoption of the metaphor of the father resonates with the political discourse that the regime propagated for a long time before the 2011 events. Qaddafi was addressed by the term *sīdī sabīb* (the knight), a Libyan expression used to convey great reverence and respect. As my interlocutors explained to me, although a father can be addressed with the word *sīdī* (my master), *sīdī sabīb* was only reserved for Qaddafi (interviews 2015–16). It also shows that the structure of political authority in Libya cohered with a traditional pattern of social relations that privileged patriarchy and was not simply imposed on society.

This can be seen in a joke about Qaddafi that unveils the dominant gendered terms structuring society. It involves Safiyya, Qaddafi's wife, who comes out of her house to throw out the garbage and encounters a man sitting on a nearby fence who calls up to her: "Safiyya! Safiyya! Do you have a pussy?" Feeling cross upon hearing such a rude question, Safiyya decides to approach her husband, Muammar, to find out how to deal with such an insolent man. Muammar suggests providing an affirmative response should she encounter the man again. The following night Safiyya goes outside to take out the garbage, and, as she starts walking back into the house, the man asks the same question. This time Safiyya confidently replies, "Yes, I do!," and the man promptly replies: "Well, tell your husband to busy himself with it because he has been screwing us in the ass for forty years!" (interview 2015).

This joke hints at Qaddafi's perverted pleasures; he appears to enjoy "screwing in the ass" the Libyan populace rather than an appropriate form of sexuality—that is, having sex with his wife. It mocks Qaddafi's power by casting doubt on his masculinity, hinting at effeminacy. Yet in positing the Libyan nation as being sodomized, Qaddafi occupies a powerful and active role vis-à-vis the powerlessness of Libyans, reproducing the same structure. According to the prevailing sexual narrative that ascribes a domineering role to the penetrator (Goldberg 2010, 202), the joke mocks the authority of the leader while simultaneously revealing the social centrality of patriarchal authority.

Libyan society has reproduced such a political vision in its interaction with the masculinist parameters of the regime that are part and parcel of (inter)national politics, as revealed by the logic of humanitarian intervention aiming to protect the lives of the Libyan people. The politics and discourses of protection—built around the binary logic of protected and protector (Young 2003)—legitimize various power relations that connect the domestic and international levels. But these are also mired in historical relations of domination, imperialism, and colonialism that served to "protect" subjected peoples by violence and silence (Nicholas and Agius 2018, 97). The logic of humanitarian intervention, or the Responsibility to Protect (R2P), is one that allows for the utilization of violence by some actors to do good while reproducing an ethos of masculinity (Orford 2003, 11). Such a vision of power via sexuality reemerged upside-down in another fundamental historical moment: Qaddafi's capture in October 2011. When the revolt took place, it emerged suddenly in the gesture of the rebels, who literally sodomized Qaddafi with a bayonet to degrade and humiliate him (Chulov 2012).[17]

Another important factor that contributed to the glorification of Qaddafi's persona was his renunciation of any official position within the

17. A video also exists showing such images (see Americaisevil1 2011).

Jamahiriya. In 1978, Qaddafi retired formally from any institutional role (Vandewalle 2006, 28), conferring upon himself only the title of "Brotherly Leader and Guide to the First of September Great Revolution of the Great Socialist People's Libyan Arab Jamahiriya." His philosophical concept was the realization of the "government of the masses" through the elimination of institutional intermediaries—political parties, parliaments, leaders or tribes—which were considered impediments to democracy (Al Gathafi 2005, 63). However, when the masses struggled to embrace the righteous revolutionary path, the "father" or other "revolutionary" organs intervened. The multiple meanings inscribed on Qaddafi's image indicate that Libyans accepted some of these meanings and denied others. For instance, while they were mesmerized by and attracted to it, they also acknowledged its unjust and at times brutal character. They did not fail to perceive those contradictions and abuses of power; rather, their everyday actions and thoughts replicated those same contradictions.

For instance, Saad told me that, when the Libyan regime was forcibly sending people to fight in Chad in the 1980s, killing or jailing those who refused to go, Qaddafi appeared on TV and acted as if he did not know what was happening: "He was the 'Leader of the Revolution' and he did not know anything about this. In fact, after three years of war, one day he came on television and said, 'I heard that you have been fighting in Chad. Can you tell me why?' Can you imagine? He asked, 'Can you tell me why?'" (interview 2017).

Saad told me that he thought Qaddafi was messing with his people. While the regime had been at war with Chad for more than ten years, recruiting (at times, forcibly) people as fighters, the Libyan leader appeared naïve and unaware of these events. Ibrahim described two similar episodes, which several other interviewees also mentioned. In 1995, under international sanctions, the Jamahiriya started importing Hyundai cars with "very bright colors—orange, green, and yellow—and a very funny shape." Ibrahim clarified that, although the regime subsidized the purchase of these cars, popular discontent grew around their color and brand to such an extent that people referred to them as "a bag of candies." In that year, during one of his speeches, Qaddafi addressed the population: "I opposed one of the People's Committees because they delivered me a car whose color I disliked. So, I started looking for someone who wanted to swap his car with mine." During the same speech, Qaddafi also said, "Can you imagine that this year I didn't have enough money to buy a goat or a lamb to slaughter for Eid al-Adha? I needed to go and borrow money from my friend, Abd al-Salam Jallud" (interviews 2015).

It is traditional to celebrate Eid al-Adha, an annual Muslim festivity, with the slaughter of a goat or lamb, but it is also a religious duty to help a fellow believer in need, which explains why Qaddafi turned to his friend Jallud for help. After presenting those episodes, Ibrahim reflected on why Qaddafi said those things and imagined two different possibilities: "Either he wanted to say, 'I am a poor person, I am like you, and I go ask my fellow citizens, I don't engage in corruption,' or, if I try to think beyond what is saying, he is just trying to fool the people, and he did not pay attention to them. He treated them like sheep, like nothing. Maybe that was the reality" (interview 2015).

The words of my interlocutors catch the contradictions of the leader, conveying a sense of cheating and disrespect, which is exemplified in other expressions they used to compare the treatment of Libyans to animals:

He treated us like sheep.

He treated Libya as his farm and the Libyans like animals. (interviews 2015–16)

In such a situation, where the exceptional stature of the leader raised disappointment and criticism, Libyans turned toward satire and humor to illustrate how they perceived Qaddafi's grandeur and charisma: "Qaddafi and *Shaīṭān* (Satan) are sitting together. *Shaīṭān* proposes to Qaddafi to organize something malicious against the people. Thrilled by such idea, Qaddafi whispers something into *Shaīṭān*'s ear, who replies, 'That's too much! You are really evil!'" (interview 2015). The benevolent and protecting father can shock the most merciless creature, the representation of evil par excellence, Satan. The joke has a religious weight because, as the Libyan leader surpasses Satan, he embodies the latter's traits, becoming a force of evil who distracts Man from goodness while showing arrogance toward God (see Esposito 2003). In addition, it echoes Islamic-derived criticisms of Qaddafi. For example, some interviewees pointed out that Qaddafi was not "a real Muslim" (interview 2015) because he prohibited people from visiting *al-Kaʿba* in Mecca for political reasons (interview 2015)—as a form of retaliation against Saudi Arabia—or devalued the relevance of the *Sunna* as a source of religious knowledge (interviews 2015).[18] Interestingly, during the period of international embargo, the Libyan government openly defied it by sending a plane of Libyan pilgrims to Saudi Arabia for hajj.

Other jokes also mock the support Qaddafi enjoyed at the popular level, unveiling its fake and forced character:

> Gamal Abdel Nasser, Saddam Hussein and Muammar Qaddafi go out hunting, and their revolutionary companions accompany all of them. As the hunting starts, the first one to shoot is Nasser. He takes his rifle, aims a bird and fires. Two birds go down. Everybody starts cheering Nasser: "He is the Greatest! He is the Greatest! He killed them all!" Then, it is the turn of Saddam Hussein, who takes his rifle, aims the target and fires. One bird is wounded. All his supporters start cheering: "He wounded a bird, the bird *will* die. He is the Greatest!" At last, Qaddafi takes his rifle, aims at the birds, and fires. His shot misses them all. At first, everybody remains silent. Then all his supporters start cheering: "Look, the birds *are flying dead!*" (interview 2015; my emphasis)

In a slightly different version of this joke, the three rulers ask their supporters to sacrifice themselves by jumping from a bridge. While political support for Nasser is overwhelming and partial for Saddam, only one man jumps over the bridge for the Libyan leader. When Qaddafi immediately welcomes the man's gesture and promises to fulfill any of his wishes, the man looks at him and replies: "Bring me the one who pushed me" (field notes 2015).

---

18. The Sunna is the amount of verbally transmitted record of the teachings, deeds, and sayings of the Islamic prophet Muhammad, that—together with the Qurʾan—constitute the most important source for Islamic theology and law.

Both jokes capture the defeating trajectory of Pan-Arabism, showing how the overwhelming support for Nasser's revolution is now replaced by a fictional, almost coercive, support for Qaddafi. During the hunting expedition, he completely misses the target, but his supporters keep cheering him, based on a lie: the birds are *flying dead*.[19] The second joke stresses instead how coercion lay at the basis of people's support for Qaddafi, and—together with the joke that follows—captures more clearly the role played by surveillance: "One day Qaddafi decides he wants to go to the cinema. Since he does not want people to recognize him, he dresses up like a Bedouin and goes to the cinema. During the screening, the movie shows Qaddafi. Everybody in the cinema immediately stands up and starts cheering for him, while Qaddafi remains seated. Suddenly someone from the back row slaps his head and says, 'Hey, stand up and start cheering! Otherwise, they will come and take you!'" (interview 2015).

Humor provides a safety valve, a space for laughter that ridicules those in power without allowing them to access such a space. More importantly, they constitute a form of quotidian cynicism, because, while people are very aware of the difference between mask and reality, they continue to wear the mask.[20] Critical and derisory narratives perform the necessary work for subjects to preserve this pretense, surviving the official sphere via a conscious distance (Yurchak 1997).

This modality of political interaction offered opportunities to maneuver the codes and rituals of power. For instance, in 2000, Ali, together with other students, started organizing walks to address the university's failure to pay their scholarships on time. As he recounted, the head manager of the university not only tended to withhold those payments for several months but also kept one or two payment rates for himself. A walk, therefore, was a form of protest consisting of a group of students blocking the main road to the university, holding a picture of Qaddafi and shouting:

19. In reference to the postcolonial situation of Africa, where dissimulation appears to be the main modality of interaction between the state and society, Mbembe (2001, 120) defines this modality of political interaction as regimes of unreality, or *regime du simulacre*.

20. See note 4 in chapter 1.

"We are here by the name of Qaddafi and you cannot tell us what to do. Otherwise you are against Qaddafi." As Ali recounted, the use of Qaddafi's picture was a "red line" for everybody, from the police to the secret services: "Qaddafi's picture saved us. Qaddafi saved me [laughing]. Qaddafi loved people holding his pictures. Nobody could touch us then, neither the police nor the intelligence. It was like a red line, and they stopped harassing us because the 'Leader of the Revolution' was one of us [laughing]" (interview 2017). The students' use of Qaddafi's picture guaranteed legitimacy and protection to their protests, allowing them to challenge the power holders without being held accountable.

Similarly, Musa told me that a couple of days before the September 1 anniversary, a man came into his shop to sell pictures of Qaddafi. Although a refusal to buy such a picture could be interpreted as a sign of opposition toward the regime, Musa replied to him: "'How dare you sell those pictures! The pictures of our Father should be given for free to his people.' The man was shocked. He didn't say anything, he gave me a bad look, because I tricked him, and he left [big laugh]" (interviews 2015). The man was trying to raise money by playing on people's fears, but Musa confronted him by turning the power of the leader in his favor. Both men referred to Qaddafi and assigned to his image a certain meaning, as long as it protected their own interests.

The insistence on the figure of one man, compensating for the so-called lack of a state, or statelessness, offers a partial and historically static picture of the politics of Libya. A closer look suggests instead that Western overfocus on Qaddafi was purposefully mobilized to present a picture of the state-society relationship as completely disarticulated, rather than based on a politically conscious and engaged population. In this manner, the nature of the long-standing anticolonial practice and ideology that supported and prompted the revolution could be easily obliterated. They present a caricatural and authoritarian image of Qaddafi to avoid considering more pressing and sensitive political issues, including Western military and political interference in the Arab region. On an everyday basis, a similar dynamic developed. Whereas we might be tempted to suggest that a cult of personality was superimposed by the regime (if not Qaddafi himself) on people's lives, the narratives of my interlocutors demonstrate that the figure of the leader became a useful tool to mobilize, when needed, for reasons other than regime's authority or surveillance. People reused and reenacted certain rituals in a way that at times reproduced their symbolic meanings and at other times shifted them. In other words, they were also able to muster those practices for their own benefit. All of these actions further heightened the leader's stature and magnitude to such an extent that immortal and God-like meanings were inscribed on the body and figure of the leader, whose representation filled the space of the everyday and functioned as a nodal point.

At the same time, it is important to point out that the political magnetism of one man also related to the obstacles encountered in the institutionalization of a system of political representation, and its wealth of ideas, that aimed to challenge a state- and market-centered vision of the world. Under constant geopolitical threat of war and the grip of international sanctions, the gradual defeat of the Libyan revolution also materialized in a progressive alienation of the ruling class and the population toward its ideals and symbols. This becomes clearer when we compare the Green Book's vision of the way society could have functioned with the memories of my interlocutors.

### The Green Book and the Revolutionary Committees

> Each village in the country—and we have like 360 of them—contained a People's Committee, which were like small parliaments. And every time they made a decision, the leader of the People's Committee passed it on to the main parliament, the People's Conference, which made decisions based on all these others.
> interview with Awad, 2015

The launch of the Jamahiriya triggered the transformation of the whole of Libyan society in accordance with the philosophical directives outlined in the Green Book. The theory of direct democracy reshaped the country's decision-making process, as Awad succinctly summarizes above. The decisions made by the popular committees (*al-Lijān al-Sha'biyya*) formed the basis for those collective resolutions formulated by the People's Conference (*al-Mu'tamar al-Sha'bī*) at the national level. In so doing, the system allowed everybody to participate, bringing to light the so-called people's authority (*al-Sulṭa al-Sha'biyya*). The Green Book aimed to provide a radical philosophical and practical alternative to the state- and market-centered vision of the world, challenging the idea of parliamentary democracy. It was part of a larger ideological apparatus that aimed at mobilizing the masses and directing their political consciousness. To promote such a vision, the regime also took innovative measures such as relying on international celebrities to publicize Qaddafi's political treatise. For instance, my interlocutor Mohammed remembered seeing Bebeto, a well-known Brazilian footballer, pictured with a copy of the Green Book in the sport magazine the *Echo* (interview 2015). Also, the regime established a center for studying the Green Book (Howden 2011) where numerous symposia were organized to discuss its philosophical relevance. In addition, the regime tried to educate people about those principles from a very young age.[21] Students, for instance, were asked to replicate the People's Committees in their schools and classes, creating smaller versions of the Jamahiriya: "When I was in primary school, elections were organized to vote for a leader in the class, who would then become the class representative in the People's Political Conference (al-Mu'tamarā al-Sha'bī al-Siyasī) at the school level, and we used to call him, for example, Omar Mukhtar" (interview 2014).[22]

Also, specific modules were assigned in primary or secondary school, such as "The Society of the Jamahiriya" (al-Mujtama' al-Jamāhīrī), as well

21. Discussing the limits of educational activities planned by the Libyan government to teach revolutionary ideology, Obeidi (2001) lists three main causes: kinship, Islamist forces/ideology, and consumer culture. While insightful, her work disassociates any discussion about these factors from questions of international politics and political economy. Interestingly, while Obeidi undertook field research in 1994, nowhere in the book does she elaborate on the impact of international sanctions by the respondents. Such a consideration does not undermine her findings on the increasing sense of political alienation among Libyans, yet it shows the need to contextualize them in a more refined manner.

22. Mukhtar was the leader of the Senussi resistance in Cyrenaica against the Italian colonial authorities from the late 1920s until his capture and execution by the hands of General Rodolfo Graziani in 1931, which was carried out in the concentration camp of Solluq.

as at university—namely, "The Jamahiriya Thought" (al-Fikr al-Jamāhīrī), where students learned about the theoretical underpinnings of the Green Book. For many Libyans, the content of these modules revealed less about the world, and more about the ambitions of Qaddafi:

> It was all about a single person [Qaddafi], and the content repeats itself every year.

> All these modules were talking about Qaddafi's achievements . . . What Qaddafi did, changed, and so on. (interviews 2015–17)

Many Libyans, therefore, perceived the attempt to structure society according to the ideas of the Green Book as the leader's personal desire to leave a legacy. In this regard, Ashraf provided an everyday rumor about Qaddafi's determination to carve his place in history by sculpting one of his philosophical gems on a rock to be discovered by posterity: "I heard this story saying that he took a stone and wrote on it one sentence from the Green Book. Then he threw the stone in the desert. I am not sure if this is true, but what it means is he wanted somebody to discover his words on that rock in two thousand years. He wanted to make history" (interview 2015).[23]

Beyond the content of the course, what appears particularly interesting is, once again, the way society envisioned how the Green Book had lost appeal among Libyans in the last decades. In fact, the main modality of everyday interaction that they recounted vis-à-vis the regime's ideological modules were cynicism and, thus, alienation. Many of my interlocutors insisted that they did not share or understand the ideas in the Green Book. For many, this module was a mandatory requirement of the hierarchical structure of political authority that governed the country, and they needed to show themselves "as someone who praises Qaddafi." From this perspective, dissimulation, or acting *as if*, played an important role in reproducing dominant norms, meanings, and mechanisms in the everyday. The

23. For an understanding of the Jamahiriya structure and the division into People's Committee, see Davis (1987); and Blundy and Lycett (1987, 101–13). For a more theoretical understanding of the People's Authority, see Al-Saadi (1987).

compulsion and the necessity to repeat certain actions turned the question of belief into a matter of secondary importance for both individuals and the regime. A dissimulating community can, in fact, agree to abandon its right to question and challenge those who think and govern in its name. It is not surprising that when a question on the final exam of those modules asked students to answer "Who liberated us from slavery?," Bashar knew that a certain code and language were required: "You cannot simply reply, 'Muammar Qaddafi.' You will say, 'The leader of the revolution, the savior of the country, the brother-leader, and so on.' . . . We were pretending that we believed in these ideas" (interview 2017). In other words, quotidian practices of life normalized this use of language and ideas, albeit devoid of any belief. In this regard, the answers to the exam ("leader of the revolution, savior of the country") normalized a code used to provide a certain vision of the world, thus reproducing a structure of political authority associated with such ideological discourse. Yet, as we shall see, the reproduction of power cannot be considered the only outcome.

Teachers and staff also appeared to distance themselves from Green Book–related modules. As the head of the Accountancy Department, Mansour often held meetings with faculty members to redesign the university curricula and include all courses necessary to prepare students for graduating in economics. Yet the same problem always came up: those meetings would continue for hours because they struggled to incorporate one particular topic, "The Thought of the Jamahiriya": "The point is that everybody knew how useless such a subject was to the students. But you had to include it, otherwise you would have had problems" (interview 2015). The hours-long struggle to fit the revolutionary course into curricula exemplifies the tension between the needs of the regime to maintain its ideological messaging and the dissimulating attitude adopted by many Libyans in their everyday life. Ultimately, dissimulation and cynical distance signaled a high level of political alienation (al-Werfalli 2011, 73–120) and silent transformation of the regime's hegemonic stature. People studied the Green Book because they had to, thus feigning loyalty to its ideals to avoid raising suspicions and eventually being questioned, if not punished, by the regime. As mentioned above, people's compulsion to reenact the dominant codes and hierarchies turned the question of belief into an ancillary problem for the regime, since it nonetheless guaranteed a certain degree of authority and stability. However, the power of alienation lay in the way it gradually emptied or redirected the meaning of these rituals and categories. Thus, the question becomes, once the ideological values and principles that had guided the revolution in 1969 seemed not to appeal to the younger generations, how did alienation, cynicism, and dissimulation reshape those other mechanisms and organizations that had been created to run the country?

This process is crucial to understand, because it permits us to grasp more closely the meanings of what is political and how systems of political control compete, evolving and developing in a dialogical process. When people reproduce the precise form (how) of representations, they do not necessarily adhere to their meanings (what). Thus, it is indeed analytically valid to argue that ritualized actions help to maintain these structures of political authority. Yet, when immersed in a sense of alienation, they also reflect the changes happening at the structural level, as these same actions now ascribe new material and symbolic meanings to the revolutionary values and rituals upheld by the regime. In other words, these newly emerging meanings did not simply undermine the stability of the regime; rather, they reflected its defeat and gradual abandonment of a revolutionary agenda. As we shall see, individual gains and economic corruption became the most dominant ones in the last turbulent decades of the Jamahiriya.

An important symbolic and organizational element that captured those dynamics at play related to the organization of the Revolutionary Committees (RC). The RC were first established in the cities of Tripoli and Benghazi in 1977 (El-Fathaly and Palmer 1980, 202; Bearman 1986, 187–99), and they played an important, yet intermittent, role in the everyday political dynamics of the Jamahiriya (Mattes 1995). Created as a means to mobilize the masses, the RC were supposed to be the natural consequence of the workers' takeover of the factories and other means of production (Naur 1986, 94–96). The regime had fully planned this process, both at the practical and ideological level. People, in fact, "knew exactly where to go [because] it had been prepared down to the last detail" (95), and, by December 1978, workers had taken "over 180 industrial, commercial, and other firms, realizing the ideological dictum 'partners, not wage laborers'" (Deeb 1986, 451).

More generally, the regime saw the RC as legitimate organizations established to control the implementation of the revolutionary directives outlined in the Green Book. However, the RC soon became "the safety valve and sieve" of people's power (Gera 1977, 631). Since the Green Book did not mention their creation, they lacked formal organization and rules, which often permitted their members to act with impunity under the banner of protecting the revolution. In this way, the RC became a veritable state within the state. They had the power to set up revolutionary courts and to control schools, universities, factories, media, and, especially, the army and the police (Ouannes 2009, 196). Relying on their power, they also accumulated wealth through diverse illegal practices, such as the confiscation of properties, misuse of public funds, and money laundering (194). Their creation marked "the separation of formal authority—as embodied by the congress and committee system (theorised in The Green Book)—and revolutionary authority" (Mattes 1995, 94). While their first members belonged to the revolutionary generation formed in the ideological camps (Obeidi 2001, 54), who mostly came from disadvantaged classes (Djaziri 1987, 465), their ranks changed and developed over time, becoming a powerful class of military-turned-merchants by the early 2000s.

My interlocutors elaborated on all of these different aspects, starting from the more general societal perception of RC power. For instance, there was a hierarchy within the RC: those who occupied a higher position usually belonged to the "liquidation group" (jamāʿāt al-taṣfiyya), whose task in the 1990s was to annihilate "enemies of the revolution." Another recurrent reaction among the interviewees when asked about the RC was to describe them as informants or strong supporters of the regime. While those replies offered stereotypical ways of explaining their role in society, more nuanced and complex dynamics emerged for the reasons that would lead someone to join the RC, whose legitimacy appeared to be very low in the last two decades of the Jamahiriya (al-Werfalli 2011, 75–76).

This picture calls into question the RC members' staunch support and loyalty for the regime and instead focuses on those general forces and motivations at work that characterized the organization's behavior—mostly individual opportunism and corruption. Many people, in fact, joined the RC to take advantage of the system, to gain access to those opportunities that otherwise would not be available, or, more simply, for "money, power, and protection" (interviews 2015). Tareq, for instance, recounted a story, dating from the late 1980s, about his neighbor, who had managed to send his sons to study in Romania: "He was a member of the RC, and at that time they came up with this idea of being missionaries (al-mubashirīn), to spread the ideas of the Third Universal Theory abroad. This was only an excuse to go abroad, nothing else. At that time, there were no scholarships or anything like that, so they found their ways" (interview 2015). To join the group translated neither into loyalty nor into direct personal or economic benefit. Being in the RC, however, allowed you to manipulate the law to your advantage. In other words, although the regime had assigned the organization an important operational power, deeming it the ideological engine of the revolution, its members seemed more interested in obtaining personal gains by abusing their authority.

Such abuse of status and power also occurred among those who joined another RC-related institution: al-Mathāba. This institution, whose unique oval-shaped buildings spread throughout Libya, derived its name from the Qu'ran and referred to al-Ka'ba—the most sacred place in Islam, meaning "the House (al-Mathāba), a place of return for the people and [a place] of security."[24] The regime's adoption of this name was supposed to enable the RC to gain reverence and respect, turning al-Mathāba into a place of worship. Following this analogy, the volunteers working in al-Mathāba were meant to be seen as prophets or angels who tried to spread moral and revolutionary values. Just as prophets and angels love "God" without expecting anything in return, so those volunteers revered and

---

24. "The ka'bah, called Mathaba [2:125] from the lexical roots thaba, signifies a place one returns to again & again. That explains our longing. And [mention] when We made the House (al-Mathābah) a place of return for the people and [a place of] security. And take, [O believers], from the standing place of Abraham a place of prayer. And We charged Abraham and Ishmael, [saying], "Purify My House for those who perform Tawaf and those who are staying [there] for worship and those who bow and prostrate [in prayer]" (Qu'ran).

worked for the "Father" (interviews 2015). Since the purpose of those institutes was to recruit young cadres, they could often be found in universities. Al-Mathāba members coordinated the organization of all events taking place on the universities' campuses, such as cultural weeks.[25] They were not considered diligent students and continually took advantage of their social status by "threatening teachers" in order to "get good marks," "mingle with girls," and thus game the system (interviews 2015). Apart from this widespread low level of legitimacy and contempt for those young cadres' abuse of their power, my interlocutors often remarked that those who joined al-Mathāba did not necessarily support Qaddafi or were faithful to him. In other words, convenience and power motivated their decision to join the group, suggesting that alienation reigned supreme even among those who belonged to regime-affiliated organizations.

Hamid's story is indicative of how the RC opened doors for individual socioeconomic mobility. Struggling to apply for a job as assistant teacher because the dean of the university considered him "too religious," Hamid was asked for a registration certificate from the RC. Although one of the prerequisites for obtaining this certificate was to attend a series of lectures two to three times a week, Hamid found a way to get around it: "Do you know what I used to do? If the lecture was between 5 and 7 p.m., I used to arrive around 6:45, sign my attendance, and then leave" (interview 2015). Hamid joined the RC to protect himself from regime scrutiny (i.e., from being seen as "too religious"). While this passage shows Hamid's ability to maintain a certain distance from the group by interacting with them as little as possible, it also suggests how such practices legitimated the regime, while undermining its political status.

In a similar way, Musbah (interview 2015) described how he obtained the "RC card to be on the safe side," as it allowed him to apply for a scholarship to study abroad. Omar (interview 2015) offered an analogous explanation, drawing on the story of his employer: "His cousin had been arrested because he was against Qaddafi. In order to protect himself, he became an

25. This particular event took place every year around April 7, a date that also had a profound relevance for those opposing the regime's policies, as shown in chapter 2.

RC member. He prayed to Qaddafi everyday [laughing]." Moreover, after the 1996 clashes, the employer decided to change his family name because a member of the Islamist group carried his own. As Omar clarified, such a decision also related to the routine control that the regime undertook on those who wished to study abroad: "For instance, in order to get a scholarship abroad, the regime would search for your surname and, if any of your relatives has been or was in prison for political reasons, they would not allow you to go anywhere" (interview 2016). Omar's employer tried to circumvent the system by joining the RC and changing his family name. What drove people to join the organization and show loyalty toward it was a need for social security, as exemplified in the expression "money, power, and protection."

In the aftermath of 2011, people who used to work for the RC had been somewhat stigmatized as affiliates of the regime. However, as Ibrahim recounted, such popular narratives failed to capture why many people joined the RC only to get money, to gain a salary, because there were very few possibilities: "When I used to ask to one of my best friends why he was working for the RC, he used to reply, 'Ibrahim, I have to work.' This person did not have qualifications. This is why most people relied on government jobs" (interview 2015). Ahmed also raised this point, explaining how two of his friends, who occupied a good position in the RC, "did not believe one word of Qaddafi, but they needed that position, that money, so they just went for it" (interview 2016). Rabia recalled that, while jobless and trying to get married, he approached the Libyan deputy ambassador in Portugal, asking to be appointed to a high position in the RC, since there were very few opportunities to improve your life in Libya: "It was not for the sake of Qaddafi that people used to do this work, although some did. But the majority joined these organizations in order to improve their lives, as few chances were given" (interview 2015). Social mobility and protection were intertwining factors that led people to join the RC, thus requiring them to dissimulate their loyalty and faithfulness toward the regime's ideology.

These narratives also shed light on the relevance of *wāsta* (having connections) and knowing somebody within the group. For instance, Naji remembered that to study law at the university, each student was required to memorize at least one-quarter of the Holy Qu'ran. While he was "planning and studying hard" to pursue such a degree, his efforts failed to meet the requirements. Other students, nonetheless, were accepted into the program without undergoing this test, since their fathers "knew somebody in the RC." Unfortunately, as Naji said, "I had no contact with anyone in power" (interview 2015). These everyday sketches shed light on several important changes taking place in the last two turbulent decades of the Jamahiriya that marked its progressive military and ideological defeat, as well as the reversal of the more progressive and egalitarian economic policies of the early decades. First, an increasing sense of alienation spread throughout society. People kept joining revolutionary groups, such as the RC, more as a form of quotidian survival than ideological commitment. These reflections certainly call into question the degree of loyalty that such groups had developed toward the regime in the last decades, despite being considered the ideological vanguard of the masses. However, as much as ideological retreat provides an important insight into the degree of everyday political estrangement within society, a second and interconnected factor was also at play: these everyday changes reflected a considerable alteration of the material and economic conditions of the country. Under the weight of sanctions and geopolitical threat of war, revolutionary defeatism of the ruling class had triggered a reversal of the more progressive and egalitarian economic policies that had marked the initial decade of al-Fātiḥ. The launch of partial waves of economic liberalization in 1987 and in the early 1990s and the rise of socioeconomic inequalities (see chapter 4) inevitably reshaped the nature of the relationship between state and society to become largely transactional. Political and ideological allegiance to the regime now turned into a form of economic opportunity or material survival, allowing one to pursue a professional career, look for a job, or secure social protection. The shifting nature of economic conditions transmuted these organizations and the regime as a whole into a complex web of patrimonial, corrupt, and clientelist relations, wherein access to it provided unique benefits. As public money and property fell into the hands of private individuals, this sense of entitlement to collective goods did not simply emerge from the so-called cursed nature of an oil-based economy. The international burden of the economic sanctions, the fall of a most strategic ally at the geopolitical level (the Soviet Union), and the long military defeat of Arab Socialism (Kadri 2016), all contributed to Libya's gradual reintegration into the world economy. At this juncture, an endemic culture of corruption cut across all levels of society.

## The Pyramid of Corruption

During the late 1980s and early 1990s, the Green Book–envisioned society suffered several setbacks, due to military and ideological defeats following the escalating confrontation with the West. While the war in Chad contributed strongly to the dissatisfaction of the population with the regime, the clash with Western powers culminated with the imposition of international sanctions in 1992.[26] The Jamahiriya's egalitarian and anti-imperialist policies reversed, whereas popular discontent turned into armed rebellions, as discussed in the previous chapters. In order to maintain its stability, the regime launched two main measures: first, a process of economic liberalization (*infitāḥ*), or what Qaddafi termed a "Revolution within the Revolution" (Vandewalle 1991; St. John 2008); and, second, a revival of tribal, transactional, and neopatrimonial dynamics.

Starting in 1987, the regime, unable to sustain its previous level of providing goods and jobs to the population, launched waves of economic privatization and liberalization.[27] The imposition of economic sanctions, however, rapidly worsened the economic and political conditions of the country. For example, the air ban not only blocked direct access to goods (prior to sanctions, more than 30 percent of goods had reached Libya by air) but also forced the regime to rely more on the private sector; it now had to purchase previously accessible goods and equipment through

---

26. For a partial exploration of the socio-political and economic impact of sanctions on Libya, see Niblock (2001); and El Mughrabi (2005, 319–30).

27. Although political debates started in 1987, these measures were officially declared in 1988 during a General People's Congress meeting in Ras Lanuf. They included import restrictions in order to deal with deficits in the balance of trade and cutting public wages, and creation of public-private associations (Vandewalle 1991, 75–91; El Mughrabi 2005, 189–95; Otman and Karlberg 2007, 218–21).

substantial payoffs to third parties, and prices inevitably rose above the levels set by the regime (Tantoush 2010). In addition, greater dependence on the private sector meant greater power for those, such as high officers and administrators, who had the necessary capital and contacts to import foreign goods, then sold to the public at high prices (see chapter 4).

By opening up its economy, the Libyan government was not only aiming to break from its international isolation but also pushing the populace to take a more productive role in the economy, instead of expecting the state to provide for everything. For these reasons, liberalization did not translate into a speedy process of privatization; rather, the regime tried to keep it in check in order to avoid the emergence of newly enriched—and potentially threatening—elites. It seemed eager in particular to combat speculation and illicit accumulation of wealth. However, the same institutions, like the "purification committees" that were created in 1994, charged with combating those activities, ended up accepting the merchants' bribes.[28] While international sanctions were leading to currency depreciation and the steady rise of inflation, the reforms contributed further to socioeconomic inequality. As I shall discuss more deeply in the next chapter, these reforms demonstrated the reversal of the state-led developmental experience and its gradual transformation into a form of private and neopatrimonial development. Ultimately, a new military-turned-merchants class consolidated, heralding the importance of modernizing and privatizing the country as opposed to what was considered the rigidity and banality of radical-revolutionary struggle. Like many other Arab republics, those shifts marked the emergence of a merchant/comprador class (Kadri 2015, 2016), which kept extracting wealth from national resources without reinvesting it for the country's development.

According to Alaa, these changes resulted in the reorganization of Libyan society into a pyramidal structure that accommodated four main levels: (1) good food and clothing; (2) good education; (3) good jobs/money;

---

28. It is interesting to note that the purification committees soon started abusing their authority, leading to the rise of popular discontent and forcing the regime to establish "volcano committees" in order to mitigate their power (Ronen 1997, 546).

and (4) good governance.[29] While much of the population was stuck at the lowest level of the pyramid, those higher levels remained inhabited by the few, an elite that plundered the country's resources for their personal benefit and that of their relatives. Undoubtedly, the first major theme that linked corruption to people's everyday lives entailed how the regime ran the country as a family business.

### How to Run a Farm

> Ben Ali, Mubarak, and Qaddafi are standing in the desert, and each one of them is asked to divide their country's money between themselves and their own people. Ben Ali starts. He draws a line in the sand, he takes the money and says, "I will throw the money in the air, what ends up on the right side of the line goes to the people, what falls on the left side goes to me." Then it's the turn of Mubarak, and he draws a circle in the sand, saying, "I will throw the money in the air and what falls in the circle goes to the people, what stays outside of it goes to me." Then Qaddafi goes. He draws a line in the air and says, "What falls goes to me. What remains in the air goes to the people."
> interview with Salem, 2017

As a way to express popular perceptions, jokes captured brilliantly not only how the Libyan leader made a fair distribution of resources impossible among his people but also how corruption spread like a virus and infected his affiliates, presenting the regime as controlled by a dishonest and selfish inner circle. In one joke, when Qaddafi sends Abu Bakr Younis and Abd al-Salam Jallud on a diplomatic mission to Saudi Arabia and the king invites them for dinner, the two affiliates do not fail to unveil their magical and corrupt tricks: "Sitting at the royal table, Younis realizes that all the cutlery is made of gold. Without hesitation, he grabs a fork and puts it in his pocket. However, Jallud, who has been witnessing the whole scene, suddenly decides to entertain the guests at the table and says, "Look, I will now put this fork into my pocket, and you will find it back in the pocket

29. As he was working on a doctoral degree in economics, Alaa's explanation drew loosely on Abraham Maslow's pyramid theory, as he confirmed (interview 2015).

of my colleague, Abu Bakr Yunis" (interview 2015). Here, two of the most important regime officials, Abu Bakr Younis and Abd al-Salam Jallud, compete in stealing golden cutlery from a Saudi Arabian royal table. This establishes a thematic continuum with other jokes and narratives that highlight the corrupt nature of Qaddafi and his family, expressing both disdain and outrage over their conduct.

According to many of my interlocutors, the country was managed as a family business, where Qaddafi's sons ended up having the most lucrative positions, controlling resources, and possessing privileges of which ordinary Libyans could only dream. All of Qaddafi's sons, in fact, occupied important positions at financial, political, and military levels. For instance, his eldest son, Muhammad Muammar, was the head of the Libyan Olympic Committee and of three national telecommunication companies (Almadar, Telecom, and General Post). Hannibal was the head of the General National Maritime Transport company, which specialized in oil exports; Khamis controlled one of the most powerful military brigades in the country, called "Khamis Brigade"; Mutassim and Saif al-Islam, who were considered possible heirs to the government, were heavily involved in the political dynamics of the country.[30] The Panama Papers further revealed that "insiders" of the regime had embezzled large sums of public funds, originally allocated to build hospitals and public infrastructures, in order to buy luxury properties in England and Scotland (Garside, Pegg, and Mahmood 2016). In 2010, Global Witness (2011) leaked a document proving the poor management by prominent American and European investment funds, ranging from HSBC and Goldman Sachs to UniCredit and France Société Générale, of hundreds of millions of dollars of the Libyan Investment Authority (LIA). While producing low returns, these funds charged millions of dollars in fees (Rohde 2011). While Libyan money entered the circuits of Western capital, financial regulators had no interest in investigating whether the banks that held LIA funds were diverting state funds for the Qaddafi family's private benefit.

---

30. For a more detailed explanation of all the siblings' involvement in the country affairs, see Chorin (2012, 103–6).

In such a scenario, many interviewees described how the whims of Qaddafi's sons determined political decisions that, in turn, impacted the lives of other Libyans, yet with no regard or respect for them. Hakim, for instance, explained to me how one day the regime closed down the motorway linking Libya to Tunisia "just because Saadi wanted to try out his new motorcycle" (interview 2015). Hussein remembered when the regime forced him to relocate from Tripoli to Tarhuna University because Aisha, Qaddafi's daughter, decided to study law in Tripoli, and the university stopped allowing men to attend (interview 2015). Particularly curious was the amount of resentment and disdain expressed toward Saadi, who was allowed to run the Libyan Football Federation and to play for a famous Italian team, Perugia, only because "he was the son of Qaddafi."[31] In this regard, my interlocutors directed me to an online video of an official football match in Libya, which starts by showing Saadi discussing with the referee and about to take a penalty kick. Once he shoots, it is very clear, despite the poor quality of the video, that the ball hits the post and ends up in the hands of the goalkeeper. In other words, Saadi has missed the penalty, yet politics emerge in this precise moment. Although Saadi has missed the penalty, he keeps acting as if he scored it (see Bouchra jad 2016). Celebrating, he takes his shirt off, leaving the commentator and fans incredulous, and the referee assigns the goal to his team. The special character of this episode lies in its ordinary nature, revealing an intense discontent about the ways Qaddafi's sons abused their power.

However, as much as the narratives convey this discontent, they also reveal the popular cynicism of society, now capable of joking about the incompetence and corruption of Qaddafi and his son Saadi:

> After having played a football game and missed a penalty at the last minute, Saadi goes back home and tries to sleep. He is, however, restless. It is 2 o'clock in the morning and he cannot sleep. His mother, Safiyya, noticing that her son is up in the middle of the night, approaches him and asks, "My son, what's going on? Why aren't you sleeping?" The son

---

31. Saadi also participated in other lucrative activities. He controlled the Libyan film industry and tried to develop a free-trade zone in Zuwara (documented in WikiLeaks 2009).

goes, "The referee gave me a penalty at the last minute, but I wasted it." So, his mother replies, "Go to sleep! Your father wasted the whole country, and he has been sleeping since 8 o'clock." (interview 2015)

The joke plays on Saadi and his family's legacy of "wasted" possibilities. Like his father, who failed the country, the son wastes an important and almost unthinkable ("at the last minute") chance for his team to win. We could say that the joke assigns to Safiyya the function of Reason, which does not fail to underline quickly that "wasting chances" is a family trait, so that there is no reason to be restless. The joke stresses not only the Qaddafi's family's corrupt control of Libya but also those underlying contradictions that characterized their authority. For instance, the Green Book considered football a deceitful sport for the masses, and, as many interviewees recounted, football commentators were not allowed to call players by their names (see yasser mas 2014).[32] Saadi, however, disregarding such rules, appointed himself the "king of football," while rumors circulated about the regime and, particularly, Qaddafi's son not allowing more skillful Libyan football players, such as Tareq Al-Tayeb, to join prestigious European clubs (interviews 2015).

Overall, many of my interlocutors sustained that a mafia-like management of the country existed, where the country and its people had been turned into a farm with its animals. Mansour, for example, said: "They used to treat Libya like their home and treat all others like goats . . . We were like animals. The corruption was in a closed circle of people. We called them 'the fat cats'" (interview 2014). The colloquial expression "fat cats" (*al-qṭāṭ al-simān*) refers to a class of revolutionaries-turned-merchants that abused their institutional power to protect their own economic and political interests. To distinguish between true revolutionary subjects and those regime-affiliated members that embezzled state money for their own private profit, some interviewees referred to the latter not as

32. "It is unconceivable for crowds to enter athletic fields and stadiums to watch one or more players, without practicing the game themselves. . . . Sport, like power, should be for the masses, and just as wealth and weapons should be for the people, sport as a social activity should also be for the people" (Al Gathafi 2005, 79–80).

*thawrī* (revolutionary) but as *thūwārjī* (liar, hypocrite, profiteer) (interviews 2015–17). Having administered the process of gradual privatization, they exploited their political connections to enrich themselves and become more powerful via informal commerce, currency speculation, takeover of state's factories, and capital flight, as we shall see in the next chapter. While those activities boosted their power, particularly during the sanctions period, it trickled down to the population in the form of rising socioeconomic inequalities and more repressive policies. Overall, the fat cats had been the first ones to abandon the revolutionary pillars of egalitarianism and anticolonialism.

It is therefore not surprising that other stories, such as the one that Rajab recounted, provide insight into people's growing outrage toward a corrupt regime. Rajab, a man in his early forties, belonged to a large family, in which only two brothers were working, with the rest either students or living at home. The family's main source of income was his mother, who worked as a cleaner for the People's Committees in Zawiya. Because she was old and suffered from severe rheumatism, Rajab often helped her to carry out the hardest tasks, such as cleaning toilets and bathrooms: "There was this big picture of Qaddafi on the wall at the entrance of the building. Whenever I passed that picture, I cleared my throat and spat on him. Every time . . . He is rich, we are poor. In rich countries like Libya, people . . . I am not saying that they should not work . . . but they should have a better life, a better salary" (interview 2015). The rasping sound of a cleared throat and the timely cadence of spitting on Qaddafi's picture convey Rajab's disgust and dissatisfaction with the conditions of his life as well as the regime's abuse of power. The discontent lies in the obstacles faced by a young man to find a job and his mother's need to hang on to her profession as a cleaner, which was the main source of income for the entire family. This story is indicative of the wider popular discontent that grew in these years, from the attempted military coup in 1993 to various popular protests and clashes erupting in stadiums and squares. In such a scenario, where the international embargo suffocated the Libyan economy and the Islamist challenge gained traction in the eastern part of the country, corruption also translated into a revival of tribal allegiances.

The Green Book defines the tribe as a "social umbrella" and disapproves of its involvement in the realm of political affairs (Al Gathafi 2005, 63). Yet, in the mid-1990s, the regime reactivated those existing social connections and embedded them into a larger set of politics of patronage and corruption (Cherstich 2014) whose ultimate aims were to secure its rule and stability. For instance, the combination of international sanctions and domestic instability led the regime to establish the Popular Social Leadership. This decision came in reaction to the October 1993 attempted coup by a group of military officers, mostly belonging to an allied and prominent tribe, the Warfalla, which occupied a leading position in the armed and security forces, together with Megharha and the Qadhdhafa. This new institution was composed of the "respected natural leaders" of the local communities, and, although the policy text did not specify who those leaders were, "the authorities were seeking to draw in . . . tribal leaders, and the emphasis was on rural rather than urban areas" (Niblock 2001, 89). The reactivation of tribal allegiances is important to understand, because it reveals how certain forms of kinship remerged as a tool of control in a moment of geopolitical threat and local discontent, rather than representing the unchanging nature of Libya.

Ihsan described how this new mechanism was adopted to govern the population. He relates the way the regime interfered in the election process of the People's Committee's leader, who was usually appointed by each village collectively. The regime instead began appointing the leader from its most loyal tribes, offering small favors in exchange, such as a new car, a monthly salary, and a trip to Sirte for the "respected leader": "It was a Mazda 323, then a Mitsubishi, and then a Toyota HiLux. After that, they delivered a new car, a Nubira. The government subsidized half its price and, if you would pay the other half, you could keep it . . . Small corruption, but people liked it [laughter]" (interview 2015). As Ihsan described, the interference of the regime created conflicts and tensions, such as the one between two tribes, the Obeidat and the Ghaity, in his town, Tobruk. The fight arose because the position of leader was socially important: it allowed one to help relatives or people from the same tribe to find a job or access other benefits.

Those tribal mechanisms, however, neither represented the essence of Libyan society nor replaced the power of an absent state, as many contemporary analysts would like us to believe. While tribalism was important, it only constituted a configuration of power relations, which was intimately connected to the larger culture of *wāsta*, or corruption (al-Werfalli 2011, 82–83), favors, and bribes that characterized Libyan society from the 1990s onward. For instance, the usual definition of *wāsta* has negative undertones and invokes tropes of archaic and traditional practices, thus seeking its origins in tribal and stateless structures. I would argue instead that, as Mabrooka al-Werfalli (2011, 103) writes, corruption was certainly the most important element that has "undeniably deepened the crisis of confidence in the political system as a whole," translating into political apathy and alienation. The people's condemnation of the regime as a corrupt entity explains not only how many Libyans perceived the nature of the relationship between state and society but also why political alienation became a dominant modality of interaction in the everyday. However, as much as Libyans talked about corruption and presented stories in which they depict themselves as critics or victims of the regime, they nevertheless participated actively in the reproduction of a system that drove predation and abuse of state resources.

## "If You Don't Steal, You're Dumb!"

> Everybody was guilty of this corruption.
> interview with Ashraf, 2015

> It is instilled in us. The corruption is inside us!
> interview with Nuri, 2016

> To be honest, it was not just the family of Qaddafi, his relatives, supporters, and loyalists from different tribes. It was everybody.
> interview with Yousef, 2016

Corruption can assume different meanings and take numerous forms, and, as Hamza told me, smuggling (see Meddeb 2011, 2012) is one of them. Coming from the tribe of al-Qadhdhafa, Hamza recounted a visit by Saif al-Islam, the reformist son of Qaddafi, to the city of Sebha. While the purpose of Saif's visit was to address the youth, his speech turned into a series of strong accusations against the tribe for smuggling subsidized products to neighboring countries. However, as Hamza related, one member of the audience stood up and replied: "Yes, it is true, we smuggle products! The government gave me a job that has nothing to do with my qualifications and the salary is peanuts. So, I smuggle to make more money. And yes! We smuggle instead of having other people doing it. Because we are not against you or your father, we don't want to bring problems. You are our blood" (interview 2016). The reaction of the people and the reference to "blood" lines were a reminder to Saif al-Islam of the constitutive and necessary function of corruption for the stability of the regime. People stood up and defended this system, stressing that its permissibility represented the basis of popular consensus for the same regime. Because they benefited from it, they supported the regime as long as the regime allowed it. For instance, the reduction of subsidies was a critical issue for those communities, which strongly opposed it because it took away one of the main sources of profit: the smuggling of heavily subsidized food items into neighboring countries, which cost three or four times more if compared to Libya. To counter such activities therefore meant questioning the regime's stability at its core, since its legitimacy relied greatly on those informal exchanges that also made possible the provision of those goods and jobs that it could not deliver. Even as the regime reinforced its controlling, supervisory capacity by involving the entire population in such everyday activities, people turned into its best defenders.

As discussed previously about the social role of the RC, this everyday economy of favors, benefits, and exchanges comprised the entire population and was often the best available method to materialize personal and mundane ambitions. For instance, Zahy explained that "in Libya you get what you want through the right people." In 2006, looking for a job as lecturer, Zahy approached a very a young man, Mohammed, who belonged to the al-Qadhdhafa tribe and, together with him, paid a visit to the head of the university to talk about jobs: "We went there, and the secretary told us that the head of the university was in a meeting ... Mohammed told her to go inside the meeting room and tell him that 'Mohammed al-Qaddafi is outside, waiting for him.' As soon as she went inside, the head, who was a very old professor, came out immediately and said, 'Hello, Mohammed! How are you? I am in a meeting, could you please come inside?' We entered the room, Mohammed spoke to him, and I got the job" (interview 2015). The responsiveness of the "old professor" to the call of a "very young man" may have stemmed from the willingness of the head of the university to avoid any problems vis-à-vis the regime, thus reinforcing the existing mechanisms of surveillance. This connection allowed Zahy to circumvent the problem of unemployment and succeed in finding a job within the university structure. As he claimed, Zahy did not support Qaddafi or the regime, but he found these practices necessary to survive. In so doing, however, he reiterated a dominant structure that placed Qaddafi and his tribe at the top of the social pyramid.

Another interviewee, Khaled, offered an important and intricate explanation of the same phenomenon. While looking for a job after his graduation, Khaled described approaching one of his friends ("a minister") and asking whether there was any chance of working at the Audit Bureau within the Ministry of the Economy: "He said 'Yes.' As long as I had my military service done . . . I went for the military service, but I attended only for two weeks because I had a relative there who sorted out my position. I got this job offer only in twenty days" (interview 2016). Like Zahy, Khaled relied on the "right people" to obtain a job in the public sector, as well as to avoid military service. The latter was a practice that Libyans often recounted (interviews 2015–18). As Khaled went on to explain, however, corruption can assume different meanings. In 2009, the Ministry of the Economy assigned him—together with two other colleagues—to work for a public construction company located in the south of Libya. As soon as they arrived, the owner of the company tried to offer favors or money in order to stop them from looking too carefully into the company's documents. Refusing these proposals, the team soon realized that more than one million LYD of public funds were missing from the company's records in the last year alone. Such a discovery, however, did not trigger an enquiry or investigation; rather, it only managed to create more problems and concerns for Khaled and his colleagues. Since the owner of the company was married to the sister of a very close affiliate of Qaddafi, when Khaled visited the company a month later the manager urged him to leave and threatened to shoot him. Fearing for his life, Khaled phoned the minister: "He told me, 'Khaled, get out immediately. The Ministry is not responsible for anything that might happen to you, even if the manager decides to shoot you.' But I asked him, 'What about the papers and reports?' He told me, 'We do not need papers or reports. Get the driver with you and leave the city.' That is what I did" (interview 2015).

Khalid's narrative presents *wāsta* as a form of "checked-illegality" (Hibou 2011, 274), a mode of governing that prevents people from speaking out about or criticizing the regime, offering in exchange the means to survive. The second passage nonetheless shows the dysfunctional symptoms of a power structure that acquires legitimacy through patronage and neopatrimonial dynamics. Those official institutions created to report illegal activities—or, more simply, to serve the people—completely lose their value, contributing further to the spread of political alienation and thus reducing the regime's popular legitimacy. It is important to understand how *wāsta* (Ramady 2016) functioned in a very similar manner to the Soviet Union economy of *blat* after its liberalizing reforms (Ledeneva 1998). In other words, while *wāsta* exploited state resources, the state depended on informal solutions to the problems of distributing scarce resources. In such a way, those informal exchanges reproduced and maintained the power of the regime that required them, yet they subverted its ideological pillars, contributing to the pillage of its wealth and resources. Moreover, Khaled's struggle to report corruption echoes the earlier narrative of the visit of Saif al-Islam to Sebha and the ill-fated story of the journalist and RC member Daif al-Ghazal. After criticizing the state of corruption in Libya while urging Libyan intellectuals to form a civil society committee against such endemic problems (Reporters Without Borders 2005; al-Watanona 2006), al-Ghazal was abducted on May 21, 2005, by members of the regime's internal security.[33] A few days later, his dead body was found, showing signs of torture and with a bullet wound in the head.

---

33. The government jailed another writer, Abd al-Raziq Mansuri, for similar reasons (Human Rights Watch 2005).

In such a situation, while citizens condemn the regime as "corrupt," they also participate in this economy of favors and bribes. In this regard, Ahmed told an emblematic story that captures the doubleness of such informal mechanisms, about how the dean of the university, who used to own a computer shop, took advantage of public funds. While any university order would normally take months to be fulfilled, computers arrived the day after: "Why? Because he owns a computer shop, and the money goes directly into his pocket. He gains more money through commissions. Corruption was without limits. As my father used to say, 'Even the sea needs more water'" (interview 2016). This anecdote shows the intricate relationship between public procurement and corruption that existed in Libya. Public procurement refers to government purchasing of goods and services from the private sector, in the form of, for instance, equipment, machinery, and technology.

The culture of corruption consisted of those quotidian and wasteful expenditures of public funds that permitted people to make extra profit. While reliable procurement practices turn public funds into functioning infrastructure and services, this narrative demonstrates how, from the regime to society, the farm/family model was replicated, creating a strong individualist culture that opposed and rejected the egalitarian and collective vision of the people's power. Everyday corruption entailed the misappropriation of public funds for personal gain, as Abdul Aziz discussed in relation to the hydrocarbon sector, where the inflated cost of spare parts allowed one to make profits on state resources: "Those purchases took place via Italy, UK, US, Germany, and the corruption was in between, with the supplier. It was an easy way to make money. You buy something whose price is worth one LYD, and you pay 400 LYD. You get a cash back of 300 LYD. The public company pays" (interview 2015).

It is important to emphasize that these ordinary yet lucrative deals that took place to capitalize on public money and property did not happen in isolation from the international and national economic context in which they occurred. In other words, corruption—like tribalism—is not an inherent characteristic of the Libyan government or population; rather, its growth took place in a context that fostered and encouraged this type of predatory behavior. From the early 1990s to the 2000s, when the international sanctions were imposed on Libya, corruption spread from the local to the international level, and vice versa. During the sanctions, the Libyan oil industry, which relied heavily on imported refining technology, witnessed a change in the relationship between Libyan buyers and foreign suppliers. The suppliers, in fact, had increased power and advantage over the buyers and could command and change prices as it pleased them (Tantoush 2010). In the early 2000s, the everyday plundering of national resources continued. The head of crude oil contracts, Najwa al-Beshti, has documented the existence of oil contracts between foreign oil companies and public officials, showing how the latter sold oil or even entire refineries—such as the case of Ras Lanuf (Donati and Gumuchian 2018)—to the latter for a price considerably below market. The result of those contracts was the disappearance of huge sums, which were pocketed by officials (Faucon, Said, and Moloney 2012). Therefore, the scale of corruption, which lowered public confidence toward the government and thus enabled political alienation, reflected the gradual reversal of state-led capitalist policies and the gradual reintegration of Libya's market into the world market. The everyday interacted with these changes: while Libyans condemned those corrupt officials whose behavior went unpunished, they also engaged in similar practices, but as heroes who steal from the real thief—the state (al-Werfalli 2011, 102–3).

## Opening Cracks

The grip of the international embargo, together with the military bombings and the Chadian debacle, produced major changes in the ideological, political, and economic structure of the Jamahiriya. As shown in the previous chapter, the fight against imperialism exposed the regime's limitations and (ultimately) its defeat, since the Jamahiriya found itself cornered and disciplined by major international powers. As a result, the previous more progressive and egalitarian policies were reversed, triggering the emergence of socioeconomic inequalities, as well as the rise of a military-turned-merchant class. In such a scenario, we delved into the everyday not to explore a place where global dynamics deterministically unfold, but, rather, to grasp the pace and modalities that processes of political change assume and require. Whether cynicism or humor, alienation or corruption, this chapter traced the mundane nature of these political changes through the stories and eyes of Libyans, highlighting how these efforts to maintain a sphere of agency—albeit minimal and scattered—heightened slowly the evolving contradictions within the regime in the last two turbulent decades.

From the perspective of the regime, people's quotidian participation in and dissimulation of these imposed rituals signaled their capacity to reiterate an officially sanctioned vision of life. People admired and revered the exceptional traits of the father, Qaddafi, through a circuit of emotions that ranged from awe and wonder, while simultaneously mocking and criticizing his magical status. While interacting with the Green Book, they performed certain actions in a condition of complete nonbelief and utter necessity, as did many of those who joined the RC. Overall, political alienation and a lack of genuine support characterized their relationship with the regime, and the forces at work that motivated their behavior frequently pointed to a desire for money, power, and protection—what seemed to distinguish the character of the fat cats. With or without belief, at last the regime seemed to stand firmly on its feet, despite the need to unleash more repressive measures of control. Yet these political changes, albeit slowly, eroded the government's legitimacy and stability from within.

From a bulwark of a nation eager to oppose imperialist powers and propose a new model of local and international development, these changes gradually turned Libya into everybody's farm. A culture of corruption, including bribes, personal and tribal connections merged, which people lived as simultaneous victims and critics. They condemned and mocked corruption within the regime while replicating it in their everyday interactions, stealing money from the government or trying to pursue their careers. At this critical juncture, we now move to trace how people's aspirations and fantasies for the future of the country changed accordingly once again, reflecting and negotiating a process of political change at global, national, and everyday levels.

# 4

# Oil, Consumerism,
# and Capitalist Modernity

The richest country, the poorest people.
interview with Ali, 2016

Despite possessing 6 percent of the world's proven oil reserves and being
the third largest producer in Africa after Angola and Nigeria (OPEC
2018), with one of the highest per-capita income in the continent, many
Libyans nonetheless believed they had not benefited from oil and its revenues during the last decades of the Jamahiriya. They not only felt poor
but they also perceived their country as being underdeveloped compared
with other resource-rich states in the Arab region, particularly the Persian
Gulf. Their expectations of what the economy could provide and what the
government should offer did not match their everyday reality. In order to
explain this frustration, academic exponents of the "paradox of the plenty"
(Karl 2007) theory have argued that Libya represented the perfect cautionary tale of the resource curse theory. The discovery of oil had encouraged the rejection of modern state structures as well as the creation of a
private-led economy. After the 1969 revolution, an abundance of oil led to
the rise of an authoritarian leader and rent-seeking elites (Martinez 2012),
who ended up controlling the population via systems of subsidies and co-
optation, also called "coercive distribution" (Albertus, Fenner, and Slater
2018). That is, the Jamahiriya regime opted for buying its loyalty from the
population, favoring specific tribes or regions over others. Such copious-
ness of resources also had repercussions at the international and regional
level, because it helped the regime to initiate conflicts or to disrupt existing regional balances. The "pariah" status of oil (Bridge 2008) reflected

103

the rogue international status of the Libyan regime, since it provided the material grounds for pursuing aggressive and irrational behavior, both domestically and beyond. Finally, when the regime faced internal dissent, the most obvious response was to increase repression against internal enemies. In other words, while oil allowed the authoritarian leader to continue driving the country along a path of statelessness, turning it into a political and economic laboratory of mismanagement and aggressive foreign policy, the people remained poor, repressed, and exploited. In *Petro-aggression: When Oil Causes War,* Jeff Colgan (2013) endeavors to study the causal mechanisms between petro-states, conflicts, and aggressive foreign policies, which leads him to conclude "that oil powerfully shaped Libya's domestic politics by creating a clientelistic political culture whereby the leader of the state was able to offer economic benefits in exchange for political quiescence. This political culture reduced Qaddafi's risk of domestic punishment for foreign policy adventurism. . . . Consequently, the modern history of Libya offers considerable support to the argument that revolutionary governments that arise in petrostates constitute a special threat to international peace" (151).

We might be tempted to say that such an explanation aligns perfectly with the narratives and everyday experiences that this book so far has recounted, discussing the role of surveillance, the mechanisms of corruption, and people's overall discontent. At the same time, those narratives and experiences did not emerge in a void, and their nature was much more ambiguous—most importantly, tied to larger international political dynamics, which, as they affected the national politics of the regime, reverberated in the everyday. As discussed in previous chapters, the RCC weaponized oil to fight imperialist control both in the region and beyond. The nationalization of the oil industry became a paradigmatic moment of postcolonial resistance for Libya, as for many other countries of the region, such as Algeria or Iran (Dietrich 2017; Garavini 2019). However, oil was also a double-edged sword. While becoming a tool for pursuing radical political goals, its centrality to the world economy made its power vulnerable and volatile, as, first, the United States, and, later, international sanctions demonstrated. Therefore, we might need to go beyond the oil-curse frame to see how social imaginaries, desires, and hopes for the future intertwined with those national and supranational dynamics, including the role of oil, and the rise of capitalist modernity worldwide. Once again, this will take us on a journey across regional and international politics and political economy, which will ultimately enable us to discover how these processes interacted with the everyday politics of the Libyan Arab Jamahiriya.

## Consumerist Desires under International Sanctions

From the early 1970s, the regime embarked on a program of sponsored economic development, effectively commandeering the entire Libyan economy. The state-capitalist class, whose core was the group of army officers who had carried out the 1969 coup d'état, took control of the national resources, allocating them through economic reforms in support of political goals—namely, the national and anti-imperialist struggle. The regime embraced a development model characterized by a process of "state-led capitalism" (Djaziri 1987, 104; Matar 2013). Investment policies became instruments for building a new state and society by empowering marginalized and poorer classes as well as social identities. For instance, the RCC expelled the Italian nationals, confiscating their assets, and shut down Western military bases. By pursuing a policy of production cuts and increasing oil prices, the Libyan government not only laid the basis for other oil producers to renegotiate their own agreements with foreign companies but also turned oil into a political weapon used to pursue revolutionary goals in the realm of foreign policy, such as pressuring Western countries over the Palestinian issue. A massive process of nationalization of those foreign and domestic exploitative businesses, from oil to retail industry, took place in order to reduce social inequalities and return ownership to the Libyan people (Otman and Karlberg 2007, 218).

Following the ideas outlined in the Green Book, the role of the regime as guarantor and distributor of the country's wealth was consolidated with the launch of the Jamahiriya, as discussed in chapter 1. There was so much money coming from oil revenues that it was not difficult to follow a policy of "all things to all people" (Ghanem 1987, 65). The government created an extensive program of subsidies that covered basic staples such as flour, rice, and sugar, as well as electronic equipment and petrol (Food and

Agriculture Organization 2011; Sehib 2013, 22–25). A nationwide organization, the National Supply Corporation (NASCo), was created in 1971 to manage the importation of all these products, protect consumers from fluctuations in international prices, and minimize inflation (Otman and Karlberg 2007, 143). By the early 1980s, the regime had fulfilled many of its promises and boosted the economic development of Libya, while raising the general standard of living.

However, from the late 1980s, the anti-imperialist and redistributive premises of the revolution gradually came under attack, and the progressive gains started to reverse. This period was marked by an escalating confrontation with the West, particularly the United States, which began deploying military, legal and economic measures to curb the perceived threatening ambitions of the Libyan revolution. This tension evolved into a full-scale military confrontation that materialized in a variety of forms: most notably, at first, through the Chadian Civil War (1978–87), which quickly became a perfect arena for an international struggle between Libya and Western-led geopolitical forces. Other examples included the US bombing of Tripoli in 1986, and the UN's international sanctions (1992–2003). These changing international conditions brought about a gradual military-ideological defeat for the Libyan revolution, which began to lose its hold over economic policies. Many members of the state-led capitalist class withdrew their support for anti-imperialist policies and aligned themselves with dollarized financial capital. As the government began to slowly open the economy with the *infitāḥ* program, social imaginaries among Libyans aspiring to a different kind of future that mirrored the defeat of the al-Fātiḥ Revolution gradually emerged. That is, people's personal and quotidian horizons cohering with ideals of individual freedom, consumerism, and capitalist modernity.[1]

Discussions around shopping for food and other consumer goods encapsulated these new clusters of desires. Abdullah, for instance, described how people had lost total control over access to goods during their journey

---

1. The term "capitalist modernity" refers to the wealth of ideas and values upholding capitalism as the most apt political path for satisfying human material needs and for advancing individual freedom and agency.

to the public supermarkets: "It was like a lottery! You stood in a long queue for hours, you paid a small amount of money and then received a bag. But you did not even know what it contained. For big families, this system was OK, because you could get all kinds of clothing sizes. For small families, it was impossible, and you ended up secretly exchanging them with other families" (interview 2014). When scarcity becomes a norm, people perceive it as a form of political control operated by the state. Musa pointed out that the scarcity of goods did not even allow people to observe the tradition of buying new clothes for religious festivities. Rather, it created conflict: "Sometimes two people could catch the same bag and they would start fighting over it . . . We could get clothes that we did not need, so we exchanged them with somebody else who could give you something back" (interview 2015).

In discussing the shortage of electronic equipment, Ismail explained that, in 1984–85, the regime established the Popular Cooperatives (al-Jam'iyyāt al-Ta'āwuniyya), which required every family to register in order to receive a ration book that, in turn, allowed monthly access to food and other goods. An electronics department existed in the Popular Cooperatives, but its stock was rather limited. Ismail described how people tried to get around such a scarcity: "Let's say one thousand people were registered under one cooperative, which only had two or three televisions, one or two freezers. What would those families do? They organized a drawing to assign those goods to somebody. And in all my life, I remember we got only a TV from these cooperatives" (interview 2015). These stories of deprivation align with common scholarly descriptions of socialist economies as "economies of scarcity" (Verdery 1991; Kornai 1992) or of coercive distribution (Albertus, Fenner, and Slater 2018).

According to these arguments, socialist authoritarian regimes engineer deprivation among the population to keep desires for consumption alive yet never fully realize them. At the same time, they rely on a system of coercive distribution, which translates into the provision of benefits and services used to render ordinary citizens dependent and enmesh them in relationships of material dependency vis-à-vis the state. Consequently, as soon as oil revenues decline, the country's economy plummets, creating popular discontent. These analyses, however, reproduce too closely the ways in which the CIA reports described the impact of sanctions on Libya during that same period: "The recent drop in world oil prices and US economic sanctions are the latest jolts to hit the Libyan economy. They come at a time of unprecedented popular discontent over Libyan leader Qadhafi's misguided economic policies and penchant for costly foreign adventures . . . would confront Qadhafi with an unmanageable cash shortage unless he makes politically risky cuts in consumer imports or swallows his pride and borrows on the international market" (Central Intelligence Agency 1986). By equating Libya's experimental strategies for decolonization with misguided economic policies and foreign policy adventurism, these analyses—willingly or not—disregard two main elements. First, they water down the anti-imperialist policies of al-Fātiḥ, and, second, they disregard the role and interests of the West to curb these aspirations.

I argue that the popular discontent around the failure of Libya's social programs and its economy more broadly were linked to two interrelated contradictions, one primary and one secondary. Of the first of these, shortages in Libya were the direct result of US and allied states' international policies designed to punish the Libyan government and hurt its entire population. The US unilateral sanctions on Libya, applied as early as 1982, had triggered major operational difficulties and led to a reduction in investments due to the risky geopolitical conditions surrounding the country. Sanctions raised the costs of technological equipment and goods, since procurers now sold them at inflated prices, adding risk premiums to invoices (Central Intelligence Agency 1987). The US ban on spare parts related to the aviation industry, for instance, had a major impact on the nascent Libyan sector: "The unjustified financial cost, the damaged image and distortion suffered by Libya's national airline in routes and fleet development, are sacrifices as natural as are scars after every battle" (Dabaaj Marghani 1988, 553). The US monopoly over the aerospace industry functioned as part of the process of unequal exchange of technology and impeded the healthy development of a service that was vital to Libya's economy.[2] Moreover, the

---

2. Developed in the 1970s by dependency theorists (Amin 1976; Emmanuel 1972), the concept of unequal exchange continues to be adopted (Ajl 2021; Hickel et al. 2022; Ricci 2021) to explain the persistence of developmental inequalities between countries

constant reference to the decline of oil prices due to international oil gluts does not account for the control of oil prices always having been a US foreign policy tool.[3]

Scholars (Mitchell 2011; Di Muzio 2015) have argued that the 1973 oil crisis was engineered to weaken the industrial capacities of Europe and Japan and frame the Arab states as a threat to US energy security. Similarly, the gluts in the 1980s coincided with the worldwide launch of a neoliberal political agenda, forcing countries of the Global South into a cycle of major debt (Harvey 2003). Hence, Saudi Arabia's decision to break with OPEC and flood the market should be linked to the US attempts to counter the USSR. In 1985, when oil production in Saudi Arabia increased fourfold, oil prices collapsed by approximately the same amount in real terms (Wright 2021). Whether or not the Saudis acted at the behest of the United States is not the crux of the matter, but this maneuver nonetheless cemented US global power. Libya was not only one of the two smaller oil exporting countries—together with Iran—to Eastern European states but was also thought to be colluding with the USSR in undermining US interests in MENA and Africa, at least since 1979 (Central Intelligence Agency 1979).

The second contradiction entails the reduction in oil rents, the main revenue source used to fund the national budget and its social programs. Although the state-capitalist experience had led to better welfare-enhancing and developmental outcomes, by the end of the 1980s the Jamahiriya had

---

of the North and South of the world at the level of trade, ecology, technology, and so on. In this case, the concept is utilized to refer to the way the unequal transfer of technology from the North to the South remains a contentious issue, one that countries of the Global South had tried to overcome when calling for the establishment of a New International Economic Order (Hope 1983).

3. While the 1973 oil embargo provided a unique moment for many Arab countries and OPEC members to turn oil into a powerful foreign policy weapon, it also sanctioned the beginning of a new globalized regime of oil production, and the change of US policy toward the region. The introduction of a market-oriented control of oil prices (Hanieh 2021) did not allow many Arab states to maintain control over prices, and the increasing military-security alliance of the United States with Saudi Arabia (and the Gulf monarchies) created tensions and divisions between them and the Arab progressive republics.

shown important limitations in terms of planning and development. It had failed to develop an economy that could sustain Libya's population beyond the use and extraction of oil rent, which would make the country economically self-sufficient. The agricultural and industrial sectors had not thrived and were largely dependent on foreign labor because nationals traditionally working in the agricultural sector were more attracted by higher-paid, part-time jobs provided by the government or the oil industry (Alawar 1985). Since oil was the country's main source of revenue, the government assumed a purely distributive role, providing imported goods and public-sector jobs to the population. In the mid-1980s, international oil prices repeatedly collapsed, inducing a decline of Libyan revenues and negatively affecting budget planning. Considering that the cost of imports had tripled from $5.311 billion in 1979 to $15.466 billion in 1981 (Ghanem 1987, 67–68), the reduction of oil prices forced the government to push for maximum production and minimum consumption to remedy the situation. At the same time, being under constant threat of war and sanctions, it maintained development of light and heavy industry, since the procurement of arms to defend itself and support other revolutionary movements remained a priority.[4] Consequently, while several commodities—such as cars, televisions, and videos—were deemed unnecessary and their import stopped (67–68); food queues became longer, and a thriving black market developed.

When the government announced the launch of the *infitāḥ*, it began to lift restrictions on state import and export monopoly, introduce the concept of *tashruqiyya*, or self-management (Vandewalle 2006, 161), and open up the private sector. As mentioned in the previous chapter, many members of the security apparatuses (i.e., police, intelligence, military) began investing abroad the private capital that they had gained in past

---

4. It is interesting to note that some scholarly analyses of the impact of sanctions on Libya (O'Sullivan 2003; Vandewalle 2016), similar to CIA reports, impute economic difficulties to the bizarre procurements of weapons under imperialist assault, while avoiding discussion of the engineered recycling of Gulf state petrodollars into arms deals and US treasury bonds.

decades. The generation of young revolutionaries had gone on to accumulate wealth and power through misuse of public funds, appropriation of properties, and marital alliances with the families of rich businessmen from the old monarchical regime (see Ouannes 2009, 248). While the initial launch of egalitarian economic policies imposed strict legal limits on foreign dollarized capital (Naur 1986), this wave of liberalization had opened up the gates of investment and provided new ways to profit. The burden of international sanctions and the constant threat of war with the United States brought about a geopolitical uncertainty that also affected the intertemporal preferences of those who had the power to invest capital.[5] Therefore, it was not simply an individual decision that determined where to direct one's own investment, but the overall geopolitical context (see chapter 2). These changes moved across space and time, affecting people's lives and the structure of the regime at large. Military defeat generated ideological defeatism that served as an alibi for the increasing appearance of working-class underconsumption and conspicuous consumption by elites—in other words, socioeconomic inequalities. Starting with the elites, the population distanced itself from the goals and ambitions of the revolution, including the ways in which it had devised its economic strategy, and aimed instead to emulate the richer strata.

In such a context, quotidian commodities assumed even greater symbolic meaning, orienting people's imaginaries of both happiness and well-being. Fantasies about consumer desires represented an attempt by the lower classes to imitate the patterns of consumption of the upper classes. For instance, Omar described how the appearance on the market of fruit—in particular, bananas—which would normally be not available, could and did provoke an overly enthusiastic reaction from the population: "People used to fight over them. Some people died for one or two kilos of bananas. Can you imagine? You sacrifice yourself for a kilo of bananas!" (interview 2015). The British author and wife of a Libyan diplomat Susie M. Sandover

5. Above all, as Kadri (2016, 4) puts it, "Do investors think they make more or less money in the future?" Investment lodges in finance or short-gestation projects.

recounts a similar episode in her autobiography, in which she signals the symbolic importance of bananas after the US bombing of Libya in 1986 as well as their association with death: "Gaddafi made an order of bananas from Nicaragua and the shelves of the government stores were filled with boxes of this imported fruit. The Libyans rushed to the stores to acquire a box and in the ensuing mayhem, it is said that two women were crushed to death and many injured. It was a source of pride to offer people bananas when guests came for tea. People wanted to give their children a treat by letting them taste and see an actual banana and for that they had to queue for hours and fight" (2016, 97).

When compared with their symbolic qualities, the physical qualities of goods are usually of secondary importance (Beckert 2016). Indeed, the demand for bananas being capable of sparking a social craze in Libya should be interpreted vis-à-vis the imaginative and positional value that people accorded to them. In other words, consumers add to goods qualities that exist only through ascription of meaning (Beckert 2016, 194–96; Murillo 2017). The positional value of bananas, for instance, refers to the attempts of the lower classes to imitate the patterns of consumption of the upper classes; the imaginative dimension relates to the way everyday commodities embody an alternative vision of the world and the future. For these reasons, when the interviewees talked about the arrival of bananas in Libya for the first time in the 1990s, they recalled rumors that nobody knew how to eat them or what they were:

> There are stories that people would throw away the inside and eat the skin. (interview 2015)

> I heard a story about a guy who brought one kilo of bananas back from Malta. When his little brother saw them, he asked, "Oh, Khalifa, what's that? What is that thing?" Can you imagine? (interview 2015)

Bananas conferred social status on those who possessed them and questioned the dominant values and political agenda pursued by the regime, while creating a new vision of the good life (Luthar and Pušnik 2010, 346). The consumerist power of banana enabled people to move beyond the state-led measures and imagine an alternative structure of the everyday where abundance qua agency replaced shortages qua control.[6] However, when discussing the notion of scarcity in Hungary, Kristzina Fehérváry (2009, 432) argues that such an idea does not capture fully the manifold functioning mechanisms of state-led economies. We should acknowledge how these conceptual and empirical reflections on the notion of shortage and scarcity are constructed from the perspective of a society characterized by abundance (Verdery 1996, 434). In this light, the general lack of goods tells us less about the goods' quality and quantity and more about the standard by which many Libyans measured the fortunes of state-socialist modernity—that is, by setting the West, and thus capitalist modernity, as a threshold.

Chocolate and chewing gum also captured those emerging fantasies. Ibrahim and Nabil discussed the lack of sweets during their childhood in the 1980s:

I never had a bar of chocolate when I was a child. Not even an ice cream.

When I was growing up, we struggled to find some sweets. You could not find chocolate or chewing gum. It was impossible.

These tiny and seemingly unimportant instances of lack do not caricature the everyday lives of Libyans; rather, they acquire political significance because the inaccessibility of these items turned them into powerful tools for imagining a different future. What such statements signal, then, are the markers and standards used to gauge their society, meaning abundance of consumer choices and individual agency.

6. Those associations of the social craze for bananas with death and ignorance reveal another important function of rumors. As discussed in chapters 2 and 3, rumors mainly aligned with a larger structure of surveillance and control, thus ultimately reproducing the power of the regime. However, as those stories show, rumors also contain and reveal the pleasure of common imagining, which "exceeds the meagre satisfactions of truth" (Butler 2018). The rumor-like stories and gossip ask another to imagine along, build a reality, and make it true, thereby entering a parallel world that aims to escape everyday reality.

The most emblematic example is the comparison that Hassan provided when discussing how chewing gum had turned into something addictive and prohibited, like "hashish": "People were selling it like hashish in the streets. They approached you and said: 'Come here, I have chewing gum, do you want some?' It was something secret and not available at all" (interview 2015). Comparing chewing gum to hashish, Hassan conveys both the secretive and addictive elements of such product. Although there were numerous obstacles to obtaining them, people's clandestine and quotidian desire for it countered regime control of imported products. The desire for chocolate and chewing gum questioned the status of normality that people experienced in their everyday lives.

The book *Chewing Gum* (*al-'ilka*) by the Libyan writer Mansour Bushnaf, whose distribution in Libya was initially banned, allows us to contextualize and grasp further the role chewing gum played in the everydayness of Libyans.[7] Bushnaf writes that chewing gum summed up the social significance of those years of failing state-led capitalist policies and burdening international sanctions: "Libya fell into the grip of chewing-gum mania. In pursuit of this latest craze, citizens applied for passports, purchased dollars on the black market and queued up in front of airline offices to gain the right to travel overseas and bring back the precious commodity" (2008, 3). Bushnaf depicts chewing gum as "a philosophical project," which compelled and was debated by an entire society, "embodying aesthetic values that were translated into theatre, music, art, pop culture, doctoral dissertations in economics and political science and a classified top-secret dossier that caused much trouble to the security forces. It was debated by rightists, leftists, centre leftists, centre rightist, and so on, to no end. In brief, gum became everyone's obsession" (61).

While Bushnaf's book discusses themes that go far beyond chewing gum, such a metonym attests to the importance of so-called happy objects in everyday life. Chewing gum was an object filled with affect (Ahmed 2010) that spurred aspirations and disappointments, philosophical debates,

---

7. See also the critical reading in Diana (2017), which explores those themes unpacked by Bushnaf in his novel.

talk about economic reforms, and challenges to the security services, and thus negotiated the normative schemes of society. The question of secrecy connects further to the wider modes of informal exchanges, favors, and economies that began to emerge when the country fell under the grip of international sanctions. Chewing gum was sold on the street like hashish because it was one of those goods that belonged to the informal economies that thrived in the 1990s.

Similarly, trips to Malta emblematized this emerging informal economy because they captured the changing expectations of a new generation of Libyans that recognized itself less in the defeated ideological pillars of egalitarianism and anti-imperialism and aspired more to a consumerist, business-oriented society. As Saif remembered, since Libyans did not require a visa to visit Malta, many people jumped on a plane or a ferry: "If you had a bit of money, you would fly to Malta. It was 42 LYD return ticket. It used to take half an hour, and you were there. There was no visa to Malta. There used to be a ferry every day as well, and in a couple of hours you arrived." He also said that young people did not simply travel to Malta for "fun": "People started to make business from there, buying chocolate, sweets, and clothes, bringing them back. We were trying to make a living, make some money" (interview 2015).

Echoing Saif's words, in his book *The Libyan Paradox* Luis Martinez further documents the centrality of those ferry trips to Malta for many young Libyans during the early and mid-1990s, representing an "infringement of political taboos": "The voyage to Malta provides an opportunity to gain an insight into certain aspects of the political outlook of these younger Libyans. They express their opinions uninhibitedly. The topic of money looms large in their conversations, unsurprisingly for a group whose central preoccupation is trade" (2007, 36). These shopping or business expeditions, as much as the desire to chew gum, captured the alternative meanings of the "good life" emerging from people's everyday experiences. However, these aspirations for international and consumer goods, while coming to rescue of the national, obfuscated more than clarified the interdependent nature of Libya's economic problems with the existing US-led international order.

As discussed by Aida Hozic (2011), Yugoslavia experienced a similar political dynamic. Faced with economic problems, including high unemployment and the need to acquire foreign currency for rebalancing its debt, the Yugoslav government since the mid-1960s decided to capitalize on the existing migratory trends, allowing workers and tourists to either emigrate and find jobs or, more simply, travel in the West. By operating within the framework defined by the state, these travel and shopping/smuggling expeditions contributed to the system rather than subverted it. However, I would argue that it is also important to point out how, for Yugoslavs as much as for Libyans, these ordinary comforts and goods were not simply trade-offs that sustained the unchanging structure of an authoritarian regime. Rather, they symbolized the capitulation of a more progressive model of economic development to the diktat of the world market and Western interests, reflecting the emergence of a new political elite that had abandoned the more egalitarian policies of the past. In fact, one might argue that state-led economies purposefully engineered these repeated shortages of consumer goods to control the population, turning them into dictatorships over people's needs. In other words, as in the Soviet Union, we might imagine that consumer fantasies ought to function as forms of popular resistance. However, such analyses ignore that these governments, like the Jamahiriya, also operated under a wider geopolitical structure that prevented the establishment of an alternative to capitalist-led development. While consumer fantasies certainly articulated popular discontent towards the government they mirrored—without necessarily revealing—existing contradictions at the structural level.

This explains the contradictory nature of the regime and the political and economic changes that the country was undergoing. The emergence of a more commercial and consumerist way of living at the social level did not translate into a full embrace of a market-friendly economy. The regime's promises to reform alluded to possibilities of change, such as the abandonment of state-led policies and the creation of a more privatized and consumerist environment. However, these changes remained largely unimplemented and instead allowed the emergence of black markets, informal exchanges (wāsta), corruption, and the enrichment of a certain class that ultimately further widened the social inequality gap. In other words, Libya did not embrace a full neoliberalization of its economy, if compared to neighboring Egypt. Nonetheless, the appearance of areas like

"Haj al-Dollar" (Niblock 2001) in Benghazi, where those who had made fortunes by acquiring dollars during the sanctions period lived, reflected not only socioeconomic inequalities but also the erosion of the official discourse of the regime at the elite level. At the same time, they indicate the positional value—in other words, the desire to imitate upper-class patterns of consumption—that ordinary people accorded to those goods and activities. Therefore, while many regime-affiliated members had been able to profit during the period of international sanctions and adopt a lifestyle that contradicted the egalitarian ideals promoted by the regime (the fat cats), ordinary people found themselves forced to resort to alternative measures. The international sanctions, in fact, led to the underperformance of the public sector and the emergence of black markets. Moreover, those years witnessed the increasing development of smuggling routes with neighboring countries, where heavily state-subsided goods, such as foodstuffs and industrial goods and equipment (e.g., tractors, trucks), were diverted and resold at three times their price with the help of civil servants (Burgat 1995, 604–5). More generally, as discussed in chapter 3, people were forced to turn to search for secondary jobs outside the public sector, as well as the use of informal contacts and kinship to realize their fantasies of upward social mobility.

Overall, when consumerist everyday desires became the realm through which Libyans could construct critical assessments of the world around them, it is not possible to reduce such a discussion to an issue of chronic shortages of state-capitalist and rentier economies. Instead it is important to understand how the revolutionary desire to regain power to shape one's economy, culture, and society clashed with the interests of Western geopolitical forces. The UN multilateral sanctions, for instance, undermined the same infrastructural development that had represented a hallmark of the al-Fātiḥ Revolution, with tremendous social, economic, and humanitarian repercussions. The health sector witnessed the increasing delay of medical supplies, as well as complications in their import and storage. By 1994, just two years into the UN sanctions' regime, as many as nine thousand medical patients had to be treated outside of the country, since Libya was not allowed access to the necessary equipment to treat them. Medical staff reductions, at the same time, had seriously impaired the functioning of the health services, which were strongly dependent on the expertise of foreign doctors. Archival documents from the United Nations reveal the extent of the impact across several industrial sectors, including oil, transportation, and agriculture.[8] Meanwhile, inflation had reached record rates, at 42 percent in 1993, peaking at 50 percent in 1994 (Haddad 2004).

In such a context, it is possible to understand Munir when he said: "When we had money, there was nothing to buy. When everything was available, we had no money" (interview 2019). When the Libyan postcolonial state had pursued a vision of development reclaiming economic sovereignty, national security and regional solidarity, which had flourished within the historical moment of decolonization, there was liquidity but no consumer goods, since the state provided them. However, as the economy opened under *infitāḥ* and geopolitical pressure, money was no longer available because of the rising inflation triggered by international sanctions and the emergence of a stratified class society. This configuration of Libya's economy had been taking place since the late 1980s and was pursued further when the country rejoined the international community in the early 2000s, and it continued to shape the ways of being and desiring in Libyans' everyday lives. More specifically, at this juncture, when the country had been rehabilitated in the international arena, the future tense for Libya aligned with the regional promise of Dubai.

## Dreaming Dubai, Building Sirte

> Shaykh Zayed came to Libya in 1970 and said that he wanted Dubai to look like Tripoli. Dubai was a desert at that time. And now it's the other way around. In 2007, I went to Dubai and it is amazing.

---

8. To gauge the extent of the international sanctions' impact on Libyan industrial/health/infrastructure/oil sectors, please see this collection of reports and letters submitted by the representative Libyan Arab Jamahiriya to the UN secretary general (in both English and Arabic), such as S/23915/1992; S/24428/1992; S/1994/921; S/1995/226; S/1996/717; S/1997/404; S/1999/457, https://digitallibrary.un.org/?ln_en (accessed August 15, 2022).

Shaykh Zayed came to visit Libya from the UAE in the 1970s and he
said that he wanted Dubai to be like Tripoli. Now it's the other way
around! Libya is stuck in the 1970s!

interviews, 2015–17

In the aftermath of the 1969 Revolution, Libya had embraced a developmental path that reflected the sociopolitical context then prevailing in the
wider African and Asian postcolonial resistance (Kadri 2016; Da'na 2019).
By the 2000s, however, Dubai and the Gulf more widely had become the
new benchmark for gauging regional development. In this regard, the
above anecdote was reiterated numerous times in the collected interviews
(2015, 2016, 2018). Although the story was recounted in different ways, the
meaning conveyed remained the same. In the 1970s, the former leader of
the UAE, Shaykh Zayed, who was visiting the country either for dental or
eye surgery (interviews 2015–16), was stunned by Libya's level of infrastructural development; in the 2000s, it was the other way around. The
Libyan wheel of modernization and development had turned in the opposite direction for more than thirty years. While Libya failed to advance,
Dubai and, more generally, the UAE had become an emblem of progress
in the region. Put simply, Dubai became for Libyans a way to measure
success and the good life compared to their country, which was lagging
behind in a state of desperation and underdevelopment. It is interesting to
examine which aspects of this fantasy my interlocutors related to in order
to imagine a different future: "People compare Libya to Gulf countries
because we have a similar good: oil. Thus, we are supposed to be very rich,
like Qatar, like Dubai. We wanted to have high salaries" (interview 2015).

The intense growth of the population (Braun and Jones 2014)—with
more than 50 percent being under the age of twenty (World Bank 2006,
8), was putting "pressure on the Libyan labor market."[9] The lack of jobs

9. As Libya reentered the international arena and began allowing international
financial experts into the country, those factors (e.g., rigidity of the labor market, cut of
state-subsidies, too large public sector) were emphasized to explain the economic problems of the Jamahiriya in the 2000s (United Nations International Labor Organization
2010; see also Abuhadra and Ajaali 2014, 9–11).

other than in the public sector (Mohamed 2014, 304) caused growth in unemployment and steadily increased the demand for social services, particularly in education and health care (African Development Bank 2009). Furthermore, there was great dissatisfaction among Libyans about Law No. 15 of 1981, which was introduced to regulate the salaries of civil servants and employees of state-owned companies. Under this law, all public companies, including private ones in which the state had a minimal percentage interest, had been required to apply its provisions—that is, salaries had been substantively frozen, with only minimal increases since 1981. The Libyan condition contrasted sharply with the Dubai model, wherein nationals enjoy a range of special allowances that, when added to their salaries, raised them to approximately twice those of non-nationals employed in the same job (Hvidt 2009). While comparisons of Libya with Arab Gulf countries stem from the abundance of a key natural resource in both, it collapses in the face of the mounting frustration that Libyans experienced regarding their country's inability to match the level of economic development and quality of life that Dubai provided for its citizens. As my interlocutors noted, Libya lacked basic infrastructure, ranging from education and health services to jobs:

Everywhere we went, we saw development. When we traveled outside Libya, we went to the Gulf, and we saw their infrastructure: airplanes, hospitals, jobs, and education. And what happened in Libya? It went backward. Can you imagine?

During the monarchy, Libya used to have a Grand Prix of F1 [Formula 1]. Now, it takes place in Doha, in Qatar. We should be like Dubai . . . and we can be like these countries in the Gulf. (interviews 2015)

Dubai embodies material elements (Kanna 2011; Kathiravelu 2016; Krane 2009) that allow us to comprehend further the significance of this metaphor (Elsheshtawy 2008, 2010) and reflect the desire for a model of modernity that Libya had once embodied but no longer did by the early 2000s. For instance, the reference to the racing circuit in Tripoli, which was set up by the Italians and lasted from 1925 to 1940, is indicative of how some interlocutors felt comfortable in going as far as praising the Italian Fascist and colonial rule of Libya rather than accepting their ordinary conditions. These sketches of simultaneous everyday frustration and aspiration explain why Dubai was upheld as a measure of success, with the scale of this measurement resting in a model of capitalist modernity oriented toward the future. Dubai's infrastructural development, comprising skyscrapers (Elsheshtawy 2010, 131–67), the largest man-made island, or enormous shopping malls (178–87) are all futuristic megaprojects that allowed the development of a corporate, consumerist-oriented image of the emirate (Kanna 2011). Dubai embodied an idea of what the state should look like and what the economy should deliver to the population.

Moreover, even though those narratives omitted problematic aspects upon which the success of Dubai was built, they did so because they aligned with the ordinary aspirations of Libyans.[10] Dubai's economic model is founded on a highly exploitative system of migrant labor, which forbids basic human rights to guest workers, onto whom the emirate could transfer the worst impacts of the 2008 economic crisis with little regard for their social consequences (Hanieh 2011, 178).[11] In Libya, while unemployment had reached levels of 20–25 percent in the 2000s (St. John 2008), the intake of foreign sub-Saharan workers in less-well-paid sectors did not diminish.[12] The social demand for public-sector jobs with higher salaries was linked to the social stigma among many young Libyans of taking less prestigious jobs, or those requiring intense labor (Mohamed 2014, 304). In addition, as other studies have discussed, there was unwillingness among Libyans to trade "the uncertain economic future of a full-scale market economy for the steady wages and subsidies, which enabled them to enjoy a standard of living envied by neighboring countries" (Otman and Karlberg

10. On the political vulnerability of Dubai and the UAE, see the work of Davidson (2005, 2009, 2015).

11. On the toxic and exploitative relationship between Dubai and the migrant work force, see Human Rights Watch (2006); and Kathiravelu (2016).

12. In 2010, according to unofficial documents, the number of foreign African workers in Libya totaled 2 million, many of them under illegal status (documented in United Nations Watch 2010).

2007, 221).[13] Moreover, in Dubai political authority is concentrated in the hands of a small familial circle, while the state, which intervenes pervasively in every aspect of society (Davidson 2009), has become increasingly oppressive toward its dissidents in recent years (Davidson 2011).

In such a light, when discussing the goals of the 2011 protests in Libya against the regime and, more broadly, in the Arab region, interlocutors also referred to Dubai as follows: "We wanted to build Libya, to have foreign companies coming to Libya. We wanted to build Libya by focusing on infrastructure, education system, and the economy. I remember most people saying: 'We want Libya to become like the UAE, like Dubai.' This was one of the sayings that summarized the goal of the revolution in 2011" (interview 2015). Similar reflections emerge more insistently and convincingly when interviewees discussed how people's material conditions, their social security, and high salaries—rather than freedom—lay at the core of the demands and struggle that many people pursued in 2011: "People demonstrated because of the economic situation, not just for freedom. They want to travel, make tourism, and get married. This is what people are looking for. We don't compare ourselves to the West, every Libyan wants to live like the citizens in Dubai or Qatar, where they have high salaries. We don't care about politics, we don't care about the regime, elections, who will be the leader. You want to be secure" (interview 2015).

While expressions of desire to improve material conditions recurred in the interviews, the issue of democracy or political representation emerged nowhere near as much as the demand for a guarantee of an economically stable and secure life. More specifically, the expression "We don't compare ourselves to the West" reveals two important and interrelated aspects. First, the fantasy of Dubai starts to distance itself from the abundance-qua-agency consumerist desires that had characterized the years of the Cold War and turned Libyans closer to the so-called West. Second, this distance from the

---

13. Such internal contradictions persist up to this day. In framing the role of the state in the economy, the documents of the ongoing national reconciliation dialogue continue to present such characteristics: while they call for more business and privatization, they insist that the Libyan government should retain a paternalist component, providing and subsidizing goods for its people (Center for Humanitarian Dialogue 2018).

West does not involve renouncing a model of modernization that characterized Western capitalist, consumerist modernity; rather, it demonstrates the success and prominence of Dubai as a regional model that had been able to reconcile more traditional cultural traits (i.e., an Arab/Islamic identity) with Western modernity, galvanizing the people of the region. Like the aspirations and hopes of Egyptians as captured by Samuli Schielke, the Gulf, and especially Dubai, "gradually gained a hegemonic status as a central site of modernity in the Middle East" (Schielke 2015, 283).

Dubai became the future tense of Libya because it encapsulated what many Libyans hoped for in terms of a better life. Those instances of aspiration and imagination represent a cultural capacity, in the sense that they emerge from within local systems of value, meaning, communication, and dissent. While aspiration is a universal practice of everyday life, its force and content relate to the values, institutional norms, and historical context in which they emerge (Appadurai 2013, 290). The fantasy of Dubai was not immune to this process; in fact, it emerged in both interaction and contestation with questions of (inter)national politics and political economy.

For instance, the fantasy of Dubai has—until now—been seen to reflect as a desire for a different model of modernization, as well as a willingness to see the state as an institution providing more to its citizens in light of its abundant resources. However, this fantasy openly refused some policies of the Libyan regime and thus became a contested terrain because its way of imagining the future clashed with the clusters of aspirations of many other Libyans. For them, to embrace this model of development embodied in the fantasy of Dubai entailed a loss, a renunciation of national sovereignty to the benefit of colonial and imperialist forces:

> For Libya to be like Dubai meant losing its sovereignty and accepting the power of the US.

> The Gulf States are the puppets of the US. In 2011, those "rebels" sold their country to them. (interviews 2015)

These statements echo the Libyan regime's long-standing confrontational stance toward the conservative Arab states of the Persian Gulf, particularly

Saudi Arabia, which Qaddafi often denounced as being "puppets of America" deliberately hindering the unity of the Arab world.[14] As already discussed, the hegemonic conception of Libyan foreign policy as rogue and unpredictable shows a profound lack of understanding of Libyan ideology, from which most of the country's strategic and tactical choices followed. For instance, the question of Arab unity lay at the center of the 1969 Revolution and its ideological underpinnings, which is why the regime often opted to adopt political and economic strategies that supported those goals: promoting the 1973 OPEC embargo to pressure Western governments over the Palestinian issue as well as numerous attempts to pursue projects of political unity and solidarity with Arab countries. The Libyan government pushed for or attempted to achieve Arab communal action for many years, yet, as Younis Lahwej (1998, 213–14) points out, "the lack of realism along with the perception of Libya in the Arab world, the accumulated problems of the Arab countries, and foreign power involvement in the region, made the idea difficult to implement." In such a context, it is possible to understand how the relationship between Libya and the Arab states in the Persian Gulf remained tense, if not openly confrontational, particularly considering the centrality of the Gulf states for the sustainment of US global dominance.

For instance, Saudi Arabia had opposed Libya's plans of expansion in Chad, supporting the coalition of Hissène Habré and aligning itself with the United States, France, Israel, and Sudan. The first Gulf War in 1990 also fueled the political dispute between Libya and those states, which radicalized the former's political position among them. Following the Iraqi invasion of Kuwait, the Libyan regime insisted on finding a resolution to the conflict among Arab states and firmly rejected the Western military presence on Arab soil in all forms, considering it a direct threat to the security of the Arab world. To this date, the logistical and infrastructural presence of the US military in the Arabian Peninsula has been a firm and long-standing feature, considered a strategic node of military transport,

14. During an Arab Summit in 2009, Qaddafi denounced King Abdullah as "a British product and American ally" (Darwish 2009) and defined the Gulf States as "puppets of the West" in one of his last speeches in 2011 (libyafirst1969 2012).

transit, and commerce (Khalili 2018). Additionally, while Libya wanted to turn oil into a weapon of foreign policy, the Saudi monarchy avoided pursuing such a strategy. As previously explained, Saudi Arabia could dictate the level of oil prices and had no interest to hurt Western economies, since such maneuvers could threaten its close political-security alliance with the United States (Vitalis 2006; Wright 2021). Overall, the remarkable transformation of the Gulf is intimately linked to its vital role in the maintenance of US power today globally (Hanieh 2018). The Gulf region has been the fulcrum around which the global economy was consolidated in the last two decades—thanks to its commodity exports providing energy (oil), its financial flows balancing the global deficits, and its acquisition of armaments and military technologies from Western countries (2018).[15] Inevitably, while controlling the Gulf region became a vital necessity for the United States, the Gulf has acquired an increasingly dominant role in the region. The so-called Arab built environment—in other words, its telecommunications sector and humanitarian, and infrastructural development—has become a key site where neoliberal reform and Gulf capital accumulation act symbiotically. The leading role of Arab Gulf countries in the region was consolidated in conjunction with the United States, which ensured their regional political power and fostered their close cooperation, via the creation of the Gulf Cooperation Council (GCC) that entered into direct competition with the project of the Arab League or the Arab Market Union (Hanieh 2011).

As such, when the fantasy of Dubai became a signifier for reconciliation with the West, it clashed with the long-standing position of the regime, which refused to become a principal host and supporter of US imperialism in the Middle East, as Ahmed also stated: "In 2009, Qaddafi spoke the truth against those big powers at the United Nations summit. He did the same among the Arab countries, but nobody ever listened to him" (interview 2015). Ahmed's words refer to two remarkable moments

15. As Kadri outlines (2015), much of regional oil revenues, especially in the Gulf, fly abroad in US T-bills, affluent consumption, and military and regime security spending; defense spending alone is twice the world share from GDP, according to the World Bank, with American military aid to the Arab region ranking highest.

in 2008 and 2009, respectively. The former took place during a meeting of the Arab League in Syria, in the aftermath of the execution of Saddam Hussein that followed the US invasion of Iraq, where Qaddafi denounced the lack of unity and efforts among Arab states to launch an investigation, bluntly suggesting that "any of you might be the next one" (in Al-Jazeera 2008; for Qaddafi's speech, see 71960). In other words, such a fate could befall any of the Arab leaders if America was not pleased with them. The latter took place at the United Nations Summit in New York, where Qaddafi proposed to rename the UN Security Council the "Terror Council."

At the national level, such a realignment of Libya with respect to Dubai was seen as in contradiction with Qaddafi's projects for the African continent. It is important to point out that cooperation with African states had always been part of the political agenda of the Libyan regime, yet the wider scope and nature of the political and economic investment that took place from the late 1990s onward coincided with the support provided by African states to Libya in its stand-off with the West, when the country fell under the grip of international sanctions following the Lockerbie case. During the 34th African summit in Ouagadougou in 1998, the Organization of African Unity (OAU) independently took the decision to end the air embargo on Libya and proclaimed "on moral and religious grounds and with immediate effect that the OAU and its members will not comply from now on with the sanctions imposed against Libya related to religious obligations, providing humanitarian emergencies or fulfilling OAU statutory obligations" (Organization of African Unity 1998). In reaction to this, the US State Department announced how "extremely disturbed by this short-sighted action" the United States was and called upon OAU members to "rescind this irresponsible decision" (Matar and Thabit 2004, 103).

As a result of this unique support vis-à-vis the passivity and fragmentation of Arab states, the Libyan regime stepped up its cooperation attempts, and in 1999 an official meeting was hosted in the Libyan city of Sirte to proclaim the establishment of the African Union (AU). As the text of the declaration reads, "inspired by the important proposals submitted by Colonel Muammar Qaddafi, Leader of the Great al-Fātiḥ Libyan Revolution, and particularly, by his vision for a strong and united Africa" (Organization of African Unity 1999), those states decided to ensure the speedy establishment of all the institutions deemed necessary for the project of the African Union, such as the African Central Bank, the African Monetary Union, the African Court of Justice, and, in particular, the Pan-African Parliament (1999). In 2002, Qaddafi also proposed the establishment of a single continental army (Alusala 2004). In this renewed spirit of regional cooperation, the city of Sirte embodied a model of economic and political development that clashed strongly with the widely shared fantasy of Dubai.

When discussing the events of 2011, Salah pointed out that Qaddafi's plans for Africa determined the fate of the country and explained the military intervention of Western countries: "The West did not like that Libya rejected the control of the IMF for Africa and Qaddafi was creating a golden currency, making it independent from the West" (interview 2015). Having abandoned the military struggle against the West, Qaddafi believed that Western imperialism now relied on the tools of economic globalization (i.e., conditional aid, debt) to subjugate Africa (Kwera 2008). This vision of globalization as an imperialist project had emerged as a result of Libya's gradual abandonment of its moral, financial, and physical support of liberation movements. During the 3rd Congress of the World Mathaba, also called Anti-Imperialist Center (AIC), Qaddafi declared that revolutionary forces should now confront "the concept of globalisation. The conflict is between us and imperialism. Imperialism wants globalisation to be an imperialist one. America wants it to be American globalisation. . . . We will fight to make globalisation an international one" (Final Call 2000).[16]

For these reasons, the Libyan regime pursued a foreign policy of diplomatic expansion and economic investment toward the African continent (St. John 2000; Boucek 2002; Amouzou 2012). These policies further hindered normalization with the United States in particular, because, for example, Qaddafi lobbied the African Union to reject the presence of the US African Command Army (AFRICOM) on African soil, forcing them to

---

16. The Mathaba, also called the Anti-Imperialist Center (AIC), was established in 1982 by the Libyan government; in 2000 Qaddafi organized a conference to mark the twentieth anniversary of the revolution (Final Call 2000).

relocate their headquarters to Frankfurt, Germany (Forte 2012). The Gulf monarchies, on the contrary, have embraced a progressively normalizing stance toward the Zionist-Israeli occupation of Palestine, encapsulated in the signing of the recent Abraham Accords. Moreover, in July 2021, the African Union readmitted Israel as an observer country, almost twenty years after ousting it from the Pan-African bloc thanks to the pressure of then-Libyan leader Qaddafi (Sokol and Lis 2021). Also, Libya sponsored and supported the launch of the first African-owned communication satellite, whose creation put an end to lucrative subcontracts for Western countries (Glazebrook 2012; Tchaleu 2014). As private emails from the account of Hillary Clinton released by WikiLeaks during the 2011 events further suggest, Libya was planning the launch of important monetary changes for the African continent. It had, in fact, accumulated 143 tons of gold that were intended to be used to establish a Pan-African currency based on the Libyan golden dinar; the plan was designed to provide the francophone African countries with an alternative to the French franc (Wikileaks 2011). The shift of the Libyan regime from armed support to revolutionary groups to a fight against globalization and the role of international institutions in pursuit of a multipolar world shared numerous aspects with the policies of the Bolivarian Republic of Venezuela under Hugo Chavez, whose collaboration with Qaddafi was once defined as "Harvard for Tyrants" (Farah 2011).[17]

One of the core elements of the fantasy of Dubai that helps explain the wider alienation people experienced in their everyday lives is the gradual rejection of the ideological pillars that sustained the regime's policies, and, more specifically, its alleged anti-imperialist positioning. This rejection sheds light on the desires of Libyans to embrace capitalist modernity, thus abandoning the policies that relegated the country to a long period of

17. Both countries were pursuing projects of political solidarity aiming to reduce the economic and political reliance of their respective continents on Western countries and international financial institutions, which included the African Union, the Community of Sahel-Saharan States (CEN-SAD), the Alianza Bolivariana para los Pueblos de Nuestra América—Tratado de Comercio de los Pueblos (ALBA-TCP), and Banco del Sur or Petro-Caribe (Capasso 2021).

isolation. As Ahmed explained, Qaddafi and Libya had essentialized the West as a way to support their own power and, consequently, to carry out the internal suppression of the people: "We had one choice; we should be friends—not enemies—with the US. Otherwise, you are the loser. . . . Qaddafi was the first one to be disillusioned but he wanted Libyans to believe in that. He wanted to be the greatest person in the world for us, Libyans . . . he used to do businesses under the table with them, as he did with Bush and Obama. Otherwise, he would have ended up like Saddam" (interview 2015). The anti-imperialist stance of the regime had lost its appeal among parts of the elites, as well as among the population. Such policies came to be seen as a failed and anachronistic ideological system that never benefited the Libyan population, only the regime. Overall, the aspiration for Dubai reflects the military-ideological defeat of the Libyan revolution, which had massively eroded social consensus and popular support for its main ideological pillars. The future did not lie in past and defeatist political approaches but in the successful model that Dubai represented.

By looking at the reaction of international development agencies, this tension further emerges. While the regime was gradually coming out of international isolation, and sanctions were being lifted in the early 2000s, the international community praised its attempt to undertake those measures deemed necessary to relaunch the country's economy, which meant privatizing it and adopting a more market-oriented model of economic governance. As IMF documents state, the Libyan authorities "were in general agreement with staff on the need for Libya to pursue more vigorously and in a coordinated manner its structural reform agenda" (International Monetary Fund 2006, 3). The IMF structural reform agenda was clear and standard. The main issues for the Libyan regime to tackle included the gradual removal of subsidies, the enacting of a privatization law, the removal of the US$50 million floor for foreign investment, and—more generally—overcoming the long legacy of centralized economic management (2006). However, official governmental willingness often translated into "slow and discontinuous progress" (International Monetary Fund 2007, 12) toward the development of a market economy. Such discontinuity notably emerged in the Libyan leader's public approach to those reforms. Popular support for the privatization of the economy

(International Monetary Fund 2005) was coupled with a strong reluctance to fully embrace those measures and often evolved into a complete antagonistic attitude.

Since the early years of the revolution, in fact, the Libyan leadership had linked such measures of economic privatization to a neocolonial, imperialist project that countries of the Arab world should have done everything to avoid: "You will see that those who have failed to resolve their economic problems in their countries and who could not mobilise popular forces for development and for the exploitation of the country's resources turn . . . toward *infitāḥ*, as in Egypt. They open the gates to foreign exploitative capital, to sumptuous palaces, to American corporations, to multinationals . . . throwing themselves into the arms of economic colonialism" (Barrada, Kravetz, and Whitaker 1984). Therefore, in the early 2000s, such rhetoric had not disappeared, and Qaddafi continued to denounce the existence of a strong neoimperialist agenda guiding the policies of international lenders like the World Bank and the IMF toward the Arab world and the African continent (Takeh 2002, 11).

By the 2000s, I argue, many Libyans perceived the regime as construing the West as Other not in order to challenge and defeat it, but in order to control the Libyan self at home. In response, a sort of anti-official Occidentalism emerged—a way in which Libyans employed the West as a category and a discourse to contest the power of the regime.[18] Like the figure of Qaddafi as discussed in the previous chapter, the West functioned as a nodal point (Laclau and Mouffe 1985), which illuminates how everyday politics in the Libyan Arab Jamahiriya interacted with global processes. The ordinary perception that Libyans had of the increasingly personalized rule of Qaddafi also signified that those Pan-African policies were understood as being the exclusive result of Qaddafi's choices. These latter points become even more glaring when my interlocutors posed a question that illustrates Qaddafi's support of Africa as another sign of his personalized

18. A similar dynamic at play existed in the USSR, particularly during those years before the final collapse, as described by Alexei Yurchak (2013), who writes about how the West was allowed to transcend the political boundaries of USSR in the collective imaginary.

and contradictory governing of Libya. More specifically, what emerges is how the "father" (Qaddafi) failed to provide for his children, focusing instead on those people "outside of the family."

The model of Sirte with its orientation toward Africa becomes a cultural marker signaling backwardness and underdevelopment, when compared to the fantasy of Dubai and its promise of modernity toward the West, which was also expressed with the use of racist stereotypes. The rejection of Qaddafi's plans for the African continent fueled social discontent, which was, in turn, directed toward sub-Saharan workers in the form of lynching or racist acts of violence.[19] Those episodes often forced the Jamahiriya to repatriate migrant workers to their native countries.[20] In this regard, the appearance of slave markets in contemporary Libya should not only appear as a surprise but also be understood as the result of racist stereotypes. As one interviewee stated: "He always repeated that Libyans should go and invest in Africa, but why was Qaddafi not the first one to marry off his daughter to an African man?" (interview 2017). This parental and familial imagery strikes important sociocultural chords, which translate into the longing for a ruler who meets his family's expectations. Dreaming of the monarchs in the Gulf, those mundane desires oppose a father (Qaddafi) who is accused of marrying his daughter (Libya) off to an African man.[21] As people sought a figure capable of providing more for them and fulfilling the dreams of his children, the political rise of Saif al-Islam gained momentum and seemed able to magnetize those clusters of desires and promises for upward social mobility, higher salaries, better infrastructure, and global ambitions articulated thus far.

19. Staub (2006) provides a good perusal of the conditions of sub-Saharan workers in Libya.

20. Many interviewees, for instance, referred to an uprising in Zawiya (though many more took place throughout the country), where lynching and protests forced them to leave. This dimension is also explored in various scholarly works. See Ouannes (2009, 280–83); and Chorin (2012, 151).

21. See also how Schatzberg (2001, 23–24) describes the moral matrix of "the father" in Middle Africa.

**Rat or Hope?**

> Many people thought that their life would improve with Saif al-Islam coming to power. That's why most people in Libya were waiting for Qaddafi to pass his power to Saif.
>> interview with Abdullah, 2015

> With Saif, we would have not reached this place. Many Libyans felt that he was better than his father.
>> interview with Abadi, 2015

> *Ibn al-kāfir kāfir*! The son of a rat will continue digging.
>> interview with Musbah, 2015

> *Hādhā al-shibl min dhāk al-asad* (A chip off the old block).
>> interview with Amina, 2017

Did Saif al-Islam represent hope for the country's future, and its people? Or was he only the spoiled son of an already authoritarian father? These questions capture the way many of my interlocutors recounted and oriented themselves toward Saif al-Islam, Muammar Qaddafi's second son with his second wife, Safiyya. While some interviewees used the Libyan sayings to describe a mentality—a tribal and blood-related continuity running through the Qaddafi family that doomed any possibility of changing Libya—many others saw the young son as somebody who was willing to steer the country in the direction of Dubai, to modernize and develop it. Yet, as this book aims to show, the debate is always more complex, ambiguous, and nuanced than the material and epistemological violence that erupted in 2011 and divided Libya into two camps.

Having received a degree in architecture in 1994 from the al-Fātiḥ University of Tripoli, Saif was known as *al-muhandis* (the engineer). From 2003 on, he rose to national and international notoriety and was increasingly considered the heir to his father's power and closely linked to numerous and important political maneuvers aiming to reform Libya (Griswold 2010; Sadiki 2014). The first international recognition of his activities came about in 2000. After having established the Gaddafi

International Charity and Development Foundation (GICDF) in 1999, Saif claimed that his foundation had provided the funds and diplomatic effort for the release of six out of twenty-one European hostages who had been captured during the Sipadan crisis in the Philippines by a splinter group of the Moro National Liberation Front (MNLF), Abu Sayyaf (Penketh 2000). The GICDF was also the only nongovernmental organization (NGO) authorized to handle human rights issues in Libya. Together with his international missions and ambitions, Saif's goals for the foundation were to develop the texture and foundation of a local civil society through various activities, while addressing very sensitive matters entailing past government abuses of power.[22] Saif relentlessly pursued open diplomacy with Western governments, the United States in particular, in order to make Libya a country of primary interest to foreign investors. In 2003, for instance, he published an article in *Middle East Policy* suggesting that Libya was "now ready to transform decades of mutual antagonism into an era of genuine friendship" (Al-Qadhafi 2003, 44) with the United States. Saif's name, therefore, came to be associated with many of those enduring tensions that had characterized both the national and international political dynamics of the country.

Shaykh Hussein, an ex-member of the Islamist opposition group LIFG, explained that Saif contributed to democratizing and relaxing the atmosphere of surveillance and suspicion that had characterized much of everyday life for Islamist-oriented groups in Libya. He recounted how, during the 1980s, the security apparatus reported Shaykh Hussein and his brother as political opponents (*zanādiqah*). This decision had major consequences for his life, since it prompted him to leave Libya for the UK after having lived in Sudan and Yemen (interview 2015). In 2006, when Saif started the negotiations for the release of more than two hundred prisoners affiliated with Islamist groups that had tried to overthrow the regime, particularly those belonging to the LIFG, Shayk Hussein's hopes began to change. Those negotiations concluded successfully in 2010 with

22. An online summary of the activities carried out in 2007–8 is still available online, in Arabic (Aljamahiria.org 2022).

the prisoners' official renunciation of jihad against the regime and the release of a formal 417-page document, entitled "Corrective Studies in Understanding of Jihad, Enforcement of Morality, and Judgement of People" that forbade armed insurgency and advocated tolerance of other ideologies and religions (Ashour 2012). While some commentators stressed that this deradicalization initiative was an attempt to boost Saif's credibility in the West (Cruickshank 2009), the book stood nevertheless as the culmination of three years of negotiations between the regime and the imprisoned/exiled leadership, with practical and important results and ramifications. For instance, the LIFG leadership split, with one faction becoming increasingly connected to al-Qa'ida. As the Sinjar Records show (Felter and Fishman 2007), many Libyans began entering Iraq around 2007 to fight the American occupation. Moreover, Saif's efforts to normalize the relationship with those who had been accused of being enemies of the revolution encouraged many people, like Shayk Hussein, to travel safely back to the country after seventeen years. More than four hundred prisoners were freed and were able to return to their homes. Interestingly, these included many of the leaders who started fighting against the regime in 2011 and whose military and operational skills, together with generous Western funds and training, contributed to its fall.

As with those negotiations, Saif was involved in two other crucial and controversial initiatives within Libya. First, he offered public support to the families of those prisoners who disappeared from the Abu Salim prison in 1996. Although the killings took place in 1996, the regime's official recognition of those events only came eight years later, in April 2008, when it acknowledged the incident and the right of the families to know what happened to their relatives. As the wall of silence was broken, and those families found the courage to challenge the regime through constant enquiries about their family members' fates (Zarrugh 2018), they were encouraged by the public calls of Saif.[23] During those years, an administrative body was

---

23. On Saif's initiatives on human rights abuses and extraordinary detentions, see Human Rights Watch (2009); and Amnesty International (2010).

established to deal with such disappearances and human rights abuses and provide information and compensation to the families, the Department of Martyrs, Prisoners, Missing Persons, and War Casualties, including those who had participated in the war in Chad. Second, Saif openly criticized the increasing politicization of the verdict of the trial against five Bulgarian nurses and a Palestinian doctor who had been sentenced to death, having been accused of infecting more than four hundred children with the HIV virus in Libyan hospitals.[24] When the nurses and the doctor were extradited to Bulgaria in 2007, it appeared that the release came about as the result of close talks between Saif and Nicolas Sarkozy, then French prime minister, over the sale of arms to Libya (Astier 2007).

For those reasons, Saif's attempts to draft a constitution and bring home Libyans who lived in exile, offering them political positions, were remarkable steps. According to Hamid, Saif's policies improved the societal perception of the regime and fed hopes for a better life, even though Libya "needed a miracle." As Rajab stated, Saif's initiatives not only raised expectations among people but also produced a tangible change in society: "After 2005, Saif changed many things and we witnessed them. Infrastructure started. Universities opened. Most Libyans thought the next president of Libya would be Saif" (interview 2015).

Considering the sense of unyielding predetermination of people's everyday lives under the Jamahiriya, one should comprehend the figure of Saif as activating hope for a better future. Focused on the younger generation, Saif appeared to be the man who was capable of steering Libyan modernization. His unique orientation toward the future was also signaled by the name of his program, "Tomorrow's Libya" or "Libya of Tomorrow" (*Libya al-Ghad*).[25] As part of the program, he sponsored the setting up of two television stations, *al-Libiyya* and *al-Shabābiyya*, and two online newspapers, *Oea* and *Quryna*, that did not refrain from tackling delicate and controversial political issues or questioning the regime

24. For some general information on the Bulgarian case, see Ronen (2007).

25. The report contains the most important points of *Libya al-Ghad* in terms of economic reforms (see Porter and Yergin 2006).

and its policies.[26] While mundane goods captured the desire for a more consumerist society, al-Islam's program of reforms drew very closely on the success story of Dubai. In documents summarized by the international research agency, Monitor Group (2007), Harvard economists Michael Porter and Daniel Yergin (2006) present the Gulf States as a key model for Libya to imitate in order to build a prosperous vision until 2019 (Wallis 2008), including the draft of a constitution, which Libya had lacked since 1977. The general narrative proposed by the two American scholars insisted on the reduction of political uncertainty in order to foster internationally risk-taking investments and entrepreneurial activities (General Planning Council of Libya 2006), repeating the same IMF tantrum discussed previously.

The figure and program of Saif not only magnetized people's aspirations but also offered concrete services, such as scholarships for studying abroad, as Mansour noted: "How did Saif al-Islam satisfy his people? Through Libya al-Ghad, he built more infrastructure, and, for instance, four thousand students got a scholarship, which meant that most Libyan families had one. To get a scholarship was such a great opportunity. Before 2007, they were only given to specific people. You needed good contacts" (interview 2014). With a focus on the building of civil society, Saif launched several educational initiatives that included the provision of one million laptops to schoolchildren, as well as the awarding of four thousand scholarships for pursuing specialized degrees abroad.[27] Mansour acknowledged how Tomorrow's Libya provided chances ("scholarships") without the need to rely on "good contacts," thus suggesting a gradual overcoming of the pyramid of *wāsta* and corruption discussed earlier. In June 2003, for instance, Qaddafi's appointment of Shukri Ghanem, a little-known oil economist, to the post of general secretary of the General People's Committee, seemed to further prove the regime's willingness to support Saif's

---

26. Those newspapers and television channels belonged to the Al-Ghad Media Group; see El Issawi (2013, 6).

27. At the time of the interviews, many interviewees (about fifteen of them) were completing a study program abroad thanks to the scholarships provided by Tomorrow's Libya.

program. Ghanem was a close friend and ally of Saif, and his appointment broke from the usual reshuffling of ministers (112 in total) that the Libyan regime had undergone in the past thirty years. Saif, together with a group of like-minded political figures—also called reformists—appeared to be on the verge of breaking from state-led economic programs in order to modernize and privatize the country, as many Libyans hoped.

Moreover, this wind of change seemed to guarantee a more equal access to social opportunities, reducing unnecessary participation in those revolutionary organizations that often represented the only chances to realize fantasies of upward social mobility. As Hamza explained: "It's not my age, it's not in my time because, honestly, in 2006, when Saif al-Islam started his project of Libya al-Ghad, all these roles were not so important anymore. Things started changing in Libya, no more need to join RC or strict dealing with employees. . . . It was the best time ever of the Qaddafi's regime . . . in 2006 to 2010" (interview 2015). The narrative juxtaposes the arbitrariness and corruption of the past with the appearance of a more relaxed environment in the country, thus suggesting that the regime was providing what the people wanted.

Saif, in fact, persistently criticized the level of institutional corruption and accused the old revolutionary "fat cats" (Al-Arabiya 2006; Reuters 2009) of looting the country's resources and money: "People are imprisoned and tortured 'in the name of the people.' . . . Decisions and recommendations are forged 'in the name of the people.' The only beneficiaries are those groups of employees in the state and some fat cats that have appeared recently in Libya. The whole story has been clarified: there is an un-sacred marriage between the fat cats and technocrats in the state. There is coordination between them in what is described as the Libyan Mafia" (Afrol News 2006). In the same speech, delivered in August 2006, Saif, not mincing words, openly criticized those who hindered any reform of the political system: "When we decided to cancel customs taxes, they considered it a sale of Libya's sovereignty, and when we decided to release prisoners from the overcrowded prisons of Libya, they considered this as sabotaging the country. . . . They considered the issuance of new legislation regulating the operation of foreign companies in Libya in a transparent manner as a conspiracy" (alWatan 2006).

Overall, Saif seemed eager to transform Libya in line with those reforms and recommendations that Western-led international financial institutions and human rights organizations had pushed the Libyan government to endorse. Despite the fact that these proposals were considered a betrayal, they nonetheless reflected the direction that a certain part of the elite had already embraced and that transpired from people's aspirations. However, while some remembered those years as "the best time ever of the Qaddafi's regime," another debate existed around the figure of Saif al-Islam, assessing the reasons why those dreams and desires that many Libyans attached to him failed to materialize.

The relationship between Saif and his father, for instance, was considered a key factor in obstructing the realization of a successful reform program in Libya. The existence of an underlying conflict of power between them, which manifested itself during the implementation of the reforms, ultimately prevented Saif from addressing larger structural problems: "Saif could not decide everything by himself, but life improved and you could feel it. It would have taken a long time, since there was so much corruption and every decision had to go back to his dad" (interview 2016). Doubtless Saif was aware of his father's unique role in the structure of the country, as well as in his own vision of its future. For instance, in 2007 Saif identified four main red lines that could not be undone, no matter how ambitious the reforms: Islamic law, the security and stability of Libya, Libya's territorial integrity, and Qaddafi himself.[28] Reverence for the father's ideas and role also comes up in the documents summarized by Monitor Group that, while attempting to make a case for the liberalization and privatization of the country's economy, provide an elaborate explanation of how the concept of market competitiveness and the Green Book shared similar principles: specifically, the welfare of society, the absence of discrimination, and individual responsibilities for economic needs (Porter 2006, 9). In other words, no matter what Saif's initiatives were and how willing he

---

28. This anecdote is also mentioned in the International Criminal Court of Justice Report in 2011.

was to reform the country, everything required carefully negotiating the role and ideas of the father.

For some of my interlocutors, however, the relationship between Saif and his father was purely instrumental:

Saif was used by his father. He could not decide anything without his father.

Saif tried to make his father change policies, but he did not let him.

He was a tool, just a tool. To be honest, Qaddafi only accepted this program because he felt he had made many mistakes. (interviews 2015)

According to these narratives, Saif's difficulties in carrying out a program of reform arose because they neither coincided with the interests of Qaddafi nor, more broadly, the regime. For instance, when Saif leaked the draft of the constitution to the press in 2008, Qaddafi came forward in outrage and stopped the project. The son, in turn, announced his immediate withdrawal from the political arena (Parteger 2016, 182). In 2009, regime-owned media channels took over al-Libiyya channel, which was part of al-Ghad Media Group, during a live program that was criticizing the role of the RC in the country's affairs. Al-Ghad Media Group was later nationalized (Black 2010). Interestingly, this interpretation emerges in the autobiography *My Story* by the leader of the Dubai emirate Shayk Mohammed bin Rashid Al Maktoum (2019). Describing his visit to Libya, where he came to meet Qaddafi, who had explicitly praised Dubai's achievements, Al Maktoum discusses how Saif seemed more knowledgeable and informed than his father, eager to undertake economic reforms in the country. Yet "Qaddafi did not want change, he only wished it. Change does not need speeches, but action" (Asharq Al-Awsat 2019). In order to rehabilitate its international image and avoid the fate of Iraq, the regime needed to develop a more dynamic and friendly approach to international powers, without altogether abandoning established ideological pillars. The regime, therefore, built a more credible and stable image of the country, particularly in the eyes of the United States, in order to attract much-needed foreign investments in the long-sanctioned oil and gas industry. Saif's initiatives enabled the functional rehabilitation of the industry, which then pumped money into the regime's coffers. As soon as this goal was achieved, however, the regime started sidelining those less convenient reforms that Saif's program aimed to address, such as freedom of the press, human rights abuses, or the drafting of a constitution. In addition, as mentioned above, the push to privatize the economy conflicted with Qaddafi's reluctance to let international lending organizations control Libya's economy. The main problem with the reform programs was that Libya was required to undergo both economic and institutional—thus political—changes at the same time. The emergence of a more oriented market-led economy could only occur with the abandonment of that system of patronage and revolutionary institutionalization that favored a specific class of military-security officers now turned merchants. More generally, such a process could reduce the power of specific elites, particularly the so-called old guard, which seemed to be more attuned to another son of Qaddafi, Mutassim, leader of the armed forces, with whom Saif had not established any alliance. Marwan explained, in fact, that there was a power struggle among Qaddafi's sons: "We didn't know what would happen if Qaddafi died, whether Saif or Mutassim would come to power, they had different visions for the country" (interview 2015).

The existence of such a conflict also appears in a 2009 US embassy cable, claiming that frictions were rising between Saif and his brothers because the proposed economic program could hurt the economic interests of the old guard, which wanted to secure its control of the most lucrative sectors in Libya (WikiLeaks 2009). Additional anecdotal evidence supporting this interpretation concerns the conditions that drove Shukri Ghanem, the oil minister and a close affiliate of Saif, to resign from his position after Mutassim approached him with a request for $1.2 million. Advised that Mutassim intended to use the money to create a militia like that of his brother Khamis, Ghanem approached Qaddafi, who told him to ignore the request. Feeling uncomfortable and caught in a crossfire, he decided to resign (WikiLeaks 2008; Mostyn 2012). Studies have explored the existence of such underlying tensions between the reformist camp and the old guard at length (Parteger 2016). Everyday narratives do not corroborate such argument, yet they provide important insights into the way people experienced such conflict in their lives, as well as its practical implications. Hamza's story helps explain how the smuggling of subsidized goods, which had become a very important and lucrative activity during those years of stagnating economy amid the international sanctions, manifested the existing arrangements of the elites with the population, thus supporting the old guard rather than the reformist camp. In the previous chapter, we discussed how Hamza recounted the people's annoyed reaction to Saif's visit to Sebha in 2008, when his speech turned into a series of indictments of smuggling. The constitutive and necessary function of these activities in the stability of the regime meant that people stood up and defended them. To counter its illegality, therefore, meant questioning the regime's stability at its core.

While these narratives illustrate the existence of conflict within the Qaddafi family, which mirrored the tensions at work within the regime, others stress a "familial" component whose essence explains the impossibility of realizing any reform in Libya. For instance, Mohammed talked about reforms as an empty discourse: "Qaddafi used to give long, long speeches. So did Saif about Tomorrow's Libya. They were just talking about their plans, people kept listening, but nothing really happened" (interview 2015).

Mohammed suggests that the discourse of reformism acted as another instrument of control used to make promises and gain time, yet without delivering any material results. In her work on Ben Ali's Tunisia, Beatrice Hibou argues that such "reformism" usually relies on two main discursive strategies: its endless perpetuation and its incomplete character (2011, 204). The government endlessly promotes a discourse of reforms ("They were just talking") without really aiming to its full realization ("Nothing really happened"). Like his father, Saif started delivering long, powerful public speeches, and he also established a date—June 19—when people would gather to celebrate his achievements. Nevertheless, the rise of Saif is also symptomatic of the strong control that a very close circle of people, particularly the Qaddafi family, had over the country. Saif had been able not only to magnetize popular everyday aspirations but also to collaborate with some of the political elites who wanted to promote a different political agenda. His rise did not occur in a political vacuum, but cohered with broader support among political elites. In this regard, the actions of Saif resemble what many of the "new sons" had initiated in many countries of the region, introducing liberalizing reforms in response to changes in the international order (Rand 2014, 71). However, the intense struggle for power among Qaddafi's sons ultimately strengthened the perception of many Libyans that their country was being run as a farm. Popular jokes conveyed such disillusionment—for instance, mocking Saif's privileged "intellectual" status, being the most educated of Qaddafi's sons and having obtained a doctoral degree from the London of School of Economics:

> The teacher asks its class to name an animal who can fly. One of the students raises his hand and says "Elephant!" The teacher, surprised, replies, "An elephant? Elephants don't fly. What's your name?" The student goes, "My name is Saif al-Islam al-Qaddafi." Immediately, the teacher replies, "Oh, yes! Elephants do fly!"

> The teacher approaches Saif al-Islam and asks him to name the country whose borders are drawn on the blackboard. Without hesitation, Saif replies, "That's my father's farm!" (interviews 2015)

The first joke captures the impunity and privileges granted to the son of Qaddafi, through the teacher's acknowledgment of an absurd idea ("Elephants do fly"). It is not relevant whether any rationale or fact exists to explain the actual statement; what matters is that nobody can oppose a Qaddafi. The second joke reflects the apparently corrupt attitude and abuse of power unveiled by Saif's reply ("That's my father's farm"), which, consequently, positions ordinary Libyans as domesticated animals (see chapter 3). Another brilliant joke reminds us not only of the underlying conflict between father and son but also how Libyans experienced and were caught up in the situation:

> Arguing over whom will rule the country, Saif and his father decide to
> go undercover into the streets and ask directly the people. While they are

walking, they stop a man and ask: "Do you want Saif or Muammar?" The man replies: "*al-ithnayn lā*" [neither of them]. Angered by this response, both Saif and his father take off their clothes and unveil their identity. The man, realizing that he is in trouble, continues, saying: "Not on Monday, not on Tuesday ['*al-ithnayn lā, al-thulātha' lā*], on Wednesday [*al-arb'ā'*] I will be able to answer this question." (interview 2015)

The joke plays on the expression *al-ithnayn lā*, which in Arabic means both "neither of them" and "not on Monday." As soon as the man realizes the real identity of his interlocutors, his answer continues in order to change the initial meaning. The joke exemplifies how people's rejection of the rule of the Qaddafi family had become the least of their concerns, assigning to the Libyan public a position of total passivity. The rules of the game were ultimately decided by the Qaddafis, who continued to rule with or without the support of the people, given the impossibility of expressing different opinions and thus the need to dissimulate the normative discourse of the regime.

## An Uncertain Future

As this chapter has shown, everyday emotional states should not merely be relegated to the sphere of the psychological; rather, their circulation and formation requires an approach that takes into account question of international politics and political economy as well (Bleiker and Hutchinson 2008; Åhäll 2018; Elias et al. 2016; Sajed 2011). This is because mundane fantasies are sustained through dominant formations and discourses, thus becoming a vehicle to contest or contribute to the status quo. Moving back and forth from the mundane to the global, a full picture of the political-economic changes of the Jamahiriya requires an organic understanding of the role of oil, the impact of international sanctions and geopolitical threat of war, the emergence of new elites, and, finally, the main contradictions stemming from these intertwined processes. Libyans' consumer desires might appear apolitical in the Global North, where consumption often is seen as a numbing practice aimed at reproducing an individualist and capitalist form of subjectivity. However, in a situation of geopolitical isolation, the desire to access goods became a way to think and imagine an alternative future. Quotidian commodities—such as bananas and chewing gum—acquired a powerful symbolic meaning, whose specific discursive configurations captured hopes and desires for a different futurity, a diverse type of modernity that would replace scarcity with abundance. Hence, at first sight these fantasies of happiness and the good life seemed to contest the political status quo, because they reveal what people hoped for and what alternative political horizons they attached to meanings of the good life.

However, these same fantasies serve also as a reminder of the rise of the global to the surface of the mundane. In fact, they were symptomatic of the gradual abandonment of another vision for the future that initially had sought to build an alternative model of development, largely reflecting the sociopolitical context then prevailing in the wider 1970s African and Asian postcolonial resistance. After this vision was defeated under the threat of war and sanctions by Western geopolitical forces, it had brought about the emergence of a military-turned-merchant class and metamorphosed into more repressive policies and rising socioeconomic inequalities. In other words, capitalist modernity was being desired, but the contribution of these same Western-led forces to the defeat of the Jamahiriya was being ignored. Those reflections became even more pertinent in the early 2000s, when everyday clusters of promises and desires crystallized in the fantasy of turning Libya into another Dubai. As discussed, the constitutive role of the Gulf in the global capitalist economy underlies the way ordinary cultural experiences called for better infrastructural development and a closer relationship with the West. Yet this simultaneously failed to consider the interests and role Western geopolitical forces played in aggravating socioeconomic inequalities in Libya historically, including Libya's reintegration into the global economy. More importantly, the success story of Dubai became the future tense of Libya, thus a model for oil-led modernization and development that both supported and opposed other existing visions within the regime. While Sirte symbolized at least the willingness to pursue a vision of regional cooperation with African states, whose support had been crucial to break out from international isolation, a large part of the ruling class had already moved toward a more

Western-oriented and market-led model of development. Undoubtedly, the everyday use of the West as a signifier to reject the anti-imperialist positioning of the regime signaled a strong sense of political alienation. In sum, everyday promises of future happiness and good life, seemingly challenging or subverting the regime, interacted with its metamorphosis, raising new opportunities for governing people's lives in the present.

Ultimately, these imaginaries heightened the intraelite tensions between the "technocrats" or "reformers," guided by Saif, who wanted to turn Libya into a version of Dubai, and the old guard, who represented the closer circle of Qaddafi's affiliates. Each camp offered a different, yet—once again—very contradictory and unclear vision of Libya's political future. On the one hand, while the old guard was building Sirte, many of its revolutionaries had progressively turned into fat cats by overseeing a slow process of privatization used to embezzle public funds in the name of the people. The reformers, on the other, more firmly believed in the possibility of building a market-led Libya. Yet, in doing so, it remained unclear how such a project—which required Libya to get closer to the West than it already was—could convince the other political group to do so. Overall, a market-oriented Libya, despite not being fully privatized, had already caused a steady deterioration of the living conditions of people since the late 1980s, as more progressive and redistributive measures had been reversed. Thus, we are left to wonder how both projects for the future of Libya, as well as what ordinary people desired, could fulfill the aspirations for better infrastructural development and improved socioeconomic conditions.

In other words, Libya was in a very uncertain position at this stage. When Saif retired from the political arena in late 2010, a large majority of Libyans could have lost their hope in his possible program of reforms, but they certainly did not stop imagining or thinking what the future could have looked like. If some knew what they wanted, they probably did not know how such goals and aims could have been achieved. The protests and uprisings that spread throughout the region complicated and, most importantly, accelerated these political changes, forcing Libyans to make choices that, for good or for bad, changed the course of their country's history.

# 5

## Revolution, Powerlessness, and War

On December 16, 2010, the *Guardian* published an article on Saif al-Islam's decision to retire from his political reformist position and dedicate his foundation to more charitable activities (Black 2010). Even though the announcement was made only a year after he had been given the second most powerful position in the country (Joffé 2010), his limited range of action directly stemmed from the competition among the intraelites that continued undisturbed, which, in turn, left little hope for the aspirations of Libya and its people. In retrospect, Saif's move was just the start of a long and twisted road. The next day, in fact, another major event took place in the neighboring country of Tunisia: a frustrated and humiliated twenty-six-year-old street vendor, Mohamed Bouazizi, after seeing his vegetable cart confiscated by a police officer, rushed to the provincial headquarters of the Sidi Bouzid governorate, where he doused his body with gasoline and set himself on fire. His action captured the symbolic significance of what unfolded in the following weeks: a mass campaign of civil resistance that demanded and achieved the resignation of Tunisian president, Zine El Abidine Ben Ali, five weeks later, on January 16, 2011. As soon as those events began to unfold, and Ben Ali went into exile in Saudi Arabia, Muammar Qaddafi gave a televised speech criticizing those protests, since they risked throwing Tunisia into chaos, with no end in sight. Proposing as an alternative the use of a referendum, he praised what Ben Ali had done for Tunisia during his twenty-year presidency (France24 2011). It is difficult to assess whether Qaddafi's words, expressing a worry that Libyans could also take to the streets and make similar demands, aimed to fend off the frustrations of his compatriots. However, it is certain that, once this pattern of protests spread

146

like wildfire to Egypt a week later and brought about the resignation of Hosni Mubarak, Libya no longer appeared immune to the possibility that something equally extraordinary was about to disrupt the ordinary patterns of people's lives.

In fact, a significant event did take place, but it is not the goal of this chapter to describe how it unfolded or to renarrate its unfolding in the everyday via the voices of its protagonists. Rather, my objective is humbler, as it investigates how my interlocutors' interpretations of the dynamics that led to the downfall of the regime interact with the everyday politics that have been analyzed thus far in the book. In other words, I aim to examine the extent to which people's interpretations and positionings over the causes and effects of the 2011 events that have marked Libya's history enter—or not—into a critical dialogue with the quotidian. This means gauging the role of violence, alienation, corruption, and capitalist modernity in igniting these protests. At the same time, I will reflect on whether these same everyday modalities of political interaction obfuscated more than clarified the possibilities of pursuing a different path. In other words, did these events undo the causes of suffering and frustration that were present in the everyday?

Since 2011, a persistent characteristic has dominated the Libyan political landscape: the recurrent presence of two main political factions, with their numerous allies, fighting for political power, which remain at war, unable to negotiate with each other. While the political actors that control today's landscape have realigned along political and ideological lines that do not correspond precisely to those that unfolded in 2011, it is nonetheless crucial to capture when and how the existence of two main camps came to the fore, what forms they took, and how they influenced the ways many Libyans interpreted the nature of those events. In this chapter I will show how this Manichean understanding of 2011, while replicating the inevitable effects triggered by the geopolitical violence inflicted on the country via the NATO-led intervention, prevented a (self)critical understanding of how Libya got to this point, which, in turn, created renewed feelings of anxiety and fear, and a deeper sense of helplessness and resignation among Libyans, as war became the new normal.

## *Taḥālib* and *Jurdhān*

> You heard both stories, you spoke to most of us. According to you, is
> what happened in Libya a revolution or a civil war?
> group interview, 2016

During my last days of field research in Italy, when I met my interlocutors
at the usual café in Perugia, and, while we were greeting each other and
sharing our future life plans, a rather unique moment took place: a reversal
of the interviewer-interviewee role. This time, it was they who had decided
to ask me a question that, I would argue, exemplified their determination
to find out my personal position on the 2011 events, thus obliterating one
or the other camp. This question did not simply seek to apply a label to
the events that had unfolded in 2011; rather, it was a less intrusive way to
find out where my allegiance lay, thus discovering whether I was "with or
against" the 2011 revolution.

The question did not surprise me. When I began undertaking this
research in 2014 Libya was—and, unfortunately, remains—locked in a
social, economic, and political crisis. There was frustration, disappointment, and disillusionment with the state of quotidian destruction and
violence in which the country had descended. It did not matter what
questions I would ask about the everyday; any inquiries about the past
always prompted a reflection on the present. A political necessity duly
arose to compare their lives in relation to both pre- and post-2011, as well
as to disclose one's own opinion over its effects and causes. This urgency
to pin down the political nature of the past kept imposing itself to such
an extent that my first question, usually to inquire about the age or profession of the interlocutor, turned into "Did you expect what happened
in 2011?" I had never felt so confident in asking such a question, because,
past politics, if to be discussed, expected one to clarify what happened in
2011.[1] So their question failed to take me aback because I had been the

---

1. Paradoxically, this final chapter deals with what was being debated right from
the start during the interviews. Yet the choice to unpack these issues at this point in the

one posing it so many times. It was probably time for me to provide an answer of my own.

However, I was fully aware of the potential pitfalls if I decided to take a side with one or the other camp. Undoubtedly, answering "with the revolution" translated into support for the suffering and sacrifice of numerous Libyans. Yet it also entailed an uncritical acceptance of the essential role played by the military might of NATO and, more broadly, of the historical Western interference in orienting the outcome of these events, destroying the national sovereignty of Libya. Similarly, the phrase "civil war" did not provide an easy way out either; it meant emphasizing the constellation of historical and neocolonial assaults against Libya. But I also knew that most interviewees would translate it into full-fledged support for the authority of Qaddafi, thus silencing the histories of fear, alienation, and frustration I had gathered up to that point. At that moment, I knew my interlocutors were looking for an easy answer, but I honestly did not have one, so I decided to deflect the question by deploying some of the same wit that Libyans had so masterfully taught me how to use when political constraints disallow going beyond binary logics. I answered: "I think about my research as a very big pot of black, dirty water. When you try to put your hands in it, sometimes you can get a *jurdhān* (rat), sometimes you can find *ṭaḥālib* (algae)."

A collective laugh followed, and I felt relieved, but their response only made tangible the underlying tension and its related difficulties that both elements of the conversation—question and answer—possessed: that violence destroys rationality, turning political events into football games and people into fans. I had had countless conversations on the nuanced nature of the past, but when it came to discussing 2011, such a nuance turned into a privilege, and what followed was the complete absence of a means of moving outside of the dichotomous and polarizing logic that most of the interviewees had used to explain what happened in 2011. In retrospect (as

---

book has nothing to do with temporality. Rather, it is my personal effort to situate such a historical moment for Libya after a careful analysis of its past political dynamics.

I unpack in the conclusion), academics, especially Western ones, should often remind themselves of the level of violence that has characterized the past and present of the politics of the Arab region.

The terms I used to reply to my interlocutors were borrowed straight from them, who had been the ones introducing me to those two main conflicting and irreconcilable camps that had characterized the events of 2011: *ṭaḥālib* (algae) and *jurdhān* (rats). Each group deployed these terms to describe or, perhaps more precisely, to stigmatize the other in a very derogatory manner. The first camp was made up of those who had supported Qaddafi and the Jamahiriya and used the term *jurdhān* (rats) to describe those people who allegedly aimed to overthrow the regime and destabilize Libya (interviews 2015–18). For them, the word *jurdhān* functioned as a synonym for "traitors," who are believed to be dirty and to destroy any place to which they gain access and to loot resources. In adopting such terminology, the so-called loyalists of the regime echoed Qaddafi's own words to describe people in the streets, "rats and mercenaries" (Reuters 2011). In opposition to the term *jurdhān*, the other camp preferred *ṭaḥālib* to describe those who had supported Qaddafi and his regime. As they explained, "algae" are as green as the regime's supporters, who go around waving the Green Flag and holding the Green Book. Yet their most identifying characteristic is that, like algae, they cling uncomfortably to the skin, making them difficult to remove. The significance of these two words did not only lie in how they functioned as cultural markers, whose rhetorical use allowed the drawing of boundaries of political inclusion and exclusion (Herzfeld 1980; Chock 1987; Brown and Theodossopoulos 2007) but also in setting the frame for understanding notions of freedom, responsibility, and power.

What characterized these two ways of interpreting the events of 2011, despite their seeming irreconcilability, was a capacity to alleviate daily experiences of limited agency and violence. Both terms functioned by displacing the multiple causes of these events onto singular spectacles and by naming Libyans innocent victims of evil forces—either the totalitarian *ṭaḥālib* or the Western-sponsored *jurdhān*. In other words, these narratives depict 2011 and its effects by employing a moral economy of good and evil to make them legible, using visceral and emotional language to describe their positionality and those actions deriving from it in a narrative whereby injured goodness leads to triumphant freedom and virtuosity.[2] The validity of such a Manichean vision of the world, albeit violent and limiting, was nevertheless asserted by the same interviewees who acknowledged their existence. For instance, when I asked Nazih whether Libyans would ever been able to reconcile their opinions regarding the country's past and, possibly, its future, his reply seemed at first quite bizarre: he asked me which football team I supported. After I hesitantly replied, "A. C. Milan," he then followed up to clarify the broader essence of his question: "I support Juventus. This is Libya now. You cannot reason with supporters!" (interview 2016).

Each discourse offered uncompromising answers to those questions of agency, freedom, and collusion with the everyday politics of the Jamahiriya, and their interdependence with global ones. Like football supporters, each camp blamed the other for how events unfolded. It is even more revealing how this insistent reliance on those discourses was presented to me as a cultural trait of Libyans, the combination of an inherent stubbornness and social pressure that some called *būnta*, or blame culture. As Latif illustrated, *būnta* is not an Arabic word but was adopted from the Italian language (pronounced as *punta*), meaning "point," or "tip." In this context, *būnta* translates as "pointing insistently at someone" to avoid taking responsibility. Various examples were provided to describe how *būnta* worked in the everyday: "People in my town are supporting that militia not because they like them. They are just doing *būnta* against the other group. It is like revenge, it is politics. I guess it works like that all over the world" (interview 2016).

2. In her book *Orgies of Feeling: Melodrama and the Politics of Freedom*, Anker (2014) describes the emergence of these opposing narratives situation as melodrama. She argues that melodrama functions in two distinct, yet interrelated, ways: first, it circumscribes "the boundaries of suffering's legibility by insisting on immutable distinctions between victimhood and villainy and between good and evil" (164). At the same time, it renders "unnecessary the work of reassessing one's own investments in and response to inequality and oppression, including those to which one may be contributing, even unintentionally" (221).

For Latif, *būnta* was the result of political violence that divided rather than reconciled people. In doing *būnta*, each camp proposed itself as morally superior to the other, insisting on an immutable distinction between good and evil, villains and victims, which obstructed any attempt to gauge one's own role and investment in the outcome of these political events. Ultimately, what emerged was a reproduction of material and symbolic violence that refused any form of self-assessment or self-criticism. Therefore, it came as no surprise when both Haitham and Mohammed stressed *būnta* as a constant trait of Libyans, who never accept their own responsibility:

> Imagine someone who is walking, trips on a stone, and falls on the ground. He would blame the stone, not himself, who failed to see it. It is always someone else's fault. Libyans are like that. It is ingrained in the social texture of society.

> If there is one thing we Libyans are good at, it's fighting. It is like preparing the dough for something. If you keep adding flour and water, you can go on and on! (interviews 2015)

The violent power of this logic lies in the way people gradually accepted and uncritically rationalized its notion of freedom, which instead obscured the political dynamics that led to the social fragmentation of the country, still unaddressed despite the fall of the regime.

Hence, what follows aims to further unpack the effects these visions produced. They charted a discourse of oppression and victimization that, in turn, paved a course of action that would restore the freedom and power of the good once villainy was annihilated. Yet, in doing so, they hindered any reassessment of one's own role in and response to forms of oppression, including those to which one might be contributing, even ambivalently, unintentionally, or ambiguously. What should become clear is the ability of these camps to pursue an idea of liberation that perpetuates, if not escalates, the modalities of interaction that defined the everyday politics in the last two turbulent decades of the Jamahiriya. These mythological narratives of both powerlessness and aggression create political subjectivities that struggle to untangle the forces of oppression that they are facing and that end up trapped in spirals of disillusionment and fear.

## A Cruel Liberation

When the Jamahiriya reached 2011, the withdrawal of Saif al-Islam from the political arena shattered the hopes of many Libyans that their country would undertake the path to capitalist modernity in the style of Dubai. This only increased the sense of popular alienation from the regime. Therefore, when thousands of people in Tunisia and Egypt flooded into the streets calling on their respective governments to resign, protests followed in Libya on February 17, 2011. For the so-called *jurdhān*, the revolution came as a historical necessity: it represented a cathartic moment that put an end to an evil rule. Adel offered an Islam-derived and mythological understanding of the events in 2011: "I expected this revolution because a change must happen every forty years, as the Holy Qu'ran shows with the story of the Prophet Musa. He reached Maydan only after forty years and then overthrew the Pharaoh" (interview 2014). Adel relies on the story of the Prophet Musa (known in the Bible as Moses) to explain the revolution as a historically predetermined event, therefore a prophecy against Qaddafi. Like Musa, the revolution grows from within the structure of the Jamahiriya and ends the corrupt rule of the pharaoh, meaning Qaddafi. At approximately the age of forty, the Prophet Musa left Egypt, the pharaoh's kingdom, and reached the city of Maydan. While he was living in the desert, God revealed Himself to Musa and asked him to travel back to Egypt and overthrow the pharaoh. According to this analogy, the revolt against Qaddafi after forty-two years of his rule assumes a divine nature.

Other interviewees, like Mohammed, explained 2011 as a revolutionary movement emerging from the growing social grievances and frustrations over malfunctioning infrastructures and the lack of education. The failure to reform the country catalyzed a revolution: "The revolution started because people felt angrier and angrier. They could not access their rights. The hospitals were very bad. People needed to travel to Tunisia for treatment. The education system was bad, and it became even worse. Then, all those things Qaddafi used to say against America, it was just empty talk" (interview 2015). Mohammed not only links the revolution to the failures of the regime to provide but also stresses the people's growing alienation from the regime's anti-imperialist ideology, now allegedly considered as contradictory. This latter point helps us to comprehend how many Libyans reacted to the words of their leader, who accused the protesters of being agents of the West and wanting to destroy the country: "We deserve Libya, we will fight those rats and agents who are being paid by secret governments. . . . Do you want Americans to come and occupy you? Like Afghanistan, Somalia, Pakistan, and Iraq? Our country will become like Afghanistan, if that's what you want" (BongoGhana 2011).

Qaddafi's cautionary rhetoric only exasperated their frustrations and turned them even further toward the West, now considered more as a friend than an enemy. Many protesters, in fact, did not recognize themselves and their aspiration in these words, because, as shown in the previous chapters, their aspirations lay elsewhere, in the orbit of capitalist modernity. They blamed the regime for the country's socioeconomic and political malaise and saw the cautionary posture of the leadership as a contradictory and empty cause. This is an aspect of utmost political significance, because it provided, for Libyans, the ideological grounds to the conscious support for a Western military intervention in their own country. Those who interpret the events of 2011 as a moment of popular resistance against the Jamahiriya envisioned a positive role for Western countries in liberating Libya. For instance, Anas saw the NATO intervention as a way for the people to realize their wishes and aspirations: "What will you do if someone says they are going to get you what you want?" (interview 2015).

The West and its military power appear as a strategic card that, if played, could allow them to get "what they wanted."[3] As previously discussed, we should keep in mind that the goals of the revolution not only entailed overthrowing Qaddafi but also transforming Libya into another

---

3. Interestingly, this position was replicated by well-established and left-leaning academics, such as Gilbert Achcar (2013, 199), who were quick to support the need for a no-fly zone led by NATO in Libya. It goes without saying that such political positioning turned out to be a disaster for Libya and its people.

Dubai. When Saif failed to fulfill this dream, people's quotidian aspirations did not fade away. The aspiration for capitalist modernity in the fashion of Dubai meant a different relationship with the West, one that could be tested in 2011; it contained a desire to reapproach Western countries in a less confrontational manner and to break away from any leftovers of anti-imperialism. For these reasons, many interviewees aligned themselves optimistically with the military intervention, regarding it as a necessary tool to modernize, develop, and reform their country. It is nonetheless important to say that the military intervention compelled a fundamental necessity for the *thuwwār* (revolutionaries): it required them to identify a main obstacle, an evil Other who impeded the materialization of the promise of freedom and the good life, which meant getting rid of all those affiliated with the Jamahiriya, the so-called loyalists or *ṭaḥālib*.

For these reasons, Reem explained, all those who wanted the fall of Qaddafi's regime experienced the NATO intervention as an imperative: "The foreign intervention was a must because we all knew that ordinary people could not make the Qaddafi regime fall. The NATO intervention, therefore, was a must. Otherwise Qaddafi would have wiped Benghazi off the face of the Earth" (interview 2015).

Appeals to humanitarian justifications combined with the sense of powerlessness that many experienced vis-à-vis the regime provided the perfect pretext for the international community to unleash the military arsenal of NATO to protect the Libyans, an umpteenth population of a Global South country, in a savior-like fashion. After all, if the West, which had relentlessly portrayed the Jamahiriya as an authoritarian and terrorist regime and often sponsored local rebellions to oust it, now had the genuine support of the population, what else could be needed? Yet this is precisely where the problems lay. The imaginative geography of the "humanitarian" intervention quickly undertaken by NATO in the wake of the Libyan protests aligned perfectly with those narratives. The moral appeal to the R2P doctrine rests on justifications similar to those that characterize the discourse of the *thuwwār*.

For instance, the interdependence between R2P and technology further shaped the idea of ethical war. Military precision lay at the heart of the virtuous war embraced by many Western powers, since technology ensured that only the bad guys would be killed while civilian lives were saved. The use of military violence became legitimate through its emphasis on surgically precise weaponry, guaranteed by technology, nobly deployed against the evil Other—in this case Qaddafi, the *ṭaḥālib*, and their allegedly mercenary soldiers. Although the practice of precision bombing is "permeated with assumptions about perfect information and the ability to be able to make distinctions from a distance" (O'Sullivan 2017, 61), such clear-cut distinctions hardly existed in Libya, as in any other society.

Moreover, the decision to resort quickly to the use of military violence was facilitated by the way Libya had been described—in both political and academic circles—in terms of problematic assumptions based on the conceptual triptych of statelessness, authoritarianism, and rogue-ness. In other words, the humanitarian intervention capitalized on a long tradition of equating Libya with a stateless laboratory for the political and economic ideas of a madman, disregarding the roles and voices of other Libyans. If, by 2011, this framework had come to represent how a large part of society related to the regime, it nonetheless meant that Western geopolitical forces did not hesitate to resort to violence to get rid of its leadership. As it took place with the frenzied (and unsupported by evidence) imposition of multilateral sanctions, there was no genuine interest in comprehending the intricacies of the country, or in respecting its sovereignty.

Therefore, the point is not to gauge whether the humanitarian intervention responded to a concrete emergency on the ground, but rather to show how those Libyans who self-identified as revolutionaries in 2011—willingly or not—opened a window for Western geopolitical forces to hijack the protests for their own interests, with dire consequences for the entire country. The revolutionary discourse and the international call for a military intervention both adopt a vision of liberation that charts the road to freedom via the eradication of evil and villainy from Libya, or—as Tareq stated—to get rid of the *ṭaḥālib*: "You will find very few people who will tell you that it was possible to oust Qaddafi without the intervention. We must recognize that Qaddafi was strong, and he had many supporters, those *ṭaḥālib*. Without the West, we could not do it. People were ready to lose their lives, but in the end they would not succeed in doing it" (interview 2015).

Oppression by the regime and its *ṭaḥālib* produced the necessity for foreign intervention, which appeared as the only viable and realistic option for the victims. By upholding 2011 as a moment for overthrowing an authoritarian regime, the 17 February Revolution became a moment that puts Libya on the path toward freedom. The rebels' desire to regain their diminished sense of agency and to fulfill their aspirations for improved economic conditions and a new government with a Western-led vision for the country required them to advocate for the violent eradication of those internal forces—Qaddafi and his *ṭaḥālib*—that impeded the realization of their dreams.

While it is important to acknowledge that these political discourses compelled people to act and interpret—perhaps narrowly—the alliances and structures around them, it is just as crucial to trace the production of a deeper sense of helplessness and powerlessness when, after the fall of Qaddafi, modernization and development did not materialize, and violence instead escalated. What transpired was the redeployment of those same discourse by some interviewees to explain this violence as a mythological continuum of Qaddafi's legacy and his master plans. For instance, Shaykh Hussein suggested that the revolution failed because Qaddafi planned the fragmentation of Libya: "I didn't expect what happened in 2011, but Qaddafi worked for forty years to get to this moment. Do you know what is happening now? He passed away four years ago. He did this, he wanted this. He was waiting for this moment. He said that 'if you finish me, you will see what happens.' So, this is what is happening" (interview 2015).

The regime fell, but the spiral of chaos and violence in Libya took place because, it was believed, of Qaddafi's supernatural powers. Because of his dividing and ruling of the population through tribal alliances, these same dynamics are now destroying the country: "He put these villages and tribes one against the other, because *he* [emphasis] did this. He was clever, he was *Shayṭān*" (interview 2015). This narrative depicts Qaddafi as a canny monster, a God-like figure, as evil as Satan, who carefully planned the disintegration of the social fabric of Libya along tribal lines, thereby plunging the country into civil war. As we saw in previous chapters, the comparison with Satan recurs in popular jokes, which demonstrate how people continue to maintain Qaddafi as a cultish figure despite his death.

Another interviewee, Salah, offered a similar explanation, indicating how Qaddafi manipulated tribes and cities: "People were kept in ignorance to make the system work. He [Qaddafi] was smart, he knew how to use and play the social fabric of Libya . . . He knew this would create problems between them. He did that!" (interview 2015).

The narratives comprehend and explain the political and geographical fragmentation of Libya into militias and cities by blaming the other party and its strategies. Mukhtar also linked the post-2011 quagmire to the evil master plan of Qaddafi and his *ṭaḥālib*, elucidating how the Libyan leader wrecked the country once he realized that the regime was about to collapse: "Libya was destroyed by the Qaddafis and those *ṭaḥālib*, who played with the tribes and bought arms from Russia, which is why everybody has weapons now. Qaddafi, once he understood that he was going to die, he made the people take the weapons. He knew what was going to happen" (interview 2014).

Independent of the substance of those narratives, be it Russian arms or the maneuvering of tribes, the act of blaming Qaddafi long after his death demonstrates how people continue to sustain those modalities of political interactions that constituted their everyday life under the regime. As Qaddafi became a nodal point in the everyday, magnetizing all blame for the country's problems or all praise for its achievements, likewise he remains accountable for the violence and infighting after 2011, despite his death. By indicating how both the military intervention and the civil war took place because of Qaddafi's powers, all these narratives ultimately reveal a strong sense of powerlessness and victimization among the rebels, which negates rather than strengthens their personal agency. While the rebels drown in the abyss of their powerlessness, Qaddafi maintains—if not acquires more—symbolical magnitude in history. This point emerges most clearly in the narrative of Emad, who holds Qaddafi accountable for a moral crime committed against the entire population, which continues to haunt any future possibility of peace: "Everybody criticized or mocked the way he looked or talked, but the real problem was how he destroyed and corrupted the Libyan man. This was the most atrocious crime he committed—destroying our humanity. How do you think this is going to impact Libya now? It is sad, tragic!" (interview 2015).

Qaddafi's ability to penetrate people's minds and behavior shaped how they now relate to one another. In so doing, the Libyan leader left no chance for the uprising to succeed. Rather, the 17 February Revolution unleashed what constituted the core of his rule and persona: infighting, moral corruption, and violence. In other words, this discourse stresses a sense of heightening impotence over the 2011 events and their aftermath, while simultaneously denying any personal involvement in the reproduction of the dynamics of inequality and oppression, thus negating the role of personal agency. This logic not only erases the complex and manifold ways people complied and reiterated certain everyday modalities of political interaction but also avoids mapping out the interdependent relationship between global and local dynamics.

For instance, the negation of agency downplays the importance of dissimulation and political alienation in society. In becoming tactics of survival that signaled a widespread sense of discontent with the regime, they allowed the reproduction of the political structure that had reigned until 2011. The narratives kept holding Qaddafi accountable for the need for foreign intervention, as well as for the subsequent failure of the uprising. In other words, Qaddafi remained the sole responsible agent for all societal failures, even after his own death, while the population stood as the victim of his dirty tricks. However, when the rebels sodomized the leader after his capture and turned his dead body into a tourist site, their actions do not reflect a marked social and political break with the past; rather, they reveal the continuity of the same practices that in part constituted their everyday life under the regime, including the largely patriarchal premises of society and the display of overt violence. Moreover, I concur with Kawther Nuri Alfasi (2017, 273) that the interpreters of the 17 February Revolution, in the process of contesting the regime's symbolic order, "propounded a utopian nationalist rhetoric that redrew fresh boundaries of exclusion, and they constructed new symbolic and material hierarchies that centred on commitment to, and involvement in, the 17 February uprising." In so doing, their representational practices did not transform the dominant symbolic classifications of the social world, but instead recapitulated the logic of exclusion. In this regard, the passage of the Political Isolation Law (Libyan General National Congress 2013), which banned from public office all those who had worked in regime-affiliated organizations, showed how the same political dynamics were sustained. Although this law aimed to break with the past, it stands in perfect continuity with the logic of the civil war that marked 2011, since the hunt for internal enemies, which built on an atmosphere of mutually reinforcing fear and surveillance, was part and parcel of the regime's capacity to maintain its control. A similar situation took place in Iraq after the US invasion of the country in 2003, when international coalitions, together with other local forces, adopted legislative measures banning from public offices all those "remnants" of and "collaborators" with the previous regime.[4] Consequently, the majority of those whose jobs required an affiliation to the Baath Party—for instance, soldiers and teachers—found themselves unemployed and unable to look for work due to the social stigma that this legislation had triggered.[5] The results were devastating. A counterinsurgency was organized against the US forces and those allied with them, since those measures disaffected a large part of the Iraqi population, who grew resentful toward the initiators of the so-called process of de-Baathification (Pfiffner 2010).

However, the most important element of this revolutionary discourse, I argue, lies in how it established a relationship of "cruel optimism" (Berlant 2011, 1), "when something you desire is actually an obstacle to your flourishing." The initial seeds for optimism blossomed as people started linking economic prosperity and modernization to capitalist modernity and better relations with the West. By turning Libya into another Dubai, the argument goes, the country could change. As the protests in 2011 erupted, this framework, on the one hand, contributed to the popular demand for a Western/foreign-led military intervention and, on the

4. According to Saghieh (2007, 117–18), it was also termed *ijtithath al-Ba'th*, meaning "eradication of Baathism." The Arabic expression is of agricultural origin and signifies completely uprooting a harmful and parasitic plant. In comparison, the term "de-Baathification" suggests a neutral, if not actually bureaucratic, matter of procedure. This mistranslation was the point at which two radically different developments converged.

5. According to a rather conservative outlet, the *Economist*, unemployment ranged between 60 and 75 percent in October 2003. The salaries of senior Baath members were frozen (David 2006, 367).

other, allowed Western geopolitical forces to hijack them. Thus, what set people on a path of revolutionary optimism gradually revealed its cruelty. Throughout this process, while the regime became viewed as the culprit of all problems, this revolutionary optimism failed to consider the role that the same Western geopolitical forces played in aggravating the socioeconomic inequalities in Libya, via international sanctions and military bombings, leading to its reintegration into the world market.

In the aftermath of the fall of the regime, however, the same interviewees now blamed the West and its neocolonial interests:

> Don't talk to me about the revolution. I was there, I fought, and I lost two brothers. [Pausing] This is not a revolution, it's just a conspiracy against Libya. Look at the country now!

> I did the revolution, but now I understand. Qaddafi could have done much more with the money of Libya. The people who went into the streets did not want a war, and they were not just Islamists. They wanted something better, but the West only wanted our gas, our reserves of oil and water. (interviews 2018)

These excerpts capture the cruelty of the disappointing realization that what seemed to promise the good life had turned Libya into a war-torn country. The West appeared to be pursuing its own interests and had no genuine desire to help build Libya's future. For these reasons, Abdul Hamid affirmed that "I understood what happened now. Rather than having Dubai in Libya, it is more likely that Dubai will turn into Libya, as long as America is pleased" (interview 2015).

The fantasy of transforming Libya as Gulf states catalyzed the hopes and desires of many Libyans, prompting them to protest in the streets and to call for a Western intervention. In so doing, they did not simply underestimate the potential dangers of allowing a foreign intervention in Libya; the same frame used to chart the path toward freedom prevented them from grasping the historical forces of oppression at work. To be more precise, as discussed in chapter 2, the West has had a long history of war and militarist intervention in colonial and postcolonial Libya, as well as in the MENA region as a whole. This history of interference and intervention hardly guaranteed the possibility of a smoothly running alliance between the rebels and the international community. It goes without saying, as some other scholars also have argued (Amin 2006; Campbell 2013; Kadri 2019), that capitalism's promise of inclusion in the Global South is inherently a trap because it is premised on the structural imperative to dominate the South of the world; thus, wars, sanctions, and liberal interventions will continue to define the promise of capitalist modernity that haunts both the present and the future of the Global South.

To rub salt in the wound, the cruelty of 2011 is further exacerbated by looking at the past and current role of the very Gulf states—the UAE, Qatar, and Saudi Arabia—to which many Libyans had looked as aspirational models of successful development and inclusion in global capitalism. From the early days of the protests, these states supported the idea of military intervention in Libya; their collective and unanimous decision provided Western powers with the needed public approval of "Arab" states to proceed with the imposition of a no-fly zone (Glanville 2013), despite other regional actors (i.e., the African Union) calling for a diplomatic solution. Consequently, the UN Security Council passed Resolution 1973 on March 13, 2011 (United Nations Security Council 2011), which provided for "all necessary measures" to establish a no-fly zone over Libya in support of the NTC. A few days later, twelve countries joined "Odyssey Dawn," the military operation to support the rebels, led by NATO. While the UNSC resolution did not allow foreign troops to occupy the country, Arab Gulf (Black 2011) and Western countries (BBC News 2011) quickly began to provide the rebels with military and logistical support in the form of weapons and training (Ulrichsen 2014). After Qaddafi was killed and the regime fell, political divisions among rebels rapidly developed as the victorious states began to support different Libyan factions to shape the future of the country and to control its natural resources and maritime routes. The fantasy of Dubai now turned into a nightmare, since all key protagonists in the war had been attempting to consolidate and formalize their gains made over the previous years. Consequently, the fantasy of turning Libya into Dubai has become more an ambition of Gulf monarchies than of Libyans themselves.

Tracing these dynamics is not simply a matter of renarrating events and reidentifying victims and perpetrators; it shows that these everyday experiences were always international, rendering legible the interdependence between local and global dynamics. For instance, Western-led strategists insisted on the surgical precision of bombing, thus assuming perfect information and the ability to make distinctions from a distance, but such clear-cut distinctions hardly existed in Libya, due to the numerous gray zones of political ambiguity and ambivalence in which the everyday was constructed and reproduced. These gray zones are not reducible to a zone that remains ambivalent about the removal of the regime, thus helping the latter to survive, as Lisa Wedeen (2019, 22) argues in her recent book on Syria. They also include people who, while wanting Qaddafi to renounce his position of power, believed in the need to maintain the sovereignty of the country, thus rejecting any form of external intervention. In other words, this gray zone really contained multiple political shades that manifested and were defined not only by the everyday as a space of ambiguity but also by the awareness that Libya remains part of the broader global South in its interaction with geoeconomic and geopolitical structures.

What happened instead is that the geopolitical violence unleashed by the international community completely obliterated the existence of those spaces. On the contrary, extending further Salwa Ismail's (2019) concept of "the rule of violence" in Syria, the military intervention revealed that the external injection of violence remains a constitutive element of the Middle East and North Africa region (Mundy 2019), its people and places, moving from the local to the global. That is, the MENA should also be understood in relation to the intensely violent practices and arrangements that "have come to constitute the fundamental conditions of its ideational and material possibility" (5). Therefore, the lack of strategic information and intelligence evident in Western governmental documents or media discourses is constitutive of this material and sociocultural space and its incorporation into global processes of accumulation and extraction that reproduce the dominance of countries of the global North. It emerged in the ways in which media outlets struggled to identify and describe the rebels, ranging from juvenile and incompetent to militarized and threatening, with potential al-Qa'ida links (O'Sullivan 2017, 116–25). Additionally, the connection between African mercenaries and the Qaddafi regime was hardly questioned; neither were the racist attitudes of the population nor the history of attacks on sub-Saharan Africans in Libya ever considered (Forte 2011). Instead, only the fact that Qaddafi had supported the African Union acquired immediate significance. Governmental investigations indicated further how this deadly mix of fantasy precision and moralism, while laying the ground for a quick and surgical operation against the evil regime-loyalists, was not informed by "accurate intelligence"; the "immediate threat to civilians was publicly overstated," and there was an "exclusive focus on military intervention" (House of Commons Foreign Affairs Committee 2016).

Why did Libyans stay attached to the fantasy of capitalist modernity, as represented in the idea of Dubai and consumerism, via foreign military intervention, when the historical record of Western involvement in the MENA region speaks otherwise? Certainly, the call for a military intervention with its related geopolitical interests, and the unique speed of its unfolding, hijacked the protests, providing very little room to envision alternative scenarios, and turned Libya into the umpteenth theater of war in the region. At the same time, the failure to grasp the structural and historical legacy of many Western states and their allies in the region also stems from another important component. To do so, we must continue to approach everyday experiences by attending to global political-economic dynamics that had compromised al-Fātiḥ and its ruling elites. This, in turn, will show how the demands voiced at the outset of the protests by many Libyans, like those of their neighbors in Tunisia and Egypt, interacted and colluded with the wider international consolidation of neoliberal capitalism.

## Revolution in (Neo)Liberal Times

> He compared them [his own people] to rats, and threatened to go door to door to inflict punishment. . . . We knew that if we wanted—if we waited one more day, Benghazi, a city nearly the size of Charlotte, could suffer a massacre that would have reverberated across the region and stained the conscience of the world.
> Barack Obama, 2011

I am your father, Aisha, I am your husband, Safiyya . . . I leave you
no shame in death. I am fighting a battle against 40 unjust countries,
I did so for forty years.

Muammar Qaddafi on True Voice TV, 2019

On March 28, 2011, the US president, Barack Obama, announced in a press conference that the world was facing a choice because of Qaddafi's merciless declarations to his own people, threatening to wipe Benghazi off the earth. Obama described the reasons that led the UN and many Western countries to intervene in Libya: the UN showed its political commitment to "end the worst forms of violence and persecution" (United Nations General Assembly 2005, 31), including genocide and ethnic cleansing, thus preventing a massacre in the eastern Libyan city. This process led to the implementation of the international doctrine R2P through UNSCR 1973 that authorized UN member states to use all necessary measures to protect civilians in Libya from pro-regime forces, short of sending ground troops to occupy the country, which did not happen. A few hours before his actual death, probably knowing he had very little chance of staying alive, Qaddafi sent a satellite-radio message to his daughter and wife in order to assure them that they would carry no shame on their shoulders after his death. As a martyr and a fighter, he had spent all his life fighting more than forty countries, and he would die continuing to do so. Do these two quotes represent the ultimate fight between an anti-imperialist leader and the neocolonial West? Do they signal the rogue status of Qaddafi vis-à-vis the liberal international order, which was about to intervene to save Libyans from a regime-led bloodbath?

Raouf suggested that political interests and the historical revenge of the West lay at the core of the humanitarian intervention. To elucidate this argument, he identified an elaborate connection between the number of the UNSC resolutions and the dates of major historical events that saw Qaddafi confronting the West and its interests: "Do you know what the number of the UN resolution that imposed a no-fly zone in Libya is? 19-73. 1973. Do you know what happened in Libya in 1973? Qaddafi got rid of the American military bases. What about the number of the resolution that was said to protect civilians? 19-70. In 1970 Qaddafi kicked out the English people." He continued elaborating this numerical logic to provide a further example of the careful and evil planning of the West against Libya, finding continuity between the invasion of Iraq and Libya: "Do you know when they [Western powers] invaded Iraq in 2003? On March 19. Guess what? They invaded Libya on March 19. On that same day. Numbers don't lie!" (interview 2017). A quasi-conspiratorial and mythological belief emerges from Raouf's statements, which nonetheless cohere with the dominant political discourse of the regime, presenting itself as a staunch opponent of Western imperialist power, fighting against colonial and neocolonial oppression.

Other interviewees explained that the regime only threatened those who were not willing to throw their weapons away, as Ahmed recounted: "In Benghazi, a group of 'nonviolent' people—those *thuwwār* [revolutionaries], as they call themselves—tried to capture a police barracks, which was full of weapons and artillery. What would your government do? Wouldn't they shoot them and try to stop them?" (interview 2015).[6] He explained that there were no grounds for allegations of an imminent massacre because, when a group of civilians aimed to take control of a weaponry deposit, the regime simply tried to stop them. Its response, therefore, aligned with what any other government would have done. In other words, those humanitarian grounds that moved the international community to intervene were fabricated. The media in general and the Qatar-based channel Al-Jazeera in particular helped to manufacture the imminent threat of a massacre in Benghazi, as Muftah stated: "What genocide in the city of Benghazi? Look, did Qaddafi massacre any other town before arriving in Benghazi? The story about the massacre does not make sense. Al-Jazeera spread all these lies" (interview 2015).[7]

Here Muftah stresses that foreign powers manipulated the nature of the 2011 events through media coverage aligned with the national and

6. Qaddafi "promised amnesty for those 'who throw their weapons away' but 'no mercy or compassion' for those who fight" (Kirkpatrick and Fahim 2011).

7. The story about the massacre of Benghazi and the bloodshed that the regime's forces were going to inflict remained a much-contested narrative mainly fought at the level of media and television news (see Bosco 2011; Forte 2011).

foreign policy interests of their home countries. Al Nahed (2015) goes further, arguing that the UK and Qatari media coverage of the Libya events was highly influenced by their political agendas. Western powers and Gulf States, as the Muftah's reference to Al-Jazeera makes clear, took advantage of this situation in order settle their political problems with the Libyan regime by getting rid of Qaddafi. As Karim explained, the media campaign valued certain of Qaddafi's words, but ignored other messages: "Qaddafi spoke on the radio, saying, 'Just throw away the weapons, even in the street. Throw them away. We will take care of them but throw away the weapons. You, my sons, go back home, I do not want you to die.' The West did not want to hear this message" (interviews 2015).[8] Karim proposes that the media contributed actively to supporting the political interests of Western and Gulf countries, thus questioning the legitimacy of those "moral concerns" upheld in Obama's speech and the UNSC resolutions. More reconciliatory messages from Qaddafi were ignored because they did not align with the ultimate interests of Western countries, and thus with their aim of overthrowing the Libyan government.

Other interviewees discussed those same dynamics in candid and colorful language. Murad, for example, started from the figure of Mohammed Bouazizi, the Tunisian street vendor who set himself on fire and sparked the Arab Spring: "You know Mohamed Bouazizi, right? Well, he is a big piece of shit." For Murad, there is no political significance in those protests that shook off the region and a Western-led strategy to bring down the entire Arab region: "They needed to bring down Tunisia and Egypt to get control of Libya, of its oil and gas. This is what they really wanted, and they mobilized its population by telling lies. This is what Al-Jazeera did. They were all lies. Lies, lies, lies!" (interview 2015). In his view, the popular uprisings in Tunisia and Egypt were strictly connected to the events in Libya, since the downfall of the regime represented the ultimate goal of Western powers and Arab Gulf states. He proposes that these states fabricated a media campaign in order to induce popular revolts in the whole

8. In this radio message, Qaddafi addresses the Libyan population and those who came into the streets to demonstrate against the regime. Karim refers to a passage starting around 8:40 until 11:00 (Jamel 2011).

region, while pursuing their real interests: controlling Libya's reserves of oil and gas.

While some interviewees like Karim hold the West and Arab Gulf states responsible for their country's destruction, another important aspect also emerges. They describe the *thuwwār* as the infamous enemies of the revolution discussed in the previous chapters. In 2011, this discourse was still alive and kicking. In fact, Anas drew on it to highlight the fact that the close alliance between foreign powers and *jurdhān* brought the fall of the regime: "There is also a military term to explain what happened in Libya. It's called 'fifth column,' which means that there was a group of people in the country working in favor of the enemy . . . These were the *jurdhān* in Libya, people who belonged to Al-Qa'ida, the Islamists. They are traitors and they will always be because they have it in their blood" (interview 2016). Drawing on these categories to reinforce his argument, Anas believes in the existence of a close alliance between the West and the rebels.

Since the end of the 1980s, under increasing geopolitical pressure, both military and economic, the Libyan government began to retreat from the social and anti-imperialist front. During this period, Western-funded Islamist groups had started challenging the political authority of the regime, which responded by launching a violent hunt for all dissenting elements of society—both Islamists and non-Islamists—accusing them of aiming to destabilize the country in collaboration with Western powers. Those elements were labeled a fifth column, "stray dogs," or *zanādīq*. For many of my interlocutors, these political groups came back to the fore in 2011: "They were exiled, now they are back, and they want to rule the country. Those *thuwwār* sold their country to the West. I will always stand with Libya" (interview 2015).

Khaled interprets 2011 as a cathartic moment for the country, where the revolutionaries sold Libya out for their own personal interests, while lacking any sense of patriotism or national pride. Those remarks hint toward a lack of a sense of belonging and kinship among the *jurdhān* with respect the *ṭaḥālib*, juxtaposing the exiled and almost foreign nature of those political opponents who joined the rebels to "will always stand for Libya." Similarly, Hamid holds Saif accountable for allowing those who were in exile to come back into the country: "Those people betrayed him. They are *jurdhān* and they have it in their blood. Now they are controlling Libya" (interviews 2015).

It is a fact that those same leaders, whom the West and Libya were trying to fight collaboratively in the last decade, had turned into revolutionary figures in 2011. In the mid-2000s, the Libyan government began cooperating with Western governments—primarily the UK and the United States—on a rendition program against terrorist groups, which allowed the abduction and extrajudicial transfer of suspects from one country to another with the purpose of circumventing the Western countries' laws on interrogation, detention, and torture. For instance, Abdel Hakim Belhadj, the leader of the Islamist group LIFG, was abducted as part of this program; the UK authorities delivered him to the Libyan government in 2006. In 2011, however, Belhadj was a leading revolutionary figure, who was going to lead the military conquest of Tripoli in collaboration with foreign troops on the ground, in complete contravention of the UN resolutions. This viewpoint, therefore, reveals an important aspect of foreign complicity in 2011, yet it also denies the internal contradictions that characterized the Jamahiriya.

For instance, the memories of fear and violence during that period resulted in the growing alienation of the population from the regime. Leaving the people almost no room to voice dissent, the struggle against anti-imperialist forces was interpreted more and more as a useful tool adopted by the leadership to maintain their privileges. Therefore, to reduce the protesters and the demands they made to agents of and collaborators with the West, a group of Islamists who aimed to overthrow the regime, meant reproducing a political mantra that for the most part no longer reflected the aspirations of the population. More importantly, when 2011 arrived, al-Fātiḥ was in a state of fragmentation and ideological defeat and lacking widespread legitimacy. While the geopolitical assault played a key role in this defeat, the regime had nonetheless abandoned those values and policies that had marked its rise to power in 1969. Its determination to rely on an anti-imperialist discourse to frame the protests of 2011 only exasperated those younger revolutionaries who sat on the other side of the spectrum. The regime's discourse claimed to defend the national integrity of the country against imperialist powers, but it did not acknowledge that this same integrity rested on very shaky ground, due to the difficulties in resolving social questions, primarily the existence of socioeconomic inequalities. From the late 1980s, the launch of economic programs aiming at liberalizing the economy reflected desertion from the regime's egalitarian and progressive values, resulting in the appearance of social inequalities, unemployment, and widespread corruption. Those processes were amplified with the imposition of the international sanctions in the 1990s and the emergence of a military-turned-merchant class (fat cats) that embezzled public funds in the name of the people. In such a context, where only a group of high-level "revolutionary" officers maintained a firm grip on most of the country's resources, the interpretation of 2011 as an imperialist plot lost traction among the population because it denied the existence of two fundamental contradictions.

First, if ordinary Libyans had begun to aspire to capitalist modernity, their dreams mirrored the metamorphosis of the regime, rather than an opposition to it; the same ruling elites had abandoned progressive policies, systematically transferring their wealth abroad instead of investing in national or regional enterprises. It is fundamental to point out that, despite its deteriorating conditions, the socioeconomic situation of Libyans in 2011 hardly resembled the one of Egypt or Tunisia, where neoliberal policies had been pursued much more aggressively in the past two decades. However, the symbolic proximity of Libya to Gulf states, due to the abundance of oil revenues, played a crucial role in spreading dissatisfaction toward the regime among a large part of the population. Second, the uncertain status of Libya reflected further the internal struggle for power between two groups (the old guard and reformists), each bearing a competing vision for the country's future, which inevitably affected the protests. These are crucial elements to understanding how the difficulties in resolving the social question affected the national question, whose metamorphosis, in turn, interacted with the consolidation of Western hegemony and neoliberal capitalism worldwide. The rise of the so-called reformist camp, guided by Qaddafi's son Saif al-Islam, not only challenged the power of the revolutionary old guard but also aligned with the population's aspirations for change and modernization. Many of those who had supported Saif's projects, like Ali Issawi or Mustapha Abdul Jalil (Gritten 2011), quickly defected to the rebel side.

Therefore, the interpretation of the events of 2011 as an imperialist plot, while rightly calling for maintaining the territorial sovereignty of the country, denied the existence of structural grievances and popular discontent, and it paid the price of alienating a large part of Libyan society. Rightly or not, many interviewees experienced the anti-imperialist discourse as a façade, a contradictory political posture used to reinforce the power of Qaddafi and his inner circle, and they only kept performing those ideological rituals in order to pursue their careers and obtain personal gains. Moreover, the renunciation of the WMD program in 2003 and the subsequent collaboration with Western countries in the fight against terrorism proved to the population the double standards of the regime's rhetoric, which instead clashed with popular memories of economic isolation and social suffering during the period while Libya was under international sanctions. The negation of other forces at work relates to those interviewees who point to the existence of an underlying conflict of interests between Libya and the West over the role of the IMF, as well as Libya's expanding role on the African continent. Their arguments do not consider that parts of the regime's ruling elite also belonged to the global financial class (Garside, Pegg, and Mahmood 2016; Munzinger and Obermaier n.d.), had long abandoned progressive ideals, and embraced consumerist and corrupt practices.

Overall, those street protests that swept across almost the entire region did not contain the radical ideological and conceptual formulations of the mass movements of the 1970s. For instance, while the 1969 coup of the Free Officers pursued a radical redistribution of wealth, the nationalization of domestic resources, and profound change in property relations, in 2011 protesters were more preoccupied with the broad issues of human rights, political accountability, and legal reform. In fact, the Libyan protests found their momentum after the arrest of Fathi Terbil, the lawyer for the families of the disappeared victims of the Abu Salim prison massacre. For these reasons, Asef Bayat uses the term "refolutions" to indicate that they were "revolutionary movements that emerged to compel the incumbent states to change themselves, to carry out meaningful reforms on behalf of the revolution" (2017, 18). While Bayat applies his analyses to Egypt and Tunisia, he additionally singles out the case of Libya and Syria, since the trajectory of those protests "assumed the form of civil wars mediated by foreign military intervention" (154). That foreign military intervention is a key element that distinguishes Libya (and Syria) from the other countries is undisputable. Yet this closer analysis of the way Libyans interpreted and rationalized the necessity of foreign intervention has demonstrated that the absence of a radical revolutionary framework should be understood vis-à-vis the victory of capitalist modernity and neoliberalism over post-colonial and anti-imperialist ideologies. In this regard, Libya is just a more radical exception. This process entailed the gradual defeat and demise of a language of national liberation, now perceived as banal and anachronistic, which became associated instead with an increasingly repressive and domestically illegitimate government. Therefore, if 2011 put the last nail in the coffin for al-Fātiḥ, it did so—and this cannot be stressed enough—because of the global triumph of (neo)liberal ideology, heavily invested in identity politics, individual rights, capitalist modernity, and the call for market-oriented economic reforms.

This is what allows us to understand that the camp of the *ṭaḥālib* raised many points, which, while stressing the dangers and reasons behind a military intervention undertaken by Western powers and their allies, had unfortunately lost their appeal to the population. In 2011, the political arena was monopolized by two discourses that not only identified principal villains but also proposed to achieve freedom through one another's heroic annihilation. In tracing responsibility for the lack of freedom or overthrow of past structures of oppression to the figure of a singular evildoer, they reduced questions of personal agency and collusion with previous political practices into a grand narrative—at times mythological—of complete powerlessness, whose main consequence was the quick obliteration of violence as a means of overcoming the situation. For the *jurdhān*, the history of anti-imperialist struggle in the Middle East and North African region was now being reinterpreted as a failure to establish liberal economic and political reforms: as a missed chance to enjoy the fruits of Western-led globalization. The *ṭaḥālib*, at the other end of the spectrum, did not realize how those anti-imperialist ideals no longer accorded with the reality on the ground; rather, they had largely become a justification for the regime to pursue repressive policies and dilute the social and economic rights of the population, while the latter acquiesced in order to obtain jobs or personal gains. Ultimately, the perfect plan for a disastrous outcome had been laid out.

# 6

# Conclusion

This book set out to provide an analysis of the everyday politics in the Libyan Arab Jamahiriya in its last turbulent decades, leading up to the 2011 events that sanctioned its fall. The book has attended to quotidian actions, emotions, and practices and woven them into the manifold elements at play that simultaneously reside in and escape the everyday. In other words, the investigation into the everyday politics of the Jamahiriya did not simply translate into an obsessive search for resistance or agency from below; it also prompted a critical engagement with those international forces that kept coming to the surface of the mundane. It brought us to consider how regional and international political dynamics had an increasing impact on the regime's ambitions, as well as on the mundane orientations and actions of Libyans. This dialectical relationship between the everyday and the international functioned as a metronome to understand the rhythms of political change that characterized the Jamahiriya since the late 1980s. It allowed identifying a set of main modalities of political interaction that shed light on the contradictory transformations following the defeat and limitations of the 1969 revolution under the geopolitical threat of war and international sanctions.

In such a scenario, the increasing use of repressive tactics played a fundamental role in affecting the legitimacy of the regime in the eyes of its population. Violence, fear, and surveillance had a long-lasting impact on society because they brought people to establish bonds based more on suspicion than on solidarity. However, this book has cautioned readers from rushing to define the Jamahiriya as an umpteenth authoritarian regime in the Arab world that crushes and controls its people. The significance of this issue lies in how the increasing repressive character of the regime inevitably reflected a wider power struggle at the international level, to which Libya was not immune. Therefore, as much as the regime's violence filled the everyday, it mirrored the geopolitical assault that was unleashed on al-Fātiḥ since the early stages of the revolution, leading to its defeat. From military bombings and attempted coups d'état to proxy wars and the imposition of a decade-long international embargo, violence was not a unique characteristic of the Jamahiriya; it permeated these political measures adopted by Western countries to discipline and control "rogue" Libya.

By seeping through the international sphere to the mundane, the uses of repressive tactics, for example, increased with the rise of Islamist groups in the country, particularly when the LIFG, together with Western support, mounted an increasing opposition against the regime during the mid-1990s. Ranging from military force to stricter surveillance, the regime successfully contained this challenge, yet the effects of these measures persisted. Both the material and affective components of fear conditioned people's actions, clouding their ability to distinguish between real and imagined threats and dangers. Moreover, my interlocutors often reflected on the widespread perception of an "invisible army" (see chapter 2) of informants, an outside structure of surveillance, a prying Orwellian "Big Brother" overseeing all aspects of their lives. Therefore, it would seem almost incomprehensible that the 2011 protests were staged against an increasingly repressive regime, considering its overarching surveillance capacities and people's involvement in it. Yet a deeper investigation into the use of *taqrīr* revealed the necessity to question such assumptions. People's capacities to manipulate and collude with such measures of state-control undermined—albeit slowly—the stability and legitimacy upon which the regime rested. By using surveillance for personal interests or as a defensive tactic, the everyday reality throws into question to what extent loyalty to and identification with the ideals of the regime pushed a person to act as an informant. In fact, as the regime gradually emerged from under the international embargo, the everyday uses of surveillance reflected a widespread culture of corruption and pursuit of personal interests that did not coincide with the regime's intended goals. In other words, people's quotidian uses of *taqrīr* linked less to the controlling desires of

the regime than to the changing socioeconomic conditions that compelled
people to act for personal gain.

To illustrate this dynamic, the book looked no further than people's
interaction with those institutionalized symbols, rituals, and organizations that sustained al-Fātiḥ's ideological vision of society, including
the figure of Qaddafi, the Green Book, and the Revolutionary Committees. Similar to the question of reporting, while people performed these
required acts or ended up joining these regime-linked organizations, the
meanings and values assigned to them changed over time. The reasons
lay in the growing sense of political distance and societal alienation in
which many Libyans lived. In such a scenario, the reversal of more progressive and egalitarian policies that had improved the lives of millions in
the previous decades, as well as the increasing centralization of the democratic structures of representation (Popular Committees), played a fundamental role. Yet, to understand the scale of these political changes, the
everyday led us to explore wider international changes. In the aftermath
of the 1969 revolution, Libya had embraced an experimental developmental path that reflected the sociopolitical context then prevalent in the
wider African and Asian postcolonial resistance. It pursued land reforms,
wealth redistribution, and the building of infrastructure accessible to all
the population, coupled with the subservience of economic policies to the
political struggle against anticolonial and anti-imperialist forces. While
the military confrontation with the West heightened, leading to the debacle in Chad and the imposition of crippling multilateral sanctions, the
increasing reliance on oil revenues failed to turn Libya into a productive
economy. Consequently, the ruling elites reversed those more progressive
policies, systematically transferring their wealth abroad instead of investing in national or regional enterprises. This process not only witnessed
the rise of a military-turned-merchant class but it also trickled down to
the population in the form of increasing socioeconomic inequalities. The
launch of programs of economic privatization, and the rise of inequalities, inevitably reshaped the nature of the relationship between state and
society. The latter, in fact, became largely oriented toward the pursuit of
individual gains and private profit, leading to a revival of clientelist connections and tribal allegiances. As many interviewees commented, the

country turned into a farm, where everybody was allowed and encouraged to steal from the state. These everyday processes of political change are fundamental to highlight for several reasons. First, as chapter 3 discusses at length, they show that tribal forms of kinship and *wāsta* remerged as a tool of control in a moment of international economic suffocation and local discontent, rather than representing the unchanging tribal nature of Libya. Second, it demonstrates that people reached a stage where they simultaneously condemned (and mocked) everything about the regime, from corruption to Qaddafi while continuing to reproduce these same practices in their everyday lives, stealing money from the government or trying to pursue their professional careers by using the right connections. In such a context, sketches of day-to-day frustration and subtle humor should be understood less as acts of resistance against the regime, and more as evidence of the heightening contradictions that developed within the Jamahiriya in its last two turbulent decades. In other words, they capture how the everyday interacted with these historical forces at play that shaped the process of political change in the Jamahiriya.

For these reasons, this investigation into the everyday helps us to rethink not only the political boundaries of authoritarianism but also the political history of the Jamahiriya, even more so when looking at the way the events of 2011 unfolded. If any interested reader picks up a book on the politics of the Jamahiriya, their overall impression will likely be that Libya has reached war due to various domestic and traditional weaknesses, mostly related to the madness of Qaddafi and the lack of modern state structures in the country. As the argument goes, the country's long rejection of modern state structures now poses major challenges for its future reconstruction, which consists of not being able to put together "a coherent national identity and public administration out of Qaddafi's shambles" (Anderson 2011, 7) because "the interim government is [was], in effect, inheriting a stateless state" (El-Katiri 2012, 23). Similarly, the analyses of think tanks explain that the current "war economy" in Libya is an effective prolongation of or return to Muammar Qaddafi's stateless and rentier Jamahiriya. Built by using income from Libya's natural resources, Qaddafi deliberately developed semi-independent economic institutions, which mirrored a complex rentier system, not a market economy. Therefore, the lack of modern state structures, supplanted by a patrimonial use of oil revenues for pursuing the whims of an authoritarian ruler, condemned Libya to a path of domestic savagery and war (Lugar, Cardin, and Maryl 2011; Lawson-Remer 2014).

Conceptually, I aimed to demonstrate that these types of analyses have simplified several aspects of the political history of the Jamahiriya. For instance, as this book shows, by reducing the question of political authority to the authoritarian figure of Qaddafi, they have overlooked the support that the regime—and Qaddafi himself—had among many Libyans, despite their numerous criticisms. Similarly, questions of political economy are also hugely misrepresented, since the history of anti-imperialist struggle in the Middle East and North African region, including Libya, is now being reinterpreted as a failure to establish liberal economic and political reforms. On the contrary, one of the key changes that marked the defeat of al-Fātiḥ was precisely the reversal of its redistributive policies and gradual reintegration into the world capitalist economy, which took place under geopolitical threat of war and sanctions. The analysis of the everyday instead shows that the seeds of an increasing corrupt economy based on the pursuit of private profit and personal gains that is so widespread and rampant today emerged precisely during the period when the Jamahiriya fell under the grip of international sanctions.

Certainly, while the study of the everyday has provided glimpses of the devastating impact of the sanctions on the infrastructures of the country, as well as on the aspirations of the population, future archival-based research could clarify further the extent of the sanction's impact on specific sectors of the economy (e.g., the oil industry, agriculture, health care). Moreover, those more conventional analyses tend to water down the role of Western geopolitical forces and their constant interference in the revolutionary ambitions of Libya. At best, their role, when mentioned, is blamed for lacking a day-after plan following the NATO-led disaster. Once again, the geopolitical specter emerged throughout my research from the very first interviews I undertook, mirroring people's increasing suspicion of its alleged government-funded research agenda—and, therefore, a Western researcher—toward Libyans and their country. Unfortunately, the insistence on embracing these categories of statelessness, rogue-ness, and authoritarianism perpetuates an ahistorical understanding of Libya's politics, which oversimplifies the manifold political dynamics surfacing in the everyday.

The failure to interact with the everyday is also present in those studies that, when analyzing the 2011 protests across the MENA region, accorded a certain validity to the notion of revolution, now being deployed to describe how the long-oppressed masses had rebelled against their authoritarian regimes. In this case, I argue that the conceptual value of events, revolutions, and ruptures can be epistemologically more romantic, but less explanatory and analytical, if lacking its dialectical partner, the everyday. The conceptual fervor linked to the notion of revolution produces a rather idealized understanding of the role played by everyday processes and practices in forming political regimes and subjectivities. The case of the two opposing discourses that starkly divided the population into *ṭaḥālib* (algae) and *jurdhān* (rats)—and, thus, pro- and anti-regime supporters—did not articulate the everyday politics of the past critically, but aimed to interpret the 2011 events in a retroactive manner. By failing to address questions of responsibility or breakdown and collusion with past political structures, those discourses located the source of oppression in moral and monological terms, refusing any form of self-criticism. Similarly, by imposing a monolithic explanation on the events of 2011, the Western-led military intervention also capitalized on its established assumption over Libya (rogue state, stateless society, mad Qaddafi) to pursue its interests. As Noam Chomsky (2006, 38) aptly describes, one of the most salient properties of rogue states is that "they do not protect their citizens from violence—and perhaps even destruction—or that decision makers regard such concerns as lower in priority than the short term power and wealth of the state's dominant sectors." This argument echoes the words of UNSC Resolution 1970 (United Nations Security Council 2011), which raised concern over the Jamahiriya's failure to protect civilians and incite violence in 2011 and prepared the grounds for the subsequent military assault. Overall, such monolithic frames provide a mutually reinforcing sense of powerlessness and victimization that disregards the nuanced nature of the everyday through the rationalization of violence and war, impeding further the possibility for a peaceful future.

The everyday, however, can provide a more reliable "index of histori-cal development than the brief, sporadically erupting event possibly can be" (Majumdar 2013, 171). It should be treated as the dialectical partner of the "event," which would have no backdrop against which to emerge. The perusal of the ordinary is fundamental for those who wish to comprehend the nature of the extraordinary. All of these connections explain why the study of the everyday matters and deserves scrutiny, particularly when an event disrupts its rhythmical pattern (Brownlee and Ghiabi 2016). Revolts and uprisings provoke the emergence of those social grievances and demands that otherwise often remain suppressed. However, to revo-lutionize the everyday means building a new ordinariness while address-ing those structures and practices that constituted its unjust nature. If focused solely on the notion of ruptures, revolution as a concept tends to obscure continuities, structural preconditions, and enabling conditions that allowed their eruption in the first place (Whitehead and Schneider 1987; Pieke 1996). In so doing, one fails to appreciate the intertwine-ment of extraordinary events with the multiple and manifold elements contained in the dimension of the mundane. Therefore, a risk exists for scholars of becoming trapped in these limitations when they deal with the study of politics and power without an adequate and appropriate grasp of the nature of the mundane, as well as the multiple political forces at work that shape the day-to-day lives of people, and vice versa.

In this regard, as I stressed from the start, while the everyday allows one to perceive and trace the complexities of processes of political change, such a focus should not be constrained by the boundaries of methodologi-cal nationalism. For instance, a surge of studies took place in the aftermath of the 2011 uprisings whose aim was to trace the seeds of subaltern discon-tent and resistance leading up to these major revolts. Undoubtedly, such a focus on the everyday that makes ordinary people regain their voices and dignity was required to counter dominant paradigms too narrowly focused on the persistence of authoritarianism. Other scholars (Ginty 2021; Koloma Beck 2012) have instead opted to peruse the everyday to grasp the complexities of people's lives in times of war and civil conflicts, particularly in the Global South. Such an approach is certainly an antidote to those studies that essentialize the Global South as a place of inherent violence, sectarian rife, unruliness, and destruction. The everyday can become a way to enter history and shift the use of dominant paradigms, engaging with the manifold and ambiguous nature of people's lives. At the same time, as I have attempted to show, focusing on the everyday might not be enough, if such an approach remains tied to methodological nationalism. In other words, the everyday cannot—and should not—be understood apart from wider international and global dynamics. As much as it allows to deessentialize the Global South, it should also be used to show the larger web of violence in which the South and the North of the world are locked.

From my interlocutors' suspicion of a foreign researcher and the regime's call to fight a neo-imperialist assault in 2011 to the NATO-led military interventions and people's aspirations for capitalist modernity, the dimension of the everyday cannot be insulated from wider world-economic and political changes (Elias et al. 2016; Hobson and Seabrooke 2009). The everyday politics of the Jamahiriya reveal the fantasies and aspirations of Libyans, providing emblematic examples that allow us to appreciate the role and influence of international political changes, as well as the rise of regional powers. In their everyday lives, Libyans showed a desire for consumerist goods or the fantasy of turning Libya into another Dubai, reflecting the extent to which their lives interacted with the rise of capitalist modernity, with its promise of happiness and global inclusion. Quotidian commodities such as bananas and chewing gum acquired a powerful symbolic meaning because they allowed Libyans to imagine a diverse type of modernity that would replace everyday scarcity with abundance. Similarly, the desire to transform Libya into a Dubai of the Mediterranean represented a call for better infrastructural development and a closer geopolitical relationship with the West. This plan was also supported at the elite level, as the reformist plans of Saif al-Islam showed (see chapter 4). Overall, we would be tempted to consider these fantasies of the good life as forms of contestation over the political status quo because they point to the alternative political horizons to which people attached meanings of a better future. On September 15, 2011, after the regime had been blocked from recapturing Benghazi, David Cameron, and Nicolas Sarkozy, prime ministers of Britain and France, respectively, arrived in the city to a rapturous welcome. In the spirit of the revolutionary festivities, both leaders announced: "Your friends in Britain and France will stand with you as you build your democracy" (BBC News 2011).

Why didn't freedom and liberation follow suit when Qaddafi was brutally captured, and the Jamahiriya fell? After all, if a revolutionary uprising was taking place, and the Western world had virtuously sided with the rebels, surely there were great things to come for Libya. Yet, at the time of writing, eleven years afterward, the country has only descended further into destruction and remains locked in a grid of violence, experiencing a massive deterioration of the most basic services, including the provision of water and electricity. Should we accept the answer provided by the David Cameron, five years after his visit to Benghazi—that the Libyan people "were given the opportunity" to build a stable democracy, and it was a matter of "huge regret" that they had not taken it (Wheeler 2016)?

The seeds of this cruel outcome lay in these fantasies, which functioned as a reminder of the rise of the global to the surface of the mundane. By linking economic prosperity and freedom to capitalist modernity, these imaginaries (as described in chapter 4) prepared the ground for revolutionary optimism while containing the seeds of its bitter outcome. They, in fact, mirrored the gradual abandonment of another vision for the future that initially had sought to build an alternative model to capitalist-led development, largely reflecting the sociopolitical context then prevailing in the wider 1970s African and Asian postcolonial resistance (see chapter 1). As this vision had been defeated under the threat of war and the imposition of sanctions, it had resulted in a military and ideological collapse that metamorphosed the Jamahiriya into more repressive policies and rising socioeconomic inequalities. In other words, capitalist modernity was being desired, yet the fact that these same Western-led capitalist forces had contributed to the defeat of the many worlds and possibilities that the Jamahiriya could have articulated was being ignored. Through the everyday, we can come to see the nuances of the international system, transcending a vision of the world configured into either methodological nationalism or stark divisions between Global North and South. The everyday, therefore, is global, regional, and local, and it doesn't compel us to get rid of those divisions; instead, it offers the conceptual space to recognize how the interminglement of those various political-economic scales exist and play out in the world.

This interconnection becomes even more important when looking at Libya and the MENA region today. In a nation devastated by years of civil war, where foreign countries continue to provide military and financial support to diverse opposing groups, the capacity to show how the local and the global feed into each other is of utmost importance at a scholarly as well as political level. Fifty-two years after the RCC had decided to evacuate two military bases occupied by US and UK military forces, Libya has gradually fallen into an infrastructure of violence and surveillance, combining development agencies, border control missions, and foreign mercenaries. Stephanie Williams, the deputy head of the United Nations Support Mission in Libya, has pointed out that there are now twenty thousand foreign forces and mercenaries in Libya, which represents a shocking violation of the country's sovereignty (UNSMIL Archives 2020). Foreign countries, both Western and non-Western, are expanding their military footprint in the region, from the construction of a border between Libya and Tunisia undertaken jointly by Germany and the United States, French military operations in the Sahel, and AFRICOM military bases to the new EU digital surveillance installation on the coast of Tunisia, "ISMariS." In this regard, the role of violence and surveillance continue to play a key role in structuring the present and future of Libya. What if, as some scholars (Kadri 2019) have argued, war and militarism have become both a central feature of the US-led international order and new forms of capital accumulation? Will these changes translate into an increase of conflicts in the South of the world? Undoubtedly, more systematic research into the nature of the relationship between these renewed instances of foreign military interference and forms of economic accumulation in Libya remains a much-needed enterprise.

While these reflections are topical, they are not meant to induce nostalgia for the previous regime in Libya, or for any other regime that was ousted in the aftermath of the tumultuous events in 2011 across the Arab region. As the disappointment of many Libyans proved to me during the interviews, post-2011 destruction and deterioration of living conditions has brought many Libyans to rediscover an attachment to the sense of stability and order that existed before 2011. While precarious and certainly problematic for several reasons, the past nonetheless appears as something to long for, as better when compared to the current war. These political configurations, however, belong to the past, and it remains impossible to rebuild or reactivate them in the present. There is no doubt that the current war has renewed a deeper sense of helplessness and resignation among Libyans, yet the future calls for a critical assessment of the past. By showing its complexities, this book could help to nuance the reasons that led to the present violence, opening a regenerative space—albeit a small one—to transcend the binaristic political camps and to think the future in a more reconciliatory way.

I witnessed those same dynamics while collecting these oral histories, which demonstrated to me both the limitations and potentialities residing in the everyday. They not only played a crucial and unique role in powering this effort to move beyond conventional approaches to the study of Libyan politics; they were also subjected to the same dialogical tensions contained in the everyday. For some of my interlocutors, these interviews allowed critical reflection on the political valence of the past, to look for better answers to the difficulties and instabilities of the present—to disrupt the linearity of time, allowing for a simultaneous shaking and rethinking of past, present, and future possibilities. Others, however, preferred to renounce the contradictions and nuances of the past and to offer a narrative that allowed them to maintain their political convictions (and material privileges) associated with the present condition of the country. In this way, the moment of remembering and historicizing became a way to confirm and further reinforce the instability of the present, with its own irreconcilable dynamics of violence. The crucial point about these collected narratives was not the facts they presented, but the dominant narratives into which the facts were fitted. Most importantly, in the intersubjective and relational space of the interview, both interviewee and interviewer negotiated each other's frameworks, privileges, and power dynamics. In a way, this book has aimed to engage with these dominant narratives, rethinking them together with my interlocutors. In fact, as much as those memories stem from the voices of Libyans, they are also refracted and sifted through my personal subjectivity.

In this process, I came to realize that the everyday indeed contains a potential for radical solidarity. By hosting so intimately those diverse yet interlinked political struggles, it inevitably reveals how their dismantlement calls for a spirit of transnational solidarity. When I began wondering how to formulate a solidarity-based response to events of such extraordinary magnitude in countries of the Global South, I became conscious that knowledge of the Other cannot—and will never—be enough, if we are not ready first and foremost to understand the historical role and economic interests that "our" governments have in shaping those narratives about "them." To be politically active at home can have a much bigger and more positive impact on the struggles of those who, more often than not, have a relation of subjugation with the Global North. The everyday, in other words, offers a space for political engagement that requires us to take into account and to ponder the various scales (individual, collective, institutional) of power, those struggles that separate while deeply linking the Global North and South. In so doing, a new space of solidarity can emerge beyond the colonial humanitarian savior trope usually activated by the privileged few to rescue subjugated people in most of the world.

This book has been a small effort to regain the complexities and voices of Libyans in the face of an increasingly repressive and domestically illegitimate regime. However, the everyday simultaneously and necessarily has forced me to consider how both Libyans and that regime operated within international and regional structures of power that influenced people's everyday lives. The challenge lies in maintaining a critical tension and assessment of these various levels of analyses and struggles that the everyday so intimately reveals. For these reasons, this book has also tried to shed light on the historical role played by international powers and foreign interventions in this country, and how they curtailed possibilities and potentialities of action for its people. Ultimately, this book is an attempt to restrain material violence from dictating or obscuring those interlinked elements that have come to determine the present of Libya. It is an effort to question simplified narratives while avoiding the dichoto-mous projection of violence in binaristic camps, with or against. It hopes that reflecting on those dynamics can assist in reorienting the present and can help bring Libya out of civil war. In this spirit of solidarity, I have nothing more to say.

*References*

*Index*

# References

Abdelrahman, Maha. 2017. "Policing Neoliberalism in Egypt: The Continuing Rise of the 'Securocratic' State." *Third World Quarterly* 38 (1): 185–202.

Abdussalam, Ali A. 1985. "The Impact of Recent Economic Changes in Libya on Monetary Aggregates." In *Planning and Development in Modern Libya*, edited by Mukthar Buru, Shukri Ghanem, and Keith McLachlan, 77–90. London: Society for Libyan Studies.

Abdussalam, Saleh Mohamed. 2006. "Privatization and Its Future Implications in Libya: A Case Study of the Libyan National Textile Company." PhD diss., Northumbria Univ.

Abuhadra, Dia Sadek, and Taher Tawfik Ajaali. 2014. *Labour Market and Employment Policy in Libya*. Torino: European Training Foundation.

Achcar, Gilbert. 2013. *The People Want: A Radical Exploration of the Arab Uprising*. Berkeley: Univ. of California Press.

AfricaGateNews. 2020. "February 15, 2011: Hisham al-Shoushan, the Cry of the Innocent." February 16, 2020. https://www.afrigatenews.net/article/15 /فبراير-2011-هشام-الشوشان-صرخة-البريء.

African Development Bank. 2009. "The Socialist People's Libyan Arab Jamahiriya: Country Engagement Note." https://www.afdb.org/fileadmin/uploads /afdb/Documents/Project-and-Operations/LIBYA_COUNTRY%20ENGAGE MENT%20NOTE_01.pdf (accessed July 12, 2022).

afrol News. 2006. "Reformists vs 'Old Mafia': Power Struggle in Libya." afrol News, September 5, 2006. http://www.afrol.com/articles/21056.

Åhäll, Linda. 2018. "Affect as Methodology: Feminism and the Politics of Emotion." *International Political Sociology* 12 (1): 36–52.

Ahlman, Jeffrey S. 2010. "The Algerian Question in Nkrumah's Ghana, 1958–1960: Debating 'Violence' and 'Nonviolence' in African Decolonization." *Africa Today* 57 (2): 66–84.

Ahmed, Sara. 2004. *The Cultural Politics of Emotions.* Edinburgh: Edinburgh Univ. Press.

———. 2006. *Queer Phenomenology: Orientations, Objects, Others.* Durham, NC: Duke Univ. Press.

———. 2010. *The Promise of Happiness.* Durham, NC: Duke Univ. Press.

Ahmida, Ali Abdullatif. 1994. *The Making of Modern Libya: State Formation, Colonization, and Resistance, 1830–1932.* Albany: State Univ. of New York Press.

———. 2005. *Forgotten Voices: Power and Agency in Colonial and Postcolonial Libya.* London: Routledge.

———. 2020. *Genocide in Libya: Shar, a Hidden Colonial History.* New York: Routledge.

Ajl, Max. 2021. *A People's Green New Deal.* London: Pluto.

Alaaldin, Ranj. 2012. "After the Arab Spring: Power Shift in the Middle East? Libya: Defining Its Future." LSE IDEAS Reports, London School of Economics and Political Science.

Al-Arabiya. 2006. "Saif al-Islam Says That Libya Is Not a Paradise." August 20, 2006. http://archive.libya-al-mostakbal.org/LibyaInThePress/August2006/alarabia_sief230806.htm.

———. 2009. "Gaddafi Spends Two Hours with 200 Italian Ladies." November 16, 2009. http://www.alarabiya.net/articles/2009/11/16/91470.html.

———. 2011. "'All My People Love Me,' Says 'Delusional' Gaddafi." March 1, 2011. https://www.alarabiya.net/articles/2011/03/01/139684.html.

Al-Barbar, Aghil M. 1994. *Political Change in Libya: A Study in the Decline of the Libyan Traditional Elite.* Palermo: Centro Culturale al-Farabi.

Albertus, Michael, Sofia Fenner, and Dan Slater. 2018. *Coercive Distribution.* Cambridge: Cambridge Univ. Press.

Alfasi, Kawther Nuri. 2017. "Political Agency and the Symbolic Legacy of Authoritarian Regimes: The Case of Libya." PhD diss., Univ. of Warwick.

Al Gathafi, Muammar. 2005. *The Green Book.* Reading: Ithaca.

Aljamahiria.org. 2022. "Aljamahiria—Gaddafi International Charity—Activities Report 2007–2008." Accessed July 12, 2022. http://aljamahiria.algaddafi.org/aljamahiria---gaddafi-international-charity---activities-report-2007---2008.

Al-Jazeera. 2008. "Gaddafi Condemns Arab Leaders." March 29, 2008. https://www.aljazeera.com/news/middleeast/2008/03/200861501453203859.html.

Al Maktoum, Mohammed bin Rashid. 2019. *My Story.* London: Explorer Group.

Al Nahed, Sumaya. 2015. "Covering Libya: A Framing Analysis of Al Jazeera and BBC Coverage of the 2011 Libyan Uprising and NATO Intervention." *Middle East Critique* 24 (3): 25167.

Al-Qadhafi, Saif Aleslam. 2003. "Libyan-American Relations." *Middle East Policy* 10 (1): 35–44.

Al-Saadi, Hameed. 1987. *Sovereignty between Delegation of Authority and the Exercise of Popular Power*. Tripoli: World Centre for the Studies and Researches of the Green Book.

Alusala, Nelson. 2004. "African Standby Force." *African Security Studies* 13 (2): 113–21.

alWatan. 2006. "Saif al-Islam Gaddafi: The Jamahiriya Is Not a Paradise and Freedom of the Press Is Non-Existent In Libya." August 21, 2006. https://www.alwatanvoice.com/arabic/news/2006/08/21/53716.html.

al-Watanona. 2006. "The Biography of a Journalist Who Stood Up To Corruption." May 10, 2006. http://www.libya-watanona.com/hrights/lhrs/lh10066c.htm.

———. n.d. "7 April 1976." Accessed August 16, 2022. http://www.libya-watanona.com/libya/7apr76c.htm.

Americaisevil1. 2011. "The New Libya—Gaddafi Sodomized with Stick before Execution." YouTube video, 0:26, October 25, 2011. https://www.youtube.com/watch?v=FdFIAIuW4HQ.

Amin, Samir. 1976. *Unequal Development: An Essay on the Social Formations of Peripheral Capitalism*. New York: Monthly Review.

———. 2006. *The Liberal Virus: Permanent War and the Americanization of the World*. New Delhi: Aakar.

Amnesty International. 1991. "Summary of Amnesty International's Concerns in Libya." Accessed July 12, 2022. https://www.amnesty.org/download/Documents/200000/mde190011991en.pdf.

———. 2006. "USA—Below the Radar: Secret Flights to Torture and 'Disappearance.'" Accessed July 12, 2022. https://www.amnesty.org/en/documents/AMR51/051/2006/en/.

———. 2010. "'Libya of Tomorrow': What Hope for Human Rights?" Accessed July 12, 2022. https://www.amnesty.org/en/documents/mde19/007/2010/en/.

Amouzou, Essè. 2012. *Mouammr Kadhafi et la realisation de l'union Africaine*. Paris: L'Harmattan.

Anderson, Lisa. 2011. "Demystifying the Arab Spring: Parsing the Differences between Tunisia, Egypt, and Libya." *Foreign Affairs* 90 (3): 2–7.

Anker, Elisabeth. 2014. *Orgies of Feeling: Melodrama and the Politics of Freedom.* Durham, NC: Duke Univ. Press.

Appadurai, Arjun. 2013. *The Future as a Cultural Fact: Essays on the Global Condition.* London: Verso.

Armbrust, Walter. 2019. *Martyrs and Tricksters: An Ethnography of the Egyptian Revolution.* Princeton, NJ: Princeton Univ. Press.

Asharq Al-Awsat. 2019. "Exclusive: In New Book, Dubai Ruler Says Offered Saddam Asylum in UAE." January 13, 2019. https://aawsat.com/english/home /article/1543876/exclusive-%E2%80%93-new-book-dubai-ruler-says-offered -saddam-asylum-uae.

Ashour, Omar. 2012. *Libyan Islamists Unpacked: Rise, Transformation and Future.* Doha: Brookings Institution.

Ashton, John. 2013. *Scotland's Shame: Lockerbie 25 Years On—Why It Still Matters.* Edinburgh: Birlinn.

Astier, Henry. 2007. "Libya Sales Deal Fuels French Row." BBC News, August 3, 2007. http://news.bbc.co.uk/2/hi/africa/6929532.stm.

Ayeb, Habib, and Ray Bush. 2019. *Food Insecurity and Revolution in the Middle East and North Africa: Agrarian Questions in Egypt and Tunisia.* London: Anthem.

Bacevich, Andrew. 2016. *America's War for the Greater Middle East.* New York: Penguin.

Baldinetti, Anna. 2012. "La Formazione Dello Stato e La Costruzione Dell'identità Nazionale" [The Formation of the State and the Construction of the National Identity]. In *Libia: Fine o Rinascita Di Una Nazione?* [Libya: End or Birth of a Nation?], edited by Karim Mezran and Arturo Varvelli, 3–20. Roma: Donzelli.

Bannon, Kevin. 2020. *How Abdelbaset Al-Megrahi Became Convicted for the Lockerbie Bombing.* Tolworth: Grosvenor House.

Barrada, Hamid, Mark Kravetz, and Mark Whitaker. 1984. *Kadhafi: Je Suis Un-opposant à l'échelon Mondial* [Qaddafi: I Am an Opponent at the Global Level]. Lausanne: Editions Pierre-Marcel Favre.

Bartu, Peter. 2015. "The Corridor of Uncertainty: The National Transitional Council's Battle for Legitimacy and Recognition." In *The Libyan Revolution and Its Aftermath*, edited by Peter Cole and Brian McQuinn, 31–54. London: Hurst.

Bayat, Asef. 2009. *Life as Politics: How Ordinary People Change the Middle East.* Stanford, CA: Stanford Univ. Press.

———. 2017. *Revolution without Revolutionaries: Making Sense of the Arab Spring.* Stanford, CA: Stanford Univ. Press.

BBC News. 2010. "Are Beards Obligatory for Devout Muslim Men?" June 27, 2010. http://www.bbc.co.uk/news/10369726.

———. 2011. "British Military Officers to Be Sent to Libya." April 19, 2011. https://www.bbc.com/news/uk-13132654.

———. 2011. "Libya Protests: Gaddafi Says 'All My People Love Me.'" February 28, 2011. https://www.bbc.com/news/world-africa-12603259.

———. n.d. "On This Day 19 December 2003." http://news.bbc.co.uk/onthisday /hi/dates/stories/december/19/newsid_4002000/4002441.stm.

Bearman, Jonathan. 1986. *Qadhafi's Libya*. London: Zed.

Becker, Jo, and Scott Shane. 2016. "Hillary Clinton, 'Smart Power,' and a Dictator's Fall." *New York Times*, February 28, 2016. https://www.nytimes.com/2016 /02/28/us/politics/hillary-clinton-libya.html.

Beckert, Jens. 2016. *Imagined Futures: Fictional Expectations and Capitalist Dynamics*. Cambridge, MA: Harvard Univ. Press.

Bensaâd, Ali, ed. 2012. "La Libye Révolutionnaire" [Revolutionary Libya]. *Politique Africaine* [African Politics] 125: 5–22.

Berlant, Laurent. 2011. *Cruel Optimism*. Durham, NC: Duke Univ. Press.

Berween, Mohammed. 2003. "The Political Belief System of Qaddafi: Power Politics and Self-Fulfilling Prophecy." *Journal of Libyan Studies* 4 (1): 49–62.

Bilgin, Pinar, and Adam David Morton. 2004. "From 'Rogue' to 'Failed' States? The Fallacy of Short-Termism." *Politics* 24 (3): 169–80.

Black, Ian. 2010. "Gaddafi's Son Retreats on Human Rights in Libya." *Guardian*, December 16, 2010. https://www.theguardian.com/world/2010/dec/16 /gaddafi-son-human-rights-libya.

———. 2011. "Qatar Admits Sending Hundreds of Troops to Support Libya Rebels." *Guardian*, October 26, 2011. http://www.theguardian.com/world/2011 /oct/26/qatar-troops-libya-rebels-support.

Blair, John Malcolm. 1978. *The Control of Oil*. New York: Vintage.

Bleiker, Roland, and Emma Hutchinson. 2008. "Fear No More: Emotions and Word Politics." *Review of International Studies* 34 (1): 115–35.

Blundy, David, and Andrew Lycett. 1987. *Qaddafi and the Libyan Revolution*. Boston: Little, Brown.

Bogaert, Koenraad. 2018. *Globalized Authoritarianism: Megaprojects, Slums, and Class Relations in Urban Morocco*. Minneapolis: Univ. of Minnesota Press.

BongoGhana. 2011. "Aljamahiriya TV Libya—Muammar Al Gaddafi's Big Full Speech February 2011, Tripoli." YouTube video, 1:04:40, December 24, 2011. https://www.youtube.com/watch?v=1n_G0vIeGqw.

Bosco, David. 2011. "Was There Going to Be a Benghazi Massacre?" *Foreign Affairs*, April 7, 2011. http://foreignpolicy.com/2011/04/07/was-there-going-to-be-a-benghazi-massacre/.

Boucek, Christopher. 2002. "Libya's Curious Relationship with Mugabe's Zimbabwe." *Journal of Libyan Studies* 3 (2): 22–31.

Bouchra jad. 2016. "Al-Saadi Gaddafi Takes a Penalty Kick, the Ball Hits the Crossbar, the Goalkeeper Picks It Up, and the Referee Announces the Goal." YouTube video, 0:42, August 16, 2016. https://www.youtube.com/watch?v=v9TNyXPC8uY.

Braun, Gerald, and Adele Jones. 2014. *Libya—Building the Future with Youth: Challenges for Education and Employability*. Bonn: Deutsche Gesellschaft für Internationale Zusammenarbeit, GIZ.

Bridge, Gavin. 2008. "Global Production Networks and the Extractive Sector: Governing Resource-Based Development." *Journal of Economic Geography* 8: 389–419.

Bright, Martin. 2004. "Gadaffi Still Hunts 'Stray Dogs' in UK." *Guardian*, March 28, 2004. https://www.theguardian.com/uk/2004/mar/28/politics.libya.

Brisard, Jean-Charles, Guillaume Dasquie, and Wayne Madsen. 2002. *Forbidden Truth: U.S.-Taliban Secret Oil Diplomacy and the Failed Search for Bin Laden*. New York: Nation.

Brown, Keith, and Dimitrios Theodossopoulos. 2007. "'Others' Others: Talking about Stereotypes and Construction of Otherness in Southeast Europe." *History and Anthropology* 15 (1): 1–22.

Brownlee, Billie Jeanne, and Maziyar Ghiabi. 2016. "Passive, Silent, and Revolutionary: The 'Arab Spring' Revisited." *Middle East Critique* 25 (3): 299–316.

Bukhari, Sahih. al-. n.d. "Volume 7, Book 72, Hadith 678, 686, 694, 696, 697, 743,744." Accessed July 12, 2022. https://www.sahih-bukhari.com/Pages/Bukhari_7_72.php.

Burdett, Charles. 2010. "Mussolini's Journey to Libya (1937): Ritual, Power, and Transculturation." In *National Belongings: Hybridity in Italian Colonial and Postcolonial Cultures*, edited by Jacqueline Andall and Derek Duncan, 151–69. Bern: Peter Lang.

Burgat, Francois. 1995. "Chronique Interieure." In *Annuaire de l'Afrique Du Nord* [Annuary of North Africa], 601–16. Paris: Centre national de la recherche scientifique.

Burgi, Michelle L. 2009. *Boundaries of Discourse in the International Court of Justice: Mapping Arguments in Arab Territorial Disputes*. Leiden: Brill.

Bushnaf, Mansour. 2008. *Chewing Gum*. London: Darf.

Butler, Judith. 2018. "Solidarity/Susceptibility." *Social Text* 36 (4): 1–20.

Campbell, Horace. 2013. *Global NATO and the Catastrophic Failure in Libya*. New York: Monthly Review.

Capasso, Matteo. 2014. "The Libyan Drawers: 'Stateless Society,' 'Humanitarian Intervention,' 'Logic of Exception,' and 'Traversing the Phantasy.'" *Middle East Critique* 23 (4): 387–404.

———. 2021. "IR, Imperialism, and the Global South: From Libya to Venezuela." *Politics* Online First.

Capasso, Matteo, and Igor Cherstich. 2014. "'Guest Editors' Note: The Libyan Event and the Part for the Whole." *Middle East Critique* 23 (4): 379–85.

CBS News. 2011. "Clinton on Qaddafi: We Came, We Saw, He Died." YouTube video, 0:12, October 20, 2011. https://www.youtube.com/watch?v=mlz3-OzcExI.

Center for Humanitarian Dialogue. 2018. "The Libyan National Conference Process: The Final Report." Accessed July 12, 2022. https://unsmil.unmissions .org/sites/default/files/ncp_report_jan_2019_en.pdf.

Central Intelligence Agency (CIA). 1979. "The USSR and Libya: Collusion in the Middle East and Africa—An Intelligence Assessment." Accessed July 12, 2022. https://www.cia.gov/readingroom/docs/CIA-RDP80T00942A0006000 80002-9.pdf.

———. [1986] 2011. "Libya: Economy under Siege." Accessed July 12, 2022. https:// www.cia.gov/readingroom/docs/CIA-RDP90G01359R000200090017-1.pdf.

———. 1986. "Libya under Qadhafi: A Pattern of Aggression." Accessed July 12, 2022. https://www.cia.gov/readingroom/docs/CIA-RDP91B00874R0002000 70001-3.pdf.

———. 1987. "International Economic and Energy Weekly." March 6, 1987. https://www.cia.gov/readingroom/docs/DOC_0000389199.pdf.

Centro Studi Libro Verde. 1984. *Libro Verde: Commenti e Recensioni*. Tripoli: Centro internazionale ricerche e studi sul libro verde—Giamahiria libica.

Chalcraft, John. 2016. *Popular Politics in the Making of the Modern Middle East*. Cambridge: Cambridge Univ. Press.

Cherstich, Igor. 2014. "When Tribesmen Do Not Act Tribal: Libyan Tribalism as Ideology (Not as Schizophrenia)." *Middle East Critique* 23 (4): 405–21.

Chock, Phyllis Pease. 1987. "The Irony of Stereotypes: Toward an Anthropology of Ethnicity." *Cultural Anthropology* 2 (3): 347–68.

Chomsky, Noam. 2006. *Failed States: The Abuse of Power and the Assault on Democracy*. New York: Metropolitan.

Chorin, Ethan. 2012. *Exit Gaddafi: The Hidden History of the Libyan Revolution.* London: Saqi.

Chulov, Martin. 2012. "Gaddafi's Last Moments: 'I Saw the Hand Holding the Gun and I Saw It Fire.'" *Guardian*, October 20, 2012. https://www.theguardian.com/world/2012/oct/20/muammar-gaddafi-killing-witnesses.

Clinton, Hillary Rodham. 2011. "Testimony Secretary of State Senate Foreign Relations Committee." United States Senate Committee on Foreign Relations, March 2, 2011. https://www.foreign.senate.gov/imo/media/doc/Clinton_Testimony.pdf.

CNN. 2011. "Witnesses Describe Violence, Chaos in Libyan Cities." February 21, 2011. http://edition.cnn.com/2011/WORLD/africa/02/21/libya.protests.scene/index.html.

Cobain, Ian. 2015. "MI5 Says Rendition of Libyan Opposition Leaders Strengthened Al-Qaida." *Guardian*, January 29, 2015. https://www.theguardian.com/world/2015/jan/29/mi5-rendition-libyan-opposton-strengthened-al-qaida.

Cojean, Annick. 2013. *Gaddafi's Harem: The Story of a Young Woman and the Abuses of Power in Libya.* London: Grove.

———. 2014. "Le viol, arme de destruction massive en Syrie." *Le Monde*, April 3, 2014. https://www.lemonde.fr/proche-orient/article/2014/03/04/syrie-le-viol-arme-de-destruction-massive_4377603_3218.html.

Colaprico, Piero, Giuseppe D'Avanzo, and Emilio Randacio. 2011. "Tutte Nude al Bunga Bunga e Quand'ero in Questura Silvio Aveva Paura" [All Naked at the Bunga Bunga and When Silvio Got Scared at the Police Station]. *La Repubblica*, Feburary 18, 2011. https://www.repubblica.it/politica/2011/02/18/news/verbali_18_febbraio-12597624/.

Cole, Peter, and Brian McQuinn, eds. 2015. *The Libyan Revolution and Its Aftermath.* London: Hurst.

Coles, T. J. 2016. *Britain's Secret Wars: How and Why the United Kingdom Sponsors Conflict around the World.* Essex: Clairview.

Cruickshank, Paul. 2009. *LIFG Revisions Posing Critical Challenge to Al-Qa'ida.* West Point: Combating Terrorism Center.

Curtis, Mark. 2018. "What Will Be the Blowback for UK Government after Libya Revelations?" Middle East Eye, April 6, 2018. http://www.middleeasteye.net/opinion/what-will-be-blowback-uk-government-after-libya-revelations.

Darwish, Adel. 2009. "Muammar Gaddafi Accuses Saudi Arabia's King Abdullah of Lying at Arab Summit." *Telegraph*, March 30, 2009. http://www.telegraph

.co.uk/news/worldnews/middleeast/qatar/5079290/Muammar-Gaddafi
-accuses-Saudi-Arabias-King-Abdullah-of-lying-at-Arab-summit.html.

David, Roman. 2006. "From Prague to Baghdad: Lustration Systems and Their Political Effects 1." *Government and Opposition* 41 (3): 347–72.

Davidson, Christopher. 2005. *The United Arab Emirates: A Study in Survival.* Boulder, CO: Lynne Rienner.

———. 2009. *Dubai: The Vulnerability of Success.* London: Hurst.

———. 2011. "The Making of Police State." *Foreign Affairs*, April 14, 2011. http://foreignpolicy.com/2011/04/14/the-making-of-a-police-state-2/.

———. 2015. *After the Sheiks: The Coming Collapse of the Gulf Monarchies.* London: Hurst.

Davies, William. 2015. *The Happiness Industry: How the Government and Big Business Sold Us Well-Being.* London: Verso.

Davis, Brian L. 1990. *Qaddafi, Terrorism, and the Origins of the U.S. Attack on Libya.* New York: Praeger.

Davis, John. 1987. *Tribe and Revolution in Libya: The Zuwara and Their Politics.* London: I. B. Tauris.

Deeb, Marius. 1986. "Radical Political Ideologies and Concepts of Property in Libya and South Yemen." *Middle East Journal* 40 (3): 445–60.

Del Monte, Stefania. 2015. *Staging Memory: Myth, Symbolism, and Identity in Postcolonial Italy and Libya.* Frankfurt am Main: Peter Lang.

Diana, Elvira. 2017. "Un Secolo Di Oppression Sociale e Culturale Nella Libia Simbolica Di Mansur Busanaf." *ArabLit* 13: 19–34.

Dietrich, Christopher R. W. 2017. *Oil Revolution: Anticolonial Elites, Sovereign Rights, and the Economic Culture of Decolonization.* Cambridge: Cambridge Univ. Press.

———. 2021. "Strategies of Decolonization: Economic Sovereignty and National Security in Libyan-US Relations, 1949–1971." *Journal of Global History,* June 9, 2021. https://www.cambridge.org/core/journals/journal-of-global-history/article/abs/strategies-of-decolonization-economic-sovereignty-and-national-security-in-libyanus-relations-19491971/29F20A3B7BDEF23E268B6619E955BA31.

Djaziri, Moncef. 1987. "La dynamique des institutions et la structure du pouvoir en Libye 1978–1987" [Institutional Dynamics and Structure of Power in Libya, 1978–1987]. In *Annuaire de l'Afrique du Nord* [Annuary of North Africa] 26: 451–76.

———. 1996. *État et société en Libye: Islam, politique et modernité* [State and Society in Libya: Islam, Politics, and Modernity]. Paris: L'Harmattan.

Donati, Jessica, and Marie-Louise Gumuchian. 2018. "Special Report: The Gaddafi Oil Papers." Reuters, December 23, 2011. https://www.reuters.com/article/us-libya-oil-corruption/special-report-the-gaddafi-oil-papers-idUSTRE7BM0JF20111223.

Dorril, Stephen. 2002. *MI6: Inside the Covert World of Her Majesty's Secret Intelligence Service.* New York: Touchstone.

Dror, Yehezkel. 1971. *Crazy States: A Counterconventional Strategic Problem.* London: Heath Lexington.

Duffy, Deirdre. 2017. "Get on Your Feet, Get Happy: Happiness and the Affective Governing of Young People in the Age of Austerity." In *Neoliberalism and Austerity: The Moral Economies of Young People's Health and Well-Being,* edited by Peter Kelly and Jo Pike, 87–101. London: Palgrave Macmillan.

Eden, Richard. 2011. "Genius Sacha Baron Cohen Makes Gaddafi: The Movie." *Telegraph,* November 6, 2011. https://www.telegraph.co.uk/culture/film/film-news/8872057/Genius-Sacha-Baron-Cohen-makes-Gaddafi-the-movie.html.

El-Fathaly, Omar, and Monte Palmer. 1980. *Political Development and Social Change in Libya.* Toronto: Lexington.

Elias, Juanita, John M. Hobson, Lena Rethel, and Leonard Seabrooke. 2016. "Everyday International Political Economy Meets the Everyday Political Economy of Southeast Asia." In *The Everyday Political Economy of Southeast Asia,* edited by Juanita Elias and Lena Rethel, 239–60. Cambridge: Cambridge Univ. Press.

El Issawi, Fatima. 2013. *Transitional Libyan Media: Free at Last?* Washington, DC: Carnegie Institute. http://carnegieendowment.org/2013/05/14/transitional-libyan-media-free-at-last-pub-51747.

El-Katiri, Mohammed. 2012. *State-Building Challenges in A Post-Revolution Libya.* Carlisle: Strategic Studies Institute–US Army War College.

El-Kikhia, Mansour. 1997. *Libya's Qadhafi: The Politics of Contradiction.* Gainesville: Univ. Press of Florida.

El Mughrabi, Marei A. 2005. "An Exploration of the Impact of International and Domestic Factors on Economic Reform Programmes in Libya, 1987–2004." PhD diss., Northumbria Univ.

Elsheshtawy, Yasser. 2008. *The Evolving Arab City: Tradition, Modernity, and Urban Development.* London: Routledge.

————. 2010. *Dubai: Behind an Urban Spectacle*. London: Routledge.

ElWarfally, Mahmoud G. 1989. *Imagery and Ideology in U.S. Policy toward Libya*. Pittsburgh: Univ. of Pittsburgh Press.

Emmanuel, Arghiri. 1972. *Unequal Exchange: A Study of the Imperialism of Trade*. New York: Monthly Review.

Esposito, John. 2003. "Satan." In *The Oxford Dictionary of Islam*. Accessed July 12, 2022. http://www.oxfordislamicstudies.com/article/opr/t125/e2108.

Fallon, James. 2011. "The Mind of a Dictator." *Psychology Today*, November 11, 2011. https://www.psychologytoday.com/intl/blog/the-psychopath-inside /201111/the-mind-dictator.

Farah, Douglas. 2011. "Harvard for Tyrants." *Foreign Policy*, March 5, 2011. https://foreignpolicy.com/2011/03/05/harvard-for-tyrants/.

Faucon, Benoît, Summer Said, and Liam Moloney. 2012. "Libya, U.S. Probe Oil-Company Deals." *Wall Street Journal*, April 8, 2012. https://www.wsj.com /articles/SB10001424052702303815404577331802347989804.

Fehérváry, Krisztina. 2009. "Goods and States: The Political Logic of State-Socialist Material Culture." *Comparative Studies in Society and History* 51 (2): 426–59.

Feldman, Ilana. 2015. *Police Encounters: Security and Surveillance in Gaza under Egyptian Rule*. Stanford, CA: Stanford Univ. Press.

Felter, Joseph, and Brian Fishman. 2007. *Al-Qa'ida's Foreign Fighters in Iraq: A First Look at the Sinjar Records*. New West Point, NY: Combating Terrorism Center.

The Final Call. 2000. "World Mathaba of Libya, Which Supported Liberation Movements, Plans Its Future." September 14, 2000. http://www.finalcall.com /international/2000/libya_mathaba09-12-2000.htm.

Fischer, Edward F. 2014. *The Good Life: Aspiration, Dignity, and the Anthropology of Well-Being*. Stanford, CA: Stanford Univ. Press.

Food and Agriculture Organization. 2011. "Food Security in Libya: An Overview." World Food Programme. Accessed July 12, 2022. https://www.wfp.org /content/libya-food-security-libya-overview-april-2011.

Ford-Rojas, John Paul. 2011. "Muammar Gaddafi in His Own Words." *Telegraph*, October 20, 2011. http://www.telegraph.co.uk/news/worldnews/africa andindianocean/libya/8838644/Muammar-Gaddafi-in-his-own-words.html.

Forte, Maximilian. 2011. "The Top Ten Myths in the War Against Libya." Counterpunch, August 31, 2011. http://www.counterpunch.org/2011/08/31/the -top-ten-myths-in-the-war-against-libya/.

———. 2012. *Slouching toward Sirte: NATO's War on Libya and Africa*. Montreal: Baraka.

Foucault, Michel. 1993. *Sorvegliare e Punire: Nascita Della Prigione* [Discipline and Punish: The Birth of the Prison]. Torino: Einaudi.

4Gaddafi. 2012. "We Are One Family and the Leader Is Our Father." YouTube video, 4:29, January 10, 2012. https://www.youtube.com/watch?v=0-sfXeriB uQ&list=RDpNE7vliLEhc&index=6.

France24. 2010. "Qaddafi Worried about the Fall of Ben Ali." France24, January 16, 2011. https://www.france24.com/ar/20110116-libya-gaddafi-achy-fall -president-tunisia-zine-elabidine-benali, (in Arabic).

Francioni, Francesco. 1984. "The Status of the Gulf of Sirte in International Law." *Syracuse Journal of International Law and Commerce* 11 (2): 311–26.

———. 1980. "The Gulf of Sirte Incident (United States v. Libya) and International Law." *Italian Yearbook of International Law Online* 5 (1): 85–109.

Gambill, Gary. 2005. "The Libyan Islamic Fighting Group." *Terrorism Monitor* 6 (3). https://jamestown.org/program/the-libyan-islamic-fighting-group-lifg/ (accessed July 12, 2022).

Garavini, Giuliano. 2019. *The Rise and Fall of OPEC in the 20th Century*. Oxford: Oxford Univ. Press.

Garside, Juliette, David Pegg, and Mona Mahmood. 2016. "Gaddafi Insider Accused of Using State Cash to Buy Luxury Scottish Hotels." *Guardian*, May 16, 2016. https://www.theguardian.com/news/2016/may/16/gaddafi-insider -accused-of-using-state-cash-to-buy-luxury-scottish-hotels.

Gatron, Jean Claude. 1989. "La Libye et Le Tchad devant la cour internationale de justice?" [Libya and Chad in Front of the International Court of Justice]. *Annuaire français de droit international* [French Annuary of International Law] 35: 205–15.

Gebauer, Matthias, John Goetz, Wiebke Hollersen, and Marc Hujer. 2011. "Der Libysche Freund." *Der Spiegel*, July 26, 2011. http://www.spiegel.de/spiegel /print/d-79175780.html.

Geha, Carmen. 2014. *Civil Society and Political Reform in Lebanon and Libya: Transition and Constraints*. London: Routledge.

General Planning Council of Libya. 2006. "Libya at the Dawn of a New Era: Improving Competitiveness in the Global Economy." Accessed July 12, 2022. https://www.hbs.edu/faculty/Publication%20Files/2006-0209_Libya_c06b 5149-bea3-44e2-a04a-f18c55a14bff.pdf.

Genugten, Saskia van. 2016. *Libya in Western Foreign Policies, 1911–2011*. London: Palgrave Macmillan.

Gera, Gideon. 1977. "Libya." In *Middle East Contemporary Survey*, edited by Colin Legum, Haim Shaked, Daniel Dishon, and Jacqueline Dyck, 526–48. Boulder, CO: Westview.

Ghanem, Shukri. 1987. "The Oil and the Libyan Economy: Past, Present and the Likely Future." In *The Economic Development of Libya*, edited by Bichara Khader and Bashir El-Wifati, 58–71. Kent: Crom Helm.

Ghubara, Abdul Baset. 2019. "The Libyan Fighting Group: The Deep Wounds of Terrorism in Libyan History." AfricaGateNews, October 24, 2019. https://www.afrigatenews.net/article/جسد-في-الغائرة-الجروح-المقاتلة-الليبية-الجماعة-الليبي-التاريخ/.

Ginty, Roger Mac. 2021. *Everyday Peace: How So-Called Ordinary People Can Disrupt Violent Conflict*. Oxford: Oxford Univ. Press.

Glanville, Luke. 2013. "Intervention in Libya: From Sovereign Consent to Regional Consent." *International Studies Perspectives* 14 (3): 325–42.

Glazebrook, Dan. 2012. "The Imperial Agenda of the US's 'Africa Command' Marches On." *Guardian*, June 14, 2012. https://www.theguardian.com/commentisfree/2012/jun/14/africom-imperial-agenda-marches-on.

Goldberg, Jonathan. 2010. *Sodometries: Renaissance Texts, Modern Sexualities*. New York: Fordham Univ. Press.

Gotachew, Adom. 2019. *Worldmaking after Empire: The Rise and Fall of Self-Determination*. Princeton, NJ: Princeton Univ. Press.

Graeff-Wassink, Maria. 1993. *Women at Arms: Is Ghadafi a Feminist?* London: Darf.

Green Rebel. 2013. "We Have Not Given You What You Deserve, Forgive Us. Exclusive to al-Khadra Channel." YouTube video, 10:08, January 28, 2013. https://www.youtube.com/watch?v=7GqyCRhSg7E.

Griswold, Elisa. 2010. "The Heir." *New Republic*, July 20, 2010. https://newrepublic.com/article/75949/the-heir.

Gritten, David. 2011. "Key Figures in Libya's Rebel Council." BBC News, August 25, 2011. http://www.bbc.co.uk/news/world-africa-12698562.

Hagger, Nicholas. 2009. *The Libyan Revolution: Its Origins and Legacy*. Ropley: Orca.

Hammond, Andrew. 2007. *Popular Culture in the Arab World: Art, Politics and the Media*. Cairo: American Univ. in Cairo.

Hanieh, Adam. 2011. *Capitalism and Class in the Gulf Arab States*. New York: Palgrave Macmillan.

———. 2018a. "Ambitions of a Global Gulf: The Arab Uprisings, Yemen and the Saudi-Emirati Alliance." *Middle East Research and Information Project (MERIP)* 289: 21–26.

———. 2018b. *Money, Markets, and Monarchies: The Gulf Cooperation Council and the Political Economy of the Contemporary Middle East.* Cambridge: Cambridge Univ. Press.

Hersh, Seymour. 1987. "Target Qaddafi." *New York Times*, February 22, 1987. https://www.nytimes.com/1987/02/22/magazine/target-qaddafi.html.

Herzfeld, Michael. 1980. "On the Ethnography of 'Prejudice' in an Exclusive Community." *Ethnic Groups* 2: 283–305.

Hibou, Beatrice. 2011. *The Force of Obedience: The Political Economy of Repression in Tunisia.* Cambridge: Polity.

Hickel, Jason, Christian Dorninger, Hanspeter Wieland, and Intan Suwandi. 2022. "Imperialist Appropriation in the World Economy: Drain from the Global South through Unequal Exchange, 1990–2015." *Global Environmental Change* 73: 1–13.

Hirschkind, Charles. 2001. "The Ethics of Listening: Cassette-Sermon Audition in Contemporary Egypt." *American Ethnologist* 28 (3): 623–49.

Hobson, John M., and Leonard Seabrooke. 2009. *Everyday International Political Economy.* London: Routledge Handbooks Online. https://www.routledgehandbooks.com/doi/10.4324/9780203881569.ch18 (accessed July 12, 2022).

Hooper, John. 2009. "Gaddafi Hires 200 Young Italian Women—to Convert Them to Islam." *Guardian*, November 16, 2009. https://www.theguardian.com/world/2009/nov/16/gaddafi-women-islam-rome.

Hope, Kempe R. 1983. "Basic Needs and Technology Transfer Issues in the 'New International Economic Order.'" *American Journal of Economics and Sociology* 42 (4): 393–403.

House of Commons Foreign Affairs Committee. 2016. *Libya: Examination of Intervention and Collapse and the UK's Future Policy Options.* Accessed July 12, 2022. https://www.publications.parliament.uk/pa/cm201617/cmselect/cmfaff/119/119.pdf.

Howden, Daniel. 2011. "Gaddafi's Green Book Study Centre Flattened." *Independent*, May 11, 2011. http://www.independent.co.uk/news/world/africa/gaddafis-green-book-study-centre-flattened-2282146.html.

Hozic, Aida. 2011. "Travel for Ordinary Comforts." *Cambridge Review of International Affairs* 24 (4): 613–27.

Huffington Post. 2015. "'Morire o Bunga Bunga?'. Silvio Berlusconi e La Barzelletta Con Protagonisti Quei 'Due Sfigati' Bondi e Cicchitto" ["Death or Bunga Bunga?" Silvio Berlusconi and the Joke with "Two Losers" Bondi and Cicchitto as Protagonists]. Huffington Post, September 27, 2015. https://www.huffington post.it/2015/09/27/silvio-berlusconi-barzelletta-bunga-bunga_n_8202924.html.

Human Rights Watch. 2005. "Before the Rule of Law Comes to Libya." November 2, 2005. https://www.hrw.org/news/2005/11/02/rule-law-comes-libya.

———. 2006a. "Building Towers, Cheating Workers: Exploitation of Migrant Construction Workers in the United Arab Emirates." Accessed November 11, 2006. https://www.hrw.org/report/2006/11/11/building-towers-cheating -workers/exploitation-migrant-construction-workers-united.

———. 2006b. "Libya: June 1996 Killings at Abu Salim Prison." June 27, 2006. https://www.hrw.org/news/2006/06/27/libya-june-1996-killings-abu-salim -prison.

———. 2009. "Truth and Justice Can't Wait: Human Rights Developments in Libya amid Institutional Obstacles." Accessed July 12, 2022. https://www .hrw.org/sites/default/files/reports/libya1209webwcover.pdf.

———. 2016. "Enabling a Dictator: The United States and Chad's Hissène Habré, 1982–1990." Accessed July 12, 2022.https://www.hrw.org/report/2016/06/28 /enabling-dictator/united-states-and-chads-hissene-habre-1982-1990.

Hvidt, Martin. 2009. "The Dubai Model: An Outline of Key Development-Process Elements in Dubai." *International Journal of Middle East Studies* 41 (3): 397–418.

Ibrahim, Azeem. 2020. *Rise and Fall?: The Rise and Fall of ISIS in Libya*. Carlisle: Strategic Studies Institute US Army War College.

Il Sussidiario. 2010. "BUNGA-BUNGA / La Web-Mania Parte Con Fede, Gheddafi e Berlusconi, Ma Finisce in Bufala" [BUNGA-BUNGA / The Web-Mania Starts with Fede, Gaddafi and Berlusconi, but Ends in Fake News]. *Il Sussidiario*, October 28, 2010. https://www.ilsussidiario.net/news/curiosita/2010 /10/28/bunga-bunga-la-web-mania-parte-con-fede-gheddafi-e-berlusconi -ma-finisce-in-bufala/122861/.

ImazighenLibya. 2013a. "The Execution Verdict of Sasi Zikri and Ahmad Sulayman / Libya Nalut City 1984." YouTube video, 1:47, September 12, 2013. https://www.youtube.com/watch?v=Dc_E47IZ7Nk.

———. 2013b. "The Execution of the Martyr Muhammad Sa'id al-Shibani 1984 (Nafusa Mountain) Tumzin Libya." YouTube video, 6:44, September 12, 2013. https://www.youtube.com/watch?v=0jH24UNYjEs.

International Criminal Court of Justice. 2011. "Situation in the Libyan Arab Jamahiriyya." Accessed July 12, 2022. https://www.icc-cpi.int/CourtRecords
/CR2011_06155.PDF.

International Monetary Fund. 2005. "Country Report No. 2005/83." https://www
.imf.org/en/Publications/CR/Issues/2016/12/31/Socialist-Peoples-Libyan
-Arab-Jamahiriya-Staff-Report-for-the-2004-Article-IV-Consultation-18109.

———. 2006. "Country Report No. 2006/136." https://www.imf.org/en/Publications
/CR/Issues/2016/12/31/The-Socialist-Peoples-Libyan-Arab-Jamahiriya-2005
-Article-IV-Consultation-Staff-Report-and-19128.

———. 2007. "IMF Country Report No. 2007/149." https://www.imf.org/en
/Publications/CR/Issues/2016/12/31/The-Socialist-People-s-Libyan-Arab
-Jamahiriya-2006-Article-IV-Consultation-Staff-Report-20679.

Ismail, Salwa. 2006. *Political Life in Cairo's New Quarters: Encountering the Everyday State*. Minneapolis: Univ. Of Minnesota Press.

———. 2019. *The Rule of Violence: Subjectivity, Memory, and Government in
Syria*. Cambridge: Cambridge Univ. Press.

Jackson, Robert H. 1990. *Quasi States: Sovereignty, International Relations, and
the Third World*. Cambridge: Cambridge Univ. Press.

Jamel Alenzi. 2013. "The Radio Speech of Leader Mu'ammar Qaddafi to the People of Benghazi—Full Version." YouTube video, March 17, 2011. https://www
.youtube.com/watch?v=JTGTDTI2YZ0&t=1s (no longer available).

Joffé, George. 1981. "Libya and Chad." *Review of African Political Economy* (21):
84–102.

———. 2010. *Saif Al-Islam: The Whole (Libyan) World in His Hands?* Washington, DC: Carnegie Institute. https://carnegieendowment.org/sada/?fa=24686.

Jureńczyk, Łukasz. 2018. "Great Britain against Libya's State Terrorism in the
1980s." *Historia i Polityka* 24 (31): 61–71.

Kadri, Ali. 2015. *Arab Development Denied: Dynamics of Accumulation by Wars
of Encroachment*. London: Anthem.

———. 2016. *The Unmaking of Arab Socialism*. London: Anthem.

———. 2019. *Imperialism with Reference to Syria*. Singapore: Springer.

Kanna, Ahmed. 2011. *Dubai: The City as Corporation*. Minneapolis: Univ. of
Minnesota Press.

Kaplan, Eben. 2007. "How Libya Got off the List." Council of Foreign Relations,
October 16, 2007. https://www.cfr.org/backgrounder/how-libya-got-list.

Karl, Terry Lynn. 2007. *The Paradox of Plenty: Oil Booms and Petro-States*. Berkeley: Univ. of California Press.

Kashiem, Mustafa Abdallah. 2010. "The Treaty of Friendship, Partnership, and Cooperation between Libya and Italy: From an Awkward Past to a Promising Equal Partnership." *Californian Italian Studies* 1 (1): 1–15.

Kathiravelu, Laavanya. 2016. *Migrant Dubai: Low-Wage Workers and the Construction of a Global City*. London: Palgrave Macmillan.

Khadduri, Majid. 1963. *Modern Libya: A Study in Political Development*. Baltimore, MD: Johns Hopkins Univ. Press.

Khalili, Laleh. 2018. "The Infrastructural Power of the Military: The Geoeconomic Role of the US Army Corps of Engineers in the Arabian Peninsula." *European Journal of International Relations* 24 (4): 911–33.

Khalili, Laleh, and Jilian Schwedler, eds. 2010. *Policing and Prisons in the Middle East: Formations of Coercion*. London: Hurst.

Khosrokhavar, Farhad. 1993. *L'utopie sacrifiée: sociologie de La Révolution Iranienne* [The Sacrificed Utopia: Sociology of the Iranian Revolution]. Paris: Presses de la Fondation Nationale des Sciences Politiques.

Kington, Tom. 2009. "Muammar Gaddafi's 'Cultural' Tours to Libya for Italian Models Revealed in Diary." *Guardian*, November 28, 2010. https://www.the guardian.com/world/2010/nov/28/muammar-gaddafi-italian-women-converts.

Kirkpatrick, David D., and Kareem Fahim. 2011. "Qaddafi Warns of Assault on Benghazi as UN Vote Nears." *New York Times*, March 18, 2011. http://www .nytimes.com/2011/03/18/world/africa/18libya.html?pagewanted=all&_r=0.

Kleist, Nauja, and Stef Jansen. 2016. "Introduction: Hope over Time: Crisis, Immobility, and Future-Making." *Journal of History and Anthropology* 27 (4): 373–92.

Kochler, Hans. 2002. "Report on the Appeal Proceedings at the Scottish Court in the Netherlands (Lockerbie Court) in the Case of Abdelbaset Ali Mohamed Al Megrahi v. H. M. Advocate." International Progress Organization. Accessed July 12, 2022. https://i-p-o.org/koechler-lockerbie-appeal_report.html.

———. 2003. "Report on and Evaluation of the Lockerbie Trial Conducted by the Special Scottish Court in the Netherlands at Kamp van Zeist." International Progress Organization. Accessed July 12, 2022. https://i-p-o.org/lockerbie -report.htm.

Köchler, Hans, and Jason Subler. 2002. "The Lockerbie Trial: Documents Related to the I.P.O. Observer Mission." Accessed July 12, 2022. International Progress Organization. http://i-p-o.org/lockerbie_observer_mission.htm.

Koloma Beck, Teresa. 2012. *The Normality of Civil War: Armed Groups and Everyday Life in Angola*. Frankfurt/AM: Campus-Verl.

Kornai, Janos. 1992. *The Socialist System: The Political Economy of Communism.* Princeton, NJ: Princeton Univ. Press.

Koskenniemi, Martti. 1994. "L'affaire du différend territorial Tchad/Libye (Arret de La Cour International de Justice Du 3 Fevrier 1994)" [The Chad/Libya Territorial Dispute Case (Judgment of the International Court of Justice of February 3, 1994)]. *Annuaire français de droit international* [French Annuary of International Law] 40: 442–64.

Krane, Jim. 2009. *Dubai: The Story of the World's Fastest City.* London: Atlantic.

Kwera, Francis. 2008. "Gaddafi Says Africans Must Reject Conditional Aid." Reuters, March 17, 2008. https://www.reuters.com/article/us-uganda-gaddafi/gaddafi-says-africans-must-reject-conditional-aid-idUSL1747216620080317?feedType=RSS&feedName=worldNews.

Laclau, Ernesto, and Chantal Mouffe. 1985. *Hegemony and Socialist Strategy.* London: Verso.

Laessing, Ulf. 2020. *Understanding Libya since Gaddafi.* London: Hurst.

Lahwej, Younis Ali. 1998. "Ideology and Power in Libyan Foreign Policy with Reference to Libyan-American Relations from the Revolution to the Lockerbie Affair." PhD diss., Univ. of Reading.

Lake, Anthony. 1994. "Confronting Backlash States." *Foreign Affairs* 73 (2): 45–55.

Lawson-Remer, Terra. 2014. "Undoing the Resource Curse." *Foreign Policy,* July 9, 2014. https://foreignpolicy.com/2014/07/09/undoing-the-resource-curse/.

Ledeneva, Alena V. 1998. *Russia's Economy of Favours: Blat, Networking, and Informal Exchange.* Cambridge: Cambridge Univ. Press.

libyafirst1969. 2012. "Qaddafi: Fuck the Fools of the Gulf." YouTube video, 1:09, March 11, 2012. https://www.youtube.com/watch?v=crRCxEPuKpE.

Libyan General National Congress. 2013. "Legislation No.13 of 2013 [on] Political and Administrative Isolation." Accessed July 12, 2022. http://muftah.org/full-text-libyas-political-isolation-law/#.WH91H9JviUk.

LibyaTV. 2013. "Phobia." YouTube video, 22:49, July 12, 2013. https://www.youtube.com/watch?v=KKlP62VZeuQ.

Lugar, Dick and Ben Cardin. 2011. "Libya: The Resource Curse Strikes Again." Huffington Post, June 20, 2011. https://www.huffpost.com/entry/libya-the-resource-curse-_b_851672.

Luthar, Breda, and Maruša Pušnik. 2010. *Remembering Utopia: The Culture of Everyday Life in Socialist Yugoslavia.* Washington, DC: New Academia.

Machon, Annie. 2005. *Spies, Lies, and Whistleblowers: M15, M16, and the Shayler Affair.* Lewes: Book Guild.

Majumdar, Saikat. 2013. *Prose of the World: Modernism and the Banality of Empire*. New York: Columbia Univ. Press.

Malinarich, Nathalie. 2001. "Flashback: The Berlin Disco Bombing." BBC News, November 13, 2001. http://news.bbc.co.uk/2/hi/europe/1653848.stm.

Manchanda, Nivi. 2020. *Imagining Afghanistan: The History and Politics of Imperial Knowledge*. Cambridge: Cambridge Univ. Press.

Mandel, Robert. 1987. *Irrationality in International Confrontation*. London: Greenwood.

Martinez, Luis. 2007. *The Libyan Paradox*. London: Hurst.

———. 2012. *The Violence of Petro-Dollar Regimes: Algeria, Iraq, and Libya*. London: Hurst.

Massad, Joseph A. 2015. *Islam in Liberalism*. Chicago: Univ. of Chicago Press.

Matar, Khalil I., and Robert W. Thabit. 2004. *Lockerbie and Libya: A Study in International Relations*. London: MacFarland.

Matar, Linda. 2013. "Twilight of 'State Capitalism' in Formerly 'Socialist' Arab States." *Journal of North African Studies* 18 (3): 416–30.

Mattes, Hanspeter. 1987. "Libya's Economic Relations as an Instrument of Foreign Policy." In *The Economic Development of Libya*, edited by Bichara Khader and Bashir El-Wifati, 81–123. Kent: Cermac.

———. 1995. "The Rise and Fall of Revolutionary Committees." In *Qadhafi's Libya: 1969–1994*, edited by Dirk Vandewalle, 89–112. New York: St. Martin's.

———. 2004. "Challenges to Security Sector Governance in the Middle East: The Libyan Case." Working paper, Centre for the Democratic Control of Armed Forces, Geneva.

Mbembe, Achille. 2001. *On the Postcolony*. Berkeley: Univ. of California Press.

McCullagh, David, Conor McMorrow, and Justin McCarthy. 2021. "Extent of Libyan Backing for IRA 'Shocked' British." RTE, December 28, 2021. https://www.rte.ie/news/2021/1228/1267955-state-papers-libya-ira/.

Meddeb, Hamza. 2011. "'L'Ambivalence de La Course à "El Khobza": Obéir et Se Révolter En Tunisie'" [The Ambivalent Search for Bread: Obedience and Revolt in Tunisia]. *Politique Africaine* 121: 35–51.

———. 2012. "Courir Ou Mourir: Course à El Khobza et Domination Au Quotidien Dans La Tunisie de Ben Ali" [Run or Die: The Search for Bread and Quotidian Domination in Ben Ali Tunisia]. PhD diss., Paris Institute of Political Studies, Sciences Po.

Mercuri, Michela, and Sergio Romano. 2017. *Incognita Libia. Cronache di un Paese sospeso*. Milano: Franco Angeli.

Meyer, Manfred G. 2012. *Gaddafi, Koks Und Knaben: Ein CIA-Mordkomplott!* Berlin: MGM Verlag.

Miles, Alex. 2003. *US Foreign Policy and the Rogue State Doctrine*. London: Routledge.

Mohamed, Ali Mohamed. 2014. "Diversification Prospects for Sustainable Libyan Economic Growth." PhD diss., Univ. of Huddersfield.

Monitor Group. 2007. "Project to Enhance the Profile of Libya and Muammar Qadhafi: Executive Summary Phase 1." Monitor Group. Accessed July 12, 2022. http://www.motherjones.com/files/project_to_enhance_the_profile _of_libya_and_muammar_qadhafi.pdf.

Moss, Dana. 2010. *Reforming the Rogue: Lessons from the US-Libya Rapprochement*. Washington, DC: Washington Institute of Near East Studies.

Mostyn, Trevor. 2012. "Shukri Ghanem Obituary." *Guardian*, May 8, 2012. https://www.theguardian.com/world/2012/may/08/shukri-ghanem.

mp3libya. 2013. "Awad al-Maliki—You Are Great." YouTube video, 8:50, April 2, 2013. https://www.youtube.com/watch?v=DBpl8KutZlM.

Mundy, Jacob. 2019. "The Middle East Is Violence: On the Limits of Comparative Approaches to the Study of Armed Conflict." *Civil Wars* 21 (4): 539–68.

Munzinger, Hannes, and Frederik Obermaier. n.d. "Lost Treasure." Panama Papers: The Secrets of Dirty Money. Accessed July 12, 2022. http://panama papers.sueddeutsche.de/articles/573aeac75632a39742ed39a0/.

Murillo, Bianca. 2017. *Market Encounters: Consumer Cultures in Twentieth-Century Ghana*. Columbus: Ohio State Univ. Press.

National Front of Salvation. 1992. *Libya under Gaddafi and the NFSL Challenge: An Anthology of the NFSL News Reports, 1989–1992*. London: NFSL.

Naur, Maja. 1986. *Political Mobilization and Industry in Libya*. Lund: Akademisk Forslag.

Navaro-Yashin, Yael. 2002. *Faces of the State: Secularism and Public Life in Turkey*. Princeton, NJ: Princeton Univ. Press.

Ness, Immanuel and Zak Cope. 2017. *Encyclopedia of Imperialism and Anti-Imperialism*. London: Palgrave Macmillan.

Niblock, Tim. 2001. *Pariah States and Sanctions in the Middle East: Iraq, Libya, Sudan*. London: Lynne Rienner.

Nicholas, Lucy, and Christine Agius. 2018. *The Persistence of Global Masculinism: Discourse, Gender, and Neo-Colonial Re-Articulations of Violence*. London: Palgrave Macmillan.

Nolutshungu, Sam C. 1996. *Limits of Anarchy: Intervention and State Formation in Chad*. Charlottesville: Univ. Press of Virginia.

Oakes, John. 2011. *Libya: The History of Gaddafi's Pariah State*. Glouchester: History Press.

Obeidi, Amal. 2001. *Political Culture in Libya*. Richmond: Curzon.

Ochman, Dafna. 2006. "Rehabilitating a Rogue: Libya's WMD Reversal and Lessons for US Policy." *Parameters* 36 (1): 63–78.

Onderco, Michael. 2014. "From a 'Rogue' to a Parolee: Analyzing Libya's 'De-Roguing.'" In *Deviance in International Relations: "Rogue States" and International Security*, edited by Wolfang Wagner, Woutner Wener, and Michael Onderco, 171–92. London: Palgrave Macmillan.

OPEC. 2018. "OPEC Share of World Crude Oil Reserves 2018." Organisation of the Petroleum Exporting Countries. Accessed July 12, 2022. https://www .opec.org/opec_web/en/data_graphs/330.htm.

Oppenheim, V. H. 1976. "Why Oil Prices Go Up: The Past, We Pushed Them." *Foreign Policy* 25: 24–57.

Orford, Anne. 2003. *Reading Humanitarian Intervention: Human Rights and the Use of Force in International Law*. Cambridge: Cambridge Univ. Press.

Organization of African Unity. 1998. "Declaration and Decisions Adopted by 34th Ordinary Session of the Assembly of Heads of State and Government." June 8–10, 1998. https://au.int/sites/default/files/decisions/9543-1998_ahg _dec_124-131_xxxiv_e.pdf.

———. 1999. "Sirte Declaration." Accessed August 16, 2022. https://archives .au.int/bitstream/handle/123456789/10157/1999_Sirte%20_Decl_%20E .pdf?sequence=1&isAllowed=y.

O'Sullivan, Susannah. 2017. *Military Intervention in the Middle East and North Africa: The Case of NATO in Libya*. London: Routledge.

Otayek, René. 1986. *La Politique Africaine de La Libye: 1969–1985* [The African Policy of Libya: 1969–1985]. Paris: Karthala.

Otman, Waniss, and Erling Karlberg. 2007. *The Libyan Economy: Economic Diversification and International Repositioning*. Berlin: Springer.

Ouannes, Moncef. 2009. *Militaires, Élites et Modernisation Dans La Libye Contemporaine* [Military, Élites, and Modernization in Contemporary Libya]. Paris: La Decouverte.

Pack, Jason, ed. 2014. *The 2011 Libyan Uprisings and the Struggle for the Post-Qadhafi Future*. London: Palgrave Macmillan.

Parra, Francisco. 2004. *Oil Politics: A Modern History of Petroleum*. London: I. B. Tauris.

Parteger, Alison. 2005. "Libya: From Rogue State to Partner." *Journal of Middle Eastern Geopolitics* 1 (2): 5–9.

———. 2012. *Libya: The Rise and Fall of Qaddafi*. New Haven, CT: Yale Univ. Press.

———. 2016. "Libya: From Reform to Revolution." In *North African Politics: Change and Continuity*, edited by Yahyia Zoubir and Gregory White, 178–95. London: Routledge.

Péan, Pierre. 2001. *Manipulations africaines. Qui sont les vrais coupables de l'attentat du vol UTA 772?* [African Manipulations: Who Are the Real Culprits of UTA Flight 772 Bombing?] Paris: Plon.

Peirce, Gareth. 2009. "The Framing of Al-Megrahi." *London Review of Books*, September 24, 2009. https://www.lrb.co.uk/v31/n18/gareth-peirce/the-framing -of-al-megrahi.

Penketh, Anne. 2000. "Libya Bids $12m to Free Hostages in Philippines." *Independent*, August 23, 2000. https://www.independent.co.uk/news/world/asia /libya-bids-12m-to-free-hostages-in-philippines-5370388.html.

Pfiffner, James P. 2010. "US Blunders in Iraq: De-Baathification and Disbanding the Army." *Intelligence and National Security* 25 (1): 76–85.

Pieke, Frank N. 1996. *The Ordinary and the Extraordinary: An Anthropological Study of Chinese Reform and the 1989 People's Movement in Bejing*. London: Kegan Paul International.

Pisa, Nick. 2008. "Silvio Berlusconi Apologizes to Libya for Colonial Rule." *Telegraph*, September 1, 2008. http://www.telegraph.co.uk/news/worldnews /europe/italy/2658703/Silvio-Berlusconi-apologises-to-Libya-for-colonial -rule.html.

Porter, Michael. 2006. *National Economic Strategy: Libya's Moment for Action*. Cambridge, MA: Monitor Group.

Porter, Michael, and Daniel Yergin. 2006. *National Economic Strategy: An Assessment of the Competitiveness of the Libyan Arab Jamahiriya*. Cambridge, MA: Monitor Group.

Prashad, Vijay. 2012. *Arab Spring, Libyan Winter*. Edinburgh: AK.

Provence, Michael. 2017. *The Last Ottoman Generation and the Making of the Modern Middle East*. Cambridge: Cambridge Univ. Press.

Puar, Jasbir K., and Rai Amit. 2002. "Monster, Terrorist, Fag: The War on Terrorism and the Production of Docile Patriots." *Social Text* 20 (3): 117–48.

Publicis Communications Schweiz AG. 2016. "Gaddafi." AdForum. Accessed July 12, 2022. https://www.adforum.com/talent/10581-urs-schrepfer/work/34521993.

The Qu'ran. *Surah Al-Baqarah, 2:12*. Accessed July 12, 2022. https://quran.com/2/125.

Ramady, Mohamed A., ed. 2016. *The Political Economy of Wasta: Use and Abuse of Social Capital Networking*. Cham: Springer International.

Rand, Dafna Hochman. 2014. *Roots of the Arab Spring: Contested Authority and Political Change in the Middle East*. Philadelphia: Univ. of Pennsylvania Press.

Ratner, Steven R. 1984. "The Gulf of Sidra Incident of 1981: A Study of the Lawfulness of Peacetime Aerial Engagements." *Yale Journal of International Law* 10 (1): 59–77.

Reagan, Ronald. 1986. "The President's News Conference." American Presidency Project, April 9, 1986. https://www.presidency.ucsb.edu/documents/the-presidents-news-conference-959.

Reporters Without Borders. 2005. "Opposition Journalist Daif Al Ghazal Tortured to Death." https://rsf.org/en/news/opposition-journalist-daif-al-ghazal-tortured-death.

Reuters. 2009. "Gaddafi's Son Appointed to Key Post." October 16, 2009. http://www.reuters.com/article/us-libya-saif-idUSTRE59F35C20091016.

———. 2011. "Defiant Gaddafi Vows to Die as Martyr, Fight Revolt." February 22, 2011. https://www.reuters.com/article/us-libya-protests/defiant-gaddafi-vows-to-die-as-martyr-fight-revolt-idUSTRE71G0A620110222.

Ricci, Andrea. 2021. *Value and Unequal Exchange in International Trade: The Geography of Global Capitalist Exploitation*. London: Routledge.

Ritchie, Carola. 2013. "Libyan Broadcasting under Al-Qadhafi: The Politics of Pseudo-Liberalization." In *National Broadcasting and State Policy in Arab Countries*, edited by Tourya Guaaybess, 150–65. New York: Palgrave Macmillan.

Robertson, Cameron, Mustapha Khalili, and Mona Mahmood. 2011. "Libya Archive Reveals Pictorial History of Gaddafi's Brutal Reign—Video [2:01–4:55]." *Guardian*, July 18, 2011. https://www.theguardian.com/world/video/2011/jul/18/libya-muammar-gaddafi.

Ronen, Yehudit. 1993. "Libya." In *Middle East Contemporary Survey 17*, edited by Amy Ayalon, 538–39. Boulder, CO: Westview.

———. 1997. "Libya." In *Middle East Contemporary Survey 21*, edited by Bruce Maddy-Weitzman, 545–46. Boulder, CO: Westview.

———. 2002. "Qadhafi and Militant Islamism: Unprecedented Conflict." *Middle Eastern Studies* 38 (4): 1–16.

———. 2007. "The HIV/AIDS Tragedy and the Bulgarian Medics Affair: A Window on State and Society in Libya." *Middle Eastern Studies* 43 (3): 341–52.

Roper, Matt. 2009. "Inside the Mad, Bad World of Colonel Gaddafi." *Mirror*, November 18, 2009. https://www.mirror.co.uk/news/uk-news/inside-the-mad-bad-world-of-colonel-431736.

Rubin, Alfred P. 1993. "Libya, Lockerbie, and the Law." *Diplomacy & Statecraft* 4 (1): 1–19.

Ryan, Eileen. 2018. *Religion as Resistance: Negotiating Authority in Italian Libya.* Oxford: Oxford Univ. Press.

Sadiki, Larbi. 2014. "In-Formalized Polity and the Politics of Dynasty in Egypt and Libya." In *Informal Power in the Greater Middle East: Hidden Geographies*, edited by Luca Anceschi, Andrea Teti, and Gennaro Gervasio, 11–23. London: Routledge.

Safire, William. 1981. "Qaddafi in Chad." *New York Times*, March 5, 1981. https://www.nytimes.com/1981/03/05/opinion/essay-qaddafi-in-chad.html.

Saghieh, Hazem. 2007. "The Life and Death of De-Baathification." *Revue des mondes musulmans et de la Méditerranée* (117–18): 203–23.

Sajed, Alina. 2011. "Everyday Encounters with the Global behind the Iron Curtain: Imagining Freedom, Desiring Liberalism in Socialist Romania." *Cambridge Review of International Affairs* 24 (4): 551–71.

Sandover, Susie M. 2016. *Libya: A Love Lived, a Life Betrayed, 9/36.* Leicestershire: Matador.

Schatzberg, Michael G. 2001. *Political Legitimacy in Middle Africa: Father, Family, Food.* Indianapolis: Indiana Univ. Press.

Shayk Kishk. "On the Anniversary of the Killing of the Tyrant Gaddafi—Sheikh Kish Predicts the Method of his Death 40 Years Ago." YouTube video, 4:00, October 21, 2014. https://www.youtube.com/watch?v=rN-7t25MK74.

Schielke, Samuli. 2015. *Egypt in the Future Tense: Hope, Frustration, and Ambivalence before and after 2011.* Bloomington: Indiana Univ. Press.

Schwartz, Jonathan. 2007. "Dealing with a 'Rogue State': The Libya Precedent." *American Journal of International Law* 101 (1): 553–80.

Scott, James C. 1990. *Domination and the Arts of Resistance: Hidden Transcripts.* New Haven, CT: Yale Univ. Press.

Seale, Patrick, and Maureen McConville. 1973. *The Hilton Assignment.* New York: HarperCollins.

Sehib, Khairia A. H. 2013. "Consumer Food Shopping Behaviour in Libya." PhD diss., Newcastle Univ.

71960. 2013. "Gaddafi Speech in Syria (2008) Warns Arab Leader They Will Be Next after Saddam Hussein Was Hanged." YouTube video, 4:01, September 1, 2013. https://www.youtube.com/watch?v=-cpiPFkL0QY.

Silj, Alessandro. 1993. "The Gulf of Sidra Incident: March–April 1986." *International Spectator* 28 (1): 75–105.

Sloterdijk, Peter. 1987. *Critique of Cynical Reason.* Minneapolis: Univ. of Minnesota Press.

Sokol, Sam, and Lis, Jonathan. 2021. "19 years after Its Ouster, African Union Reinstates Israel as Observer Country." *Haaretz*, July 22, 2021. https://www.haaretz.com/israel-news/.premium-19-years-after-its-ouster-african-union-reinstates-israel-as-an-observer-country-1.10020545

St. John, Ronald Bruce. 1983. "The Ideology of Muammar Al-Qadhdhafi: Theory and Practice." *International Journal of Middle East Studies* 15 (4): 471–90.

———. 2000. "Libya in Africa: Looking Back, Moving Forward." *Journal of Libyan Studies* 1 (1): 18–32.

———. 2004. "'Libya Is Not Iraq': Preemptive Strikes, WMD, and Diplomacy." *Middle East Journal* 58 (3): 386–402.

———. 2008. "The Changing Libyan Economy: Causes and Consequences." *Middle East Journal* 62 (1): 75–91.

———. 2015. *Libya: Continuity and Change.* London: Routledge.

Staub, Vincent. 2006. *La Libye et Les Migrations Subsahariennes* [Libya and the Sub-Saharan Migrations]. Paris: L'Harmattan.

Stocker, Valerie. 2012. *Les Enfants de La Jamahiriyya: La Jeunesse Libyenne Sous Kadhafi—Comportements Sociaux, Attitudes Politiques et Perceptions Du Discours Official* [The Children of al-Jamāhīrīyah: Libyan Youth under Qaddafi—Social Behaviors, Political Attitudes, and Perceptions of the Official Discourse]. Brussels: Éditions Universitaires Européennes.

Stork, Joe. 1975. *Middle East Oil and the Energy Crisis.* New York: Monthly Review.

Takeh, Ray. 2002. "The Fate of the Permanent Revolution." *Journal of Libyan Studies* 3 (1): 6–12.

Tantoush, Jalal. 2010. "The Impact of Sanctions on Buyer-Supplier Relationships within the Libyan Oil Industry." PhD diss., Univ. of East Anglia.

Tchaleu, Joseph Wouako. 2014. *L'agression Libyenne: La Démocratie de Guerre* [The Libyan Aggression: Democracy of War]. Paris: L'Harmattan.

*Telegraph.* 2011. "Gaddafi Speech Was Code to Begin Genocide against Libyans." February 23, 2011. https://www.telegraph.co.uk/news/worldnews/africaand indianocean/libya/8342349/Gaddafi-speech-was-code-to-begin-genocide -against-Libyans.html.

Thomas-Johnson, Amanda, and Simon Hooper. 2018. "'Sorted' by MI5: How UK Government Sent British-Libyans to Fight Gaddafi." Middle East Eye, November 7, 2018. http://www.middleeasteye.net/news/sorted-mi5-how-uk -government-sent-british-libyans-fight-gaddafi.

Toaldo, Mattia. 2013. *The Origins of the US War on Terror.* London: Routledge.

Tripp, Charles. 2014. *The Power and the People: Paths of Resistance in the Middle East.* Cambridge: Cambridge Univ. Press.

True Voice TV. "The Last Message of Colonel Mu'ammar Qaddafi—No Shame in Death." YouTube video, June 29, 2019. https://www.youtube.com/watch ?v=64WpuxzX-vo (no longer available).

Ulrichsen, Kristian Coates. 2014. *Qatar and the Arab Spring.* London: Hurst.

United Nations General Assembly. 2005. "A/RES/60/1." October 24, 2005. http:// www.un.org/en/development/desa/population/migration/generalassembly /docs/globalcompact/A_RES_60_1.pdf.

United Nations High Commissioner for Refugees. 2003. "Libya: The Significance of 7 April: Whether It Is a Day on Which Dissidents Are Hanged and If This Practice Has Been in Existence since 1970." January 7, 2003. http://www .refworld.org/docid/3f7d4dc238.html.

United Nations International Labour Organization. 2010. *BTI Libya Country Report.* Geneva: United Nations ILO.

United Nations Security Council. 1992. "Resolution 748." https://digitallibrary .un.org/record/196976?ln=en.

———. 2006. "Joint Letter on Peace and Security between the United Kingdom of Great Britain and Northern Ireland and the Great Socialist People's Libyan Arab Jamahiriya." https://digitallibrary.un.org/record/578450?ln=en.

———. 2011a. "Resolution 1970." February 26, 2011. http://www.nato.int/nato _static/assets/pdf/pdf_2011_02/20110927_110226-UNSCR-1970.pdf.

———. 2011b. "Resolution 1973." March 17, 2011. http://www.nato.int/nato _static/assets/pdf/pdf_2011_03/20110927_110311-UNSCR-1973.pdf.

United Nations Watch. 2010. "Libya Must End Racism against Black African Migrants and Others." https://web.archive.org/web/20111026161747/http://

www.unwatch.org/site/apps/nlnet/content2.aspx?c=bdKKISNqEmG&b=13
13923&ct=8411733.

Vandewalle, Dirk. 1991. "Qadhafi's" Perestroika": Economic and Political Liberalization in Libya." *Middle East Journal* 45 (2): 216–31.

———. 1995. *Qadhafi's Libya, 1969–1994*. New York: St. Martin's.

———. 2006. *A History of Modern Libya*. Cambridge: Cambridge Univ. Press.

———. 2016. *Libya since 1969: Qadhafi's Revolution Revisited*. London: Palgrave Macmillan.

Varzi, Roxanne. 2006. *Warring Souls: Youth, Media, and Martyrdom in Post-Revolution Iran*. Durham, NC: Duke Univ. Press.

Verdery, Katherine. 1991. "Theorizing Socialism." *American Ethnologist* 12 (2): 210–27.

———. 1996. *What Was Socialism and What Comes Next?* Princeton, NJ: Princeton Univ. Press.

———. 2014. *Secrets and Truths: Ethnography in the Archive of Romania's Secret Police*. Budapest: Central European Univ.

Villa, Matteo. 2012. "Un Caso Poco Studiato Di Rentier State" [A Not Well-Studied Case of Rentier State]. In *Libia: Fine o Rinascita Di Una Nazione?* [Libya: End or Birth of a Nation?], edited by Karim Mezran and Arturo Varvelli, 61–82. Roma: Donzelli.

Vitalis, Robert. 2006. *America's Kingdom: Mythmaking on the Saudi Oil Frontier*. Stanford, CA: Stanford Univ. Press.

Waddams, Frank C. 1980. *The Libyan Oil Industry*. London: Crom Helm.

Wallis, William. 2008. "New Blueprint for Overhaul of Libyan Economy." *Financial Times*, February 8, 2008. https://www.ft.com/content/35f5a62a-98d0-11da-aa99-0000779e2340.

Wedeen, Lisa. 1999. *Ambiguities of Domination: Politics, Rhetoric, and Symbols in Contemporary Syria*. Chicago: Univ. of Chicago Press.

———. 2019. *Authoritarian Apprehensions: Ideology, Judgment, and Mourning in Syria*. Chicago: Univ. of Chicago Press.

Werfalli, Mabroka al-. 2011. *Political Alienation in Libya: Assessing Citizens' Political Attitude and Behaviour*. Reading: Ithaca.

Obama, Barack. 2011. "Remarks by the President in Address to the Nation on Libya." Obama White House, March 28, 2011. https://obamawhitehouse.archives.gov/the-press-office/2011/03/28/remarks-president-address-nation-libya.

Wheeler, Brian. 2016. "David Cameron defends Libya decisions." BBC News, January 15, 2016. https://www.bbc.com/news/uk-politics-35300667.

Whitehead, John S., and William S. Schneider. 1987. "The Singular Event and the Everyday Routine: The Interplay of History and Culture in the Shaping of Memory." *Oral Historical Review* 15 (2): 43–79.

WikiLeaks. 2008. "National Oil Corporation Chairman Shukri Ghanem May Seek to Resign Soon." July 13, 2008. https://wikileaks.org/plusd/cables/08 TRIPOLI565_a.html.

———. 2009. "09TRIPOLI198." Accessed August 16, 2022. https://wikileaks .jcvignoli.com/cable_09TRIPOLI198?hl=.

———. 2011. "France's Client & Q's Gold. Sid." April 2, 2011. https://wikileaks .org/clinton-emails/Clinton_Email_December_Release/C05779612.pdf.

Wolchover, David. 2016. "Culprits of Lockerbie: A Treatise Concerning the Destruction of Pan Am 103 on 21 December 1988." Accessed July 12, 2022. www.davidwolchover.co.uk/docs/Culprits%20of%20Lockerbie.doc.

World Bank. 2006. "Socialist People's Libyan Arab Jamahiriya Country Economic Report." Accessed July 12, 2022. http://documents.worldbank.org /curated/en/918691468053103808/pdf/30295.pdf.

World Bank DataBank. n.d. Life Expectancy at Birth, Total (Years) 1960–2018. Accessed on September 24, 2019. https://databank.worldbank.org/home.aspx.

Wright, David M. 2021. *Oil Money: Middle East Petrodollars and the Transformation of US Empire, 1967–1988.* Ithaca, NY: Cornell Univ. Press.

Wright, John. 1989. *Libya, Chad, and the Central Sahara.* London: Hurst.

———. 2005. "Mussolini and the Sword of Islam." In *Italian Colonialism*, edited by Ruth Ben-Ghiat and Mia Fuller, 121–30. New York: Palgrave Macmillan.

WSWS. 1998. "ZDF-Magazin Frontal zerstört Legende vom libyschen Staatsterrorismus." World Socialist, August 28, 1998. https://www.wsws.org/de /articles/1998/08/bell-a28.html.

yasser mas. 2014. "Final Game of the Libyan Football Championship between al-Ahly and al-Ittihad Season 1993-1994 (Second Half)." YouTube video, 44:19, December 7, 2014. https://www.youtube.com/watch?v=21gleEXwAes.

Yergin, Daniel. 1991. *The Prize: The Epic Quest for Oil, Money, and Power.* New York: Simon & Schuster.

Young, Iris Marion. 2003. "The Logic of Masculinist Protection." *Signs: Journal of Women in Culture and Society* 29 (1): 1–25.

Younis, Mustafa R. A. 2014. "Il governatorato di italo Balbo nella Libia coloniale: riforme e rinnovamento delle politiche sociali (1934–1940)" [The Governorate of Italo Balbo in Colonial Libya: Reforms and Renovation of the Social Policies (1934–1940)]. PhD diss., Università degli studi di Roma Tor Vergata.

Yurchak, Alexei. 1997. "The Cynical Reason of Late Socialism: Power, Pretense, and the Anekdot." *Public Culture* 9: 161–88.

———. 2013. *Everything Was Forever, Until It Was No More: The Last Soviet Generation*. Princeton, NJ: Princeton Univ. Press.

Zarrugh, Amina. 2018. "'You Exile Them in Their Own Country': The Everyday Politics of Reclaiming the Disappeared in Libya." *Middle East Critique* 27 (3): 247–59.

Zoubir, Yahyia. 2002. "Libya in US Foreign Policy: From Rogue State to Good Fellow?" *Third World Quarterly* 23 (1): 31–53.

———. 2006. "The United States and Libya: From Confrontation to Normalization." *Middle East Policy* 23 (2): 48–70.

Zucchino, David. 2011. "Ramadan Brings Back Bitter Memories for Many Libyans." *Los Angeles Times*, July 31, 2011. http://articles.latimes.com/2011/jul/31/world/la-fg-libya-hangings-20110731.

# Index

of, 65; popularity of, 68–70; power of,
65–66, 68–69, 72; propaganda from,
44–45; protests regarding, 76–77;
quote of, 28, 39, 73–74, 126, 157,
165, 167; sexual appetite of, 62–63;
speeches of, 141, 146; support for, 149;
travels of, 65–66; United States' viewpoint regarding, 28–29; viewpoint
of, 55; words describing, 68; writings
regarding, 62–63, 157–58
Qaddafi, Mutassim, 140
Qaddafi, Saadi, 92–93, 92n31
quotidian commodities, 111, 144, 181
*Quryna* (newspaper), 135–36

Rai, Amit, 63
Ramadan, 36–37
rape, 62–63, 63n2
Ras Lanuf, 101
ration books, 107
Reagan, Ronald, 30–31, 32, 61, 62
refolutions, 171–72
reformism, 141
reformist camp, 170–71
reform programs, 140
religion, within al-Mathāba, 84–85
Reouane, Rachid, 38n9
repression, tactics for, 174, 175
Republic of the Masses, 14
Resolution 1973, 162, 165–66
Responsibility to Protect (R2P), 72,
155–56, 165
revolution, concept of, 180
Revolutionary Command Council
(RCC), 13, 28, 36, 104
Revolutionary Committees (RC), 56,
82–88, 97
revolutionary optimism, 161
Rice, Condoleeza, 70

rogueness, 5, 178–79
rogue states, 9
rule of violence, in Syria, 163
rumors, function of, 113n6

Sadat, Anwar, 32
sanctions: consumerist desires under,
105–18; dropping of, 53; effects of,
16–18, 34, 35, 37, 51–52, 88–89, 108,
170
Sandover, Susie M., 111–12
Sarkozy, Nicolas, 182
Saudi Arabia, 109, 124
scarcity, 106–7, 108
Schielke, Samuli, 123
Sebha, 96–97
self-censorship, 44
Senusi Order, 31
17 February Revolution: cruel optimism
regarding, 160–61; derogatory conversations regarding, 150; effects of, 157,
159, 169; media manipulation regarding, 166–67; NATO intervention
within, 154, 155; protesting purpose
within, 171; public opinion regarding, 148–54, 184; questions regarding,
148–49; success of, 1; Western geopolitical forces within, 156
"7th of April," 37
sexuality, 62–63, 64, 71–72
al-Shabani, Muhammad Saeed, 36n5
Shayler, David, 38n8
al-Shoushan, Hisham, 2
Shukri Ghanem, 19
Shwehdi, Sadiq Hamed, 36–37
Six-Day War, 13
smuggling, 97, 117, 141
social classes, emergence of, 12, 118
social services, demand increase for, 120

**Matteo Capasso** is Marie Curie Global Fellow between Ca' Foscari University of Venice, Italy, and Columbia University in New York City. His current project focuses on the impact of US-led imperialism on Libya. He was previously Max Weber Research Fellow at the European University Institute and visiting fellow at the University of Turin. He holds a PhD in International Relations from Durham University. Since 2013, he has been working for *Middle East Critique*, currently as managing editor. His research interests include political history, everyday politics, and international political economy, with a focus on the Middle East and North Africa and the Global South at large.

.

www.ingramcontent.com/pod-product-compliance
Lightning Source LLC
Chambersburg PA
CBHW020857270326
41928CB00006B/748